Writing, Law, and Kingship in Old Babylonian Mesopotamia

Writing, Law, and Kingship in Old Babylonian Mesopotamia

DOMINIQUE CHARPIN

Translated by Jane Marie Todd

University of Chicago Press
Chicago and London

Dominique Charpin is *directeur d'études* in the History of Science and Philology Section, École pratique des hautes études, at the University of Paris. He is the author of several books, including *Hammu-Rabi de Babylone* and *Lire et Écrire à Babylone*.

Jane Marie Todd has translated many books for the University of Chicago Press, including works by Alain Besançon, François Jullien, Jean Starobinski, Brassaï, and Mona Ozouf.

The University of Chicago Press, Chicago 60637
The University of Chicago Press, Ltd., London

Printed in the United States of America

19 18 17 16 15 14 13 12 11 10 1 2 3 4 5

ISBN-13: 978-0-226-10158-3 (cloth)
ISBN-10: 0-226-10158-4 (cloth)

Library of Congress Cataloging-in-Publication Data

Charpin, Dominique.
Writing, law, and kingship in Old Babylonian Mesopotamia / Dominique Charpin ; translated by Jane Marie Todd.
p. cm.
Includes bibliographical references and index.
ISBN-13: 978-0-226-10158-3 (cloth : alk. paper)
ISBN-10: 0-226-10158-4 (cloth : alk. paper) 1. Diplomatics, Cuneiform—Iraq—History. 2. Law, Assyro-Babylonian—Language. 3. Civilization, Assyro-Bablonian. 4. Cuneiform writing—History. I. Todd, Jane Marie, 1957– II. Title.
KL75.C48 2010
935—dc22

2009052457

♾ The paper used in this publication meets the minimum requirements of the American National Standard for Information Sciences—Permanence of Paper for Printed Library Materials, ANSI Z39.48-1992.

CONTENTS

ACKNOWLEDGMENTS

This book came into being as the result of a remark Jack Sasson made when he learned of the essay that would become chapter 2 of this book: Why not make it available to a broader public by translating it into English? Although it is true that the essay in question had been published in the *Bibliothèque de l'École des chartes,* well known to medieval specialists, no one would have thought to look for a study dealing with ancient Mesopotamia in such a publication. Since that was also the case for many of my other writings, the idea of a book published in English began to take shape. I then asked Martha Roth to put me in touch with the University of Chicago Press. At the fifty-first Rencontre Assyriologique Internationale, held in Chicago in July 2005, I was able to meet with Susan Bielstein, who received me most warmly. She proposed that I select those of my essays that had to do with law and the royal exercise of justice. So it was that this book assumed its definitive form in summer 2005, with various modifications introduced the following year.

The eight chapters that make up the core of the book emerged from work I pursued at various times: the two oldest essays date back some twenty years, but the majority are very recent, and the introduction and conclusion have never before been published. This is not a translation *ne varietur* of already-published essays. I have reworked them so as to complete or update them when necessary and to avoid repetition; when warranted, full details have been given in the preliminary note to each chapter. I have also included many cross-references to make the coherence of the approach underlying this book more apparent. In order not to discourage the willing reader, I have sometimes cut a few technical passages from the body of the text or from the notes, especially the transcription of the Akkadian texts cited. Interested specialists may refer to the original publication if need be. Nevertheless, I have insisted on retaining the fairly copious notes, which validate some of the positions I have taken and will allow those who so desire to delve deeper into one point or another. My wish above all is to provide the non-French-speaking reader access to a particular way of approaching cuneiform documentation, which culminates in a certain vision of Mesopotamian history.[1]

I extend my thanks to the individuals already mentioned; and of course to my wife, Nele Ziegler, for her encouragement and attentive rereading of my manuscript; and finally, to my translator, Jane Marie Todd.

ABBREVIATIONS

AbB	Altbabylonische Briefe
ABL	Assyrian and Babylonian Letters
ADOG	Abhandlungen der Deutschen Orient-Gesellschaft
AfO	*Archiv für Orientforschung*
AFPP	*Archives familiales et propriété privée en Babylonie ancienne: Étude des documents de "Tell Sifr"*
AHw	*Akkadisches Handwörterbuch*
AMD	Ancient Magic and Divination
Amurru 1	*Mari, Ébla et les Hourrites: Dix ans de travaux. Actes du colloque international (Paris, mai 1993)*. Vol. 1
Amurru 2	*Mari, Ébla et les Hourrites: Dix ans de travaux. Actes du colloque international (Paris, mai 1993)*. Vol. 2
AO	Antiquités Orientales, Louvre Museum
AOAT	Alter Orient und Altes Testament
AoF	*Altorientalische Forschungen*
AOS	American Oriental Society
ARM	Archives Royales de Mari
ASOR	American Schools of Oriental Research
BAH	Bibliothèque archéologique et historique
BaM	*Baghdader Mitteilungen*
BBVO	Berliner Beiträge zum Vorderen Orient
BBVOT	Berliner Beiträge zum Vorderen Orient Texte
BiMes	Bibliotheca Mesopotamica

BiOr	*Bibliotheca Orientalis*
CAD	Chicago Assyrian Dictionary
CDOG	Colloquien der Deutschen Orient-Gesellschaft
CHANE	Culture & History of the Ancient Near East
CM	Cuneiform Monographs
CNIP	Carsten Niebuhr Institute Publications
CRRAI	Comptes rendus des Rencontres Assyriologiques Internationales
CRRAI 30	*Cuneiform Archives and Libraries: Papers Read at the 30e Rencontre Assyriologique Internationale, Leiden, 4–8 July 1983*
CRRAI 33	*La femme dans le Proche-Orient antique. Compte rendu de la 33e Rencontre Assyriologique Internationale (Paris, 7–10 juillet 1986)*
CRRAI 35	*Nippur at the Centennial: Papers Read at the 35e Rencontre Assyriologique Internationale, Philadelphia, 1988*
CRRAI 36	*Mésopotamie et Elam. Actes de la 26e Rencontre Assyriologique Internationale, Gand, 10–14 juillet 1989*, vol. 1
CRRAI 38	*La circulation des biens, des personnes et des idées dans le Proche-Orient ancien, Actes de la 38e Rencontre Assyriologique Internationale (Paris, 8–10 juillet 1991)*
CRRAI 40	*Houses and Households in Ancient Mesopotamia: Papers Read at the 40e Rencontre Assyriologique Internationale, Leiden, July 5–8, 1993*
CRRAI 43	*Intellectual Life of the Ancient Near East: Papers Presented at the 43rd Rencontre Assyriologique Internationale, Prague, July 1–5, 1996*
CRRAI 44	*Landscapes: Territories, Frontiers and Horizons in the Ancient Near East: Papers Presented to the 44th Rencontre Assyriologique Internationale, Venice, 7–11 July 1997*
CRRAI 45/1	*Historiography in the Cuneiform World: Proceedings of the 45th Rencontre Assyriologique Internationale, Part I, Harvard University*
CRRAI 45/2	*Seals and Seal Impressions: Proceedings of the 45th Rencontre Assyriologique Internationale, Part II, Yale University*
CRRAI 46	*Nomades et sédentaires dans le Proche-Orient ancien. Compte rendu de la 46e Rencontre Assyriologique Internationale, Paris, 10–13 juillet 2000*
CRRAI 47	*Sex and Gender in the Ancient Near East: Proceedings of the 47th Rencontre Assyriologique Internationale, Helsinki*
CRRAI 48	*Ethnicity in Ancient Mesopotamia: Papers Read at the 48th Rencontre Assyriologique Internationale, Leiden, 1–4 July 2002*
CRRAI 49	*Nineveh: Papers of the 49e Rencontre Assyriologique Internationale, London, 7–11 July 2003*

CRRAI 51	*Proceedings of the 51st Rencontre Assyriologique Internationale Held at the Oriental Institute of the University of Chicago, July 18–22, 2005*
CRRAI 52	*Krieg und Frieden im Alten Vorderasien, Münster, 17.–21. Juli 2006*
CT	Cuneiform Texts
CTN	Cuneiform Texts from Nimrud
DCS	*Documents cunéiformes de Strasbourg conservés à la Bibliothèque Nationale et Universitaire*, vol. 1
FAOS	Freiburger Altorientalische Studien
FM	*Florilegium Marianum*
FM [I]	*Florilegium marianum. Recueil d'études en l'honneur de M. Fleury*
FM II	*Florilegium marianum II. Recueil d'études à la mémoire de Maurice Birot*
FM III	*Florilegium marianum III. Recueil d'études à la mémoire de Marie-Thérèse Barrelet*
FM IV	*Florilegium marianum IV. Le harem de Zîmrî-Lîm*
FM V	*Florilegium marianum V. Mari et le Proche-Orient à l'époque amorrite: Essai d'histoire politique*
FM VI	*Florilegium marianum VI. Recueil d'études à la mémoire d'André Parrot*
FM VII	*Florilegium marianum VII. Le culte d'Addu d'Alep et l'affaire d'Alahtum*
FM VIII	*Florilegium marianum VIII. Le culte des pierres et les monuments commémoratifs en Syrie amorrite*
HANE/S	History of the Ancient Near East/Studies, Padua
HdO	Handbuch der Orientalistik
HEO	Hautes Études Orientales
HUCA	*Hebrew Union College Annual*
IM	Iraq Museum, Baghdad
JA	*Journal Asiatique*
JAOS	*Journal of the American Oriental Society*
JCS	*Journal of Cuneiform Studies*
JEOL	*Jaarbericht van het vooraziatisch-egyptisch Genootschap* Ex Oriente Lux
JESHO	*Journal of the Economic and Social History of the Orient*
JNES	*Journal of Near Eastern Studies*
LAPO	Littératures anciennes du Proche-Orient
LAPO 16	*Les documents épistolaires du palais de Mari*, vol. 1
LAPO 17	*Les documents épistolaires du palais de Mari*, vol. 1

LAPO 18	*Les documents épistolaires du palais de Mari*, vol. 3
LAPO 19	*Correspondance des marchands de Kanish*
LAPO 20	*Textes akkadiens d'Ugarit. Textes provenant des vingt-cinq premières campagnes*
MARI	*Mari Annales de Recherches Interdisciplinaires*
MDP	Mémoires de la Délégation en Perse
Mél. Artzi	*Bar-Ilan Studies in Assyriology Dedicated to Pinḥas Artzi*
Mél. Birot	*Miscellanea Babylonica. Mélanges offerts à Maurice Birot*
Mél. Böhl	*Symbolae biblicae et mesopotamicae Francisco Mario Theodorico De Liagre Böhl dedicatae*
Mél. Borger	*Festschrift für Rykle Borger zu seinem 65. Geburtstag am 24. Mai 1994* tikip santakki mala bašmu . . .
Mél. De Meyer	*Cinquante-deux réflexions sur le Proche-Orient ancien offertes en hommage à L.De Meyer*
Mél. Finet	*Reflets des deux fleuves, Volume de Mélanges offert à André Finet*
Mél. Garelli	*Marchands, diplomates et empereurs. Études sur la civilisation mésopotamienne offertes à Paul Garelli*
Mél. Güterbock	*Anatolian Studies Presented to Hans Gustav Güterbock on the Occasion of His 65th Birthday*
Mél. Hoffner	*Hittite Studies in Honor of Harry A. Hoffner Jr. on the Occasion of His 65th Birthday*
Mél. Kienast	*Festschrift für Burkhart Kienast zu seinem 70. Geburtstage dargebracht von Freuden, Schülern und Kollegen*
Mél. Kraus	Zikir šumim: *Assyriological Studies Presented to F. R. Kraus on the Occasion of His Seventieth Birthday*
Mél. Landsberger	*Studies in Honor of Benno Landsberger on His Seventy-Fifth Birthday, April 21, 1965*
Mél. Oppenheim	*From the Workshop of the Chicago Assyrian Dictionary: Studies Presented to A. Leo Oppenheim*
Mél. Orthmann	*Beiträge zur Vorderasiatischen Archäologie Winfried Orthmann gewidmet*
Mél. Perrot	*Contribution à l'histoire de l'Iran. Mélanges offerts à Jean Perrot*
Mél. Reiner	*Language, Literature, and History: Philological and Historical Studies Presented to Erica Reiner*
Mél. Röllig	Ana šadî Labnāni lū allik. *Beiträge zu altorientalischen und mittelmeerischen Kulturen. Festschrift für Wolfgang Röllig*
Mél. von Soden2	*Vom Alten Orient zum Alten Testament, Festschrift für Wolfram Freiherrn von Soden zum 85. Geburtstag am 19. Juni 1993*

Mél. Steve	*Fragmenta Historiae Elamicae, Mélanges offerts à M.-J. Steve*
Mél. Stol	*Studies in Ancient Near Eastern World View and Society Presented to Marten Stol on the Occasion of His 65th Birthday*
Mél. Veenhof	*Veenhof Anniversary Volume: Studies Presented to Klaas R. Veenhof on the Occasion of His Sixty-fifth Birthday*
Mél. Walker	*Mining the Archives: Festschrift für Christopher Walker on the Occasion of His 60th Birthday*
Mél. Wilcke	*Literatur, Politik und Recht in Mesopotamien. Festschrift C. Wilcke*
Mém. Albright.	*The Study of the Ancient Near East in the Twenty-first Century: The William Foxwell Albright Centennial Conference*
Mém. Jacobsen	*Riches Hidden in Secret Places: Ancient Near Eastern Studies in Memory of Thorkild Jacobsen*
Mém. Sachs	*A Scientific Humanist: Studies in Memory of Abraham Sachs*
MHEM	Mesopotamian History and Environment Memoirs
MHET	Mesopotamian History and Environment Texts
MSL	Materialien zum sumerischen Lexicon
NABU	*Nouvelles Assyriologiques Brèves et Utilitaires*
NAPR	*Northern Akkad Project Reports*
NBC	Nies Babylonian Collection, New Haven
OBO	Orbis Biblicus et Orientalis
OBO 160/4	*Mesopotamien: Die altbabylonische Zeit*
OIP	Oriental Institute Publications
OIS	Oriental Institute Seminars
OLA	Orientalia Lovaniensia Analecta
OLA 109	*Economy and Society in Northern Babylonia in the Early Old Babylonian Period (ca. 2000–1800* BC*)*
OPSNKF	Occasional Publications of the Samuel Noah Kramer Fund
OR	*Orientalia*
PBS	Publications of the Babylonian Section
PIHANS	Publications de l'Institut historique et archéologique néerlandais de Stamboul
PRU	Palais Royal d'Ugarit
PSD	*The Sumerian Dictionary of the University Museum of the University of Pennslyvania*
RA	*Revue d'Assyriologie et d'Archéologie orientale*

RB	*Revue biblique*
Recueil G. Dossin	*Recueil Georges Dossin. Mélanges d'Assyriologie (1934–1959)*
RHDFE	*Revue historique de droit français et étranger*
RlA	Reallexikon der Assyriologie und vorderasiatischen Archäologie
SAA	State Archives of Assyria
SAAS	State Archives of Assyria Series
SANE	Sources from the Ancient Near East
SCCNH	*Studies on the Civilization and Culture of Nuzi and the Hurrians*
SD	Studia et Documenta ad iura Orientis antiqui pertinentia
ShA 1	*The Shemshara Archives, vol. 1: The Letters*
SLB	Studia ad tabulas cuneiformes a de Liagre Böhl collectas pertinentia
StBOT	Studien zu den Boõazköz-Texten
TCL	Textes cunéiformes du Louvre
TCS	Texts from Cuneiform Sources
TIM	Texts in the Iraqi Museum
TUAT	Texte aus der Umwelt des Alten Testaments
VAB	Vorderasiatische Bibliothek
VAB 5	*Urkunden des Altbabylonischen Zivil- und Prozessrechts*
VS	Vorderasiatische Schriftdenkmäler
WAW	Writings from the Ancient World
WO	*Die Welt des Orients. Wissenschaftliche Beiträge zur Kunde des Morgenlandes*
WVDOG	Wissenschaftliche Veröffentlichungen der Deutschen Orient-Gesellschaft
YNER	Yale Near Eastern Researches
YOS	Yale Oriental Series
YTLR	Yale Tell Leilan Research
ZA	*Zeitschrift für Assyriologie und Vorderasiatische Archäologie*
ZABR	*Zeitschrift für Altorientalische und Biblische Rechtsgeschichte*

Introduction: The Historian's Task and Sources

Next to Egypt, Mesopotamia is the most ancient civilization that the historian can know in-depth through a study of texts.[1] These writings make it possible to felicitously complement the archaeological data, the only kind available for the earlier periods. The material vestiges still retain their full importance, however. First, they make an essential contribution to the knowledge of Mesopotamian civilization. Regional surveys allow us to study the spatial distribution of the sites, and, though the dangers of that approach have recently been highlighted, it remains essential for retracing the evolution of landscapes and settlements over the long term.[2] Excavations of the tells give us information about the cities, with their temples, palaces, and living quarters; the characteristics of Babylonian urbanism are beginning to surface.[3] It is regrettable, however, that peasants' villages, not to mention nomad encampments, are still notably absent from the archaeology of historical eras.[4] Sculpted or painted monuments offer a rich iconography that is of interest not only to art historians: a knowledge of these works is irreplaceable for the study of mentalities but also for political history.[5] This list is by no means exhaustive.

If archaeology remains at the center of the historian's task, it is also because all the written data we possess have come from excavations. Mesopotamia had no uninterrupted tradition that transmitted a corpus, such as the Bible or the texts of Greek and Roman antiquity. I must insist on the importance of the context within which inscribed monuments and documents are exhumed. Their physical relationship to one another is often

For more extensive reflections on this theme, see my essay in D. Charpin, D. O. Edzard, and M. Stol, OBO 160/4 (Fribourg: 2004): 39–56; and D. Charpin and N. Ziegler, *FM* V, Mémoires de NABU 6 (Paris: 2003), 8–27.

significant, and in studying them we must absolutely take into account how they were arranged in antiquity.[6] That is why illegal excavations cause irreparable damage.

Epigraphy, Philology, and History

To understand these texts, we must first overcome the difficulties of deciphering them.[7] It is here that the qualifications of the epigraphist are essential. Most of the documents are inscribed on clay tablets. But these are rarely intact: the material fragments of a single tablet must first be pieced together. There are often lacunae remaining, and a delicate labor is required to restore them. A knowledge of parallels allows at times for clear solutions, at others for less certain hypotheses. In addition, the cursive writing is sometimes hard to read, even when the tablets are well preserved. After that, we must attempt to translate the texts. At this point, the historian must become a philologist, and there is no end of problems. Of course, the Akkadian language is now very well known. But that is not true of Sumerian, and even less so of Hurrian and Elamite, which are much less frequently attested. Even in Akkadian, the meaning of certain words is still sometimes poorly defined. But a further problem lies in the need to provide translations that avoid anachronisms. Is it possible to speak of a "state minister" for the age of Hammurabi? And if objections are raised about that term because it is anachronistic, how are we to render the Babylonian *šukkallum*? "Vizier" sounds more Oriental but does not solve the problem. We must not be so paralyzed by such considerations that we refuse to translate,[8] since we do not hesitate to speak of "ministers" for the age of Louis XIV, even though the status of such officials was very different from that of present-day ministers.

Even once all these difficulties have been overcome, the task remains delicate. We must not fall victim to a naive reading of these texts, and that is where the qualifications of the historian proper come into play.[9] We must never forget that the scribe introduces a screen between ancient reality and the historian, both revealing that reality and acting as a filter. It is therefore necessary to study the training of these scribes so as to learn the conventions that governed the composition of the various sorts of writings and thereby learn to decode them correctly. Studies in diplomatics play a crucial and often misunderstood role here. The texts must also be situated within the series to which they belong: an isolated document can easily be misleading. In this realm, prosopographical research holds a central place.

The abundance of primary sources that were preserved in Mesopotamia should not deceive us; they represent only a small fraction of what existed. Certainly, the omnipresence of the written document in the Old Babylonian period is a striking phenomenon for the historian. The authorities responsible for guarding the borders received written documents that allowed them to let messengers or merchants pass through—or, on the contrary, to stop them. Because of the randomness governing which texts in particular were preserved, at times no copy of a certain type of document has come down to us, and it is only by collating different sources that we can establish its existence. Even when a few of these texts have survived, the question of the sample's representativeness must still be raised. Significantly, we possess only one letter from Zimri-Lim, king of Mari, relating to the assignment of a field to one of his servants, versus more than a hundred from a contemporary of his, Hammurabi, king of Babylon.[10] But that is sufficient for a comparison between the systems in the two kingdoms.

In short, the historian must always keep essential questions in mind: For what purpose was this text composed? How much is left implicit? Why was it preserved, and how did it come down to us?

The Importance of the Legal Sources

Why does a historian like myself, who is not a jurist by training, take so great an interest in Babylonian law, to the point of devoting many studies to it, culminating in the present book? The answers are many. First, there is the nature of the sources. A good share of them are made up of texts that the Babylonians set down in writing in the interest of avoiding legal disputes or of ending those that had already taken place. The first four centuries of the second millennium BCE,[11] the Old Babylonian period, to which most of this book is devoted,[12] was a very interesting time in the evolution of civilizations. Written evidence occupied an important place, and the transfer of deeds when property was alienated had very "modern" aspects about it. It must not be forgotten, however, that this was still an archaic civilization where magical practices played a major role, as demonstrated by the formulation of curses and the performance of symbolic gestures upon the conclusion of contracts between private individuals or alliances between rulers.

It should be mentioned, moreover, that the written word was also in the service of power. It was used largely by kings and their administrations to control the population. In that respect, censuses played an essential role, allowing the authorities to register, locality by locality, men to be mobilized in case of conflict.[13] Only nomads escaped that system: tribal solidarity was counted on to induce such men to go to war, and their leaders were bound to the king by a special oath.[14] The control exerted by means of writing extended to property as well. The overseers of the Crown lands had large registries in which were recorded the cadastral data on the fields allocated by the sovereign in exchange for the performance of a service (*ilkum*), and the beneficiaries kept the allocation document they had been given by the royal chancellery (*ṭuppi isihtim*). The cup-bearer to whom the king's luxury tableware was entrusted took regular inventories, particularly before and after the sovereign took a journey, which he never did without his gold and silver vessels.[15] After a conquest, the booty was also carefully inventoried,[16] and the names of prisoners were recorded.[17]

Law was the foremost preoccupation of rulers. The ideology of kingship made justice the first of the monarch's duties in a civilization where religion and politics were closely associated. As a result, it is essential that the historian not simply analyze the texts we call "codes of laws" but also consider in what context they were composed and what their status was. The sovereign intervened in legal life in the capacity of judge. Hammurabi's desire to be accessible to all, transcending the limits of space but also of time, led him to compose his famous code. The king had to please the god Shamash, a sun god who oversaw justice. And in his concern to bring comfort to the poorest people, the sovereign regularly proclaimed acts of amnesty (*mīšarum*), which led to the drafting of edicts. The historian is thus confronted with a problem: to what degree were royal texts actually applied? The code and the edicts differ in that regard. And did these royal texts replace a custom that had previously remained oral? There is no dearth of questions.

Finally, a study of the political relations among the many kingdoms that coexisted in the Old Babylonian period obliges us to reflect on the legal bases for diplomatic life. The Code of Hammurabi does not address any questions of international law. For the most part, it is via correspondence, and also by means of the texts of "treaties," that we can reconstitute the rules governing war and peace in the Near East of the Amorite period. A king declared war by sending a letter to the ruler he wished to attack, after an oracular consultation had given the king the gods' approval. At the end of the conflict, the deities were guarantors of the peace accords concluded. The monarchs exchanged tablets on which each had written the text of the pledge to which he wished his counterpart to subscribe. There again, the oral and the written were very closely linked, since the only thing that ultimately mattered was the oath pronounced by each king in front of his own gods and those of the other sovereign.

It is clear that politics, law, and religion were inextricably linked in Mesopotamian civilization, so that an overall approach is absolutely necessary if we wish to avoid sterile compartmentalization. This was a civilization prior to the Greek miracle, which J.-P. Vernant has rightly defined as a "process of change that led to the emergence, as so many distinctive domains, of the realms of economics, politics, law, art, science, ethics, and philosophy."[18] Previously, all these realms had constantly overlapped. Historians must study each of them, not neglecting any, if we wish our approach to account for ancient reality.

Structure

The organization of this book is fairly simple. Chapters 1 and 2 are devoted to the written sources generally. I shall begin by examining the question of literacy in ancient Mesopotamia, with particular emphasis on the Old Babylonian period. It is not inconsequential for the evaluation of the texts to know whether the scribes were the only ones in possession of writing or whether that knowledge was shared by many members of the elite. I shall then show that the documents can be analyzed from the standpoint both of their external and internal characteristics. Historians must be very familiar with the conventions governing the production of written texts if we are to avoid falling victim to illusions while reading them.

In chapters 3 and 4, I seek to define the status of the legal texts found in the archives. I shall show that their composition corresponds to only one aspect of a larger process, which entailed the performance of symbolic gestures and the utterance of formulaic words. Nevertheless, it is clear that written evidence played an increasingly important role as the Old Babylonian period progressed, so that the transfer of property deeds became a crucial phenomenon. There again, it is essential that the historian understand how the family archives found in living quarters were constituted if we are to avoid errors when using them to reconstruct economic and social life.

The king enters the scene in chapter 5, in which I study the sovereign as promulgator of the "codes of laws." I shall present both the written sources for these collections and the uses that were made of them. In chapter 6, I shall proceed to examine the edicts that the Babylonian monarchs promulgated and the identifiable traces of their application.

The last two chapters are studies on international law. Chapter 7 focuses on diplomatic life in the age of Hammurabi. Messengers at that time often played a role similar to that of true ambassadors. Wars began with actual declarations, the text of which has sometimes come down to us. They ended with the conclusion of treaties. These texts were only proposals, not all of which were ratified. In chapter 8, I attempt to elucidate the role of borders and how control was exerted over those who, by virtue of their status, were led to cross them continually: merchants, messengers, and nomads.

CHAPTER 1

Reading and Writing in Mesopotamia: The Business of Specialists?

Mesopotamian documentation, written in cuneiform signs, displays several noteworthy characteristics.[1] First, let me insist on its longevity: it originated in about 3200 BCE, and the last dated text was written in 75 CE. From the start, clay was the privileged support. The term "cuneiform," in fact, refers to the appearance of the signs, resulting from the arrangement of wedges (in Latin, *cunei*) formed by the impression of a reed calamus on a clay tablet. There were considerable advantages to that support, beginning with its low cost, despite the length of time it took to prepare the clay. The plasticity of the material allowed for a great variety of forms, depending on the era and the kind of text. But clay also had disadvantages. The first was its weight: the larger a tablet, the thicker, and thus heavier, it had to be. Scribes also had to know in advance the length of the text to be inscribed so that they could fashion a tablet of the appropriate size. Finally, no corrections or additions could be made once the tablet had been dried in the sun.[2]

Cuneiform writing is a mixed system, entailing both logograms (one sign representing one word) and phonograms (one sign representing one syllable). There were about six hundred signs in the repertoire, and they usually had several logographic *and* phonetic values. Seen from outside, that system appears very complicated. Traditionally, Assyriologists have maintained that its use was reserved for a caste of specialists, namely, scribes, who alone could master cuneiform, and only after a long training period. I shall situate my analysis within the context of recent studies of the phenomenon of literacy, which is currently the object of a debate in

The initial version of this chapter was published under the title "Lire et écrire en Mésopotamie: Une affaire de spécialistes?" in *Comptes rendus de l'Académie des inscriptions et belles lettres* (session of March 26, 2004) (2006), 481–508.

Assyriology, as delineated in the excellent overview edited by Jack Sasson.[3] Some authors continue to embrace the traditional view. Laury Pearce, for example, notes that "scribes functioned in a society in which the vast majority of people were illiterate";[4] and Piotr Michalowski claims that "literacy was always highly restricted in the Ancient Near East, and only an elite, scribes as well as government and temple officials—could read and write."[5] A more nuanced position is expressed by Hermann Vanstiphout, who begins by declaring that "a first structural aspect of literacy can be said to consist in the social function fulfilled by literati. We know from the mass of documents that almost every aspect of life was subject to a detailed administration, much of which was, of course, kept in writing and, therefore, by literates."[6] He continues, "The spread and rate of literacy . . . is very uncertain. But the overwhelming importance of written documents in all walks of life suggests that literacy was more extensive than primary sources report." J. N. Postgate goes even further in that direction. In his overview *Early Mesopotamia* (1992), he points out that widespread literacy at the beginning of the second millennium BCE can be demonstrated on the basis of several indications: the private and often trivial content of letters as well as the frequency of inscribed clay labels, attached, for example, to the necks of animals who died accidentally. He concludes, "Writing had reached to the most mundane levels of society."[7]

1. Who Could Read and Write?

For a long time, the focus was placed on a few exceptions to what was believed to be the exclusive realm of professional scribes. I shall therefore examine, first, the case of kings, the clergy, and merchants. Next, I shall indicate what arguments Claus Wilcke has developed to show that, in the late third and the second millennia BCE, writing was more widespread than is usually believed. Finally, I will set out the arguments recently advanced in light of discoveries in the Mari archives that confirm this way of seeing things.

1.1. The Exceptions Traditionally Recognized

Three rulers in Mesopotamian history are known to have laid claim to the status of "literates": Shulgi, king of Ur, in the first half of the twenty-first century BCE; Lipit-Eshtar, king of Isin, in the second half of the twentieth century BCE; and, much later, Ashurbanipal, king of Assyria, in the mid-seventh century BCE.

Let me begin with Shulgi. In Hymn A, he exclaims, "I am the sage scribe of the goddess Nisaba!"[8] Hymn B exalts the king's mastery of writing but also of divination and music.[9]

The literacy of Lipit-Eshtar, king of Isin, is also celebrated in Hymn B, where the ruler is addressed as follows: "The goddess Nisaba, the woman who radiates joy,/The reliable woman-scribe, lady of all knowledge,/Guided your fingers over the clay,/She made your writing on the tablets beautiful,/She made your hand resplendent with a calamus of gold."[10] The case of Ashurbanipal is the best known. In a famous inscription, the neo-Assyrian king sketches his self-portrait. He claims to excel in all realms of the written word:

> The god Marduk, the sage among gods, offered me as a present vast understanding and profound intelligence. The god Nabu, scribe of the universe, gave me as a gift the precepts of wisdom. The gods Ninurta and Nergal endowed my body with heroic power and physical strength without equal. I studied the art of the sage Adapa, the hidden knowledge of the entire art of the scribe. I know the ominous signs of heaven and earth. I can discuss them in the assembly of scholars. I am able to debate the series "If the liver is the reflection of heaven" with the expert diviners. I can solve the complicated divisions and multiplications that have no solution. I have read complex texts, the Sumerian version of which is encrypted, and the Akkadian version, difficult to clarify. I have examined inscriptions on stone from before the flood, whose meaning is hidden, obscure, and murky.[11]

Ashurbanipal presents himself as an expert in divination, mathematics, ancient languages, and epigraphy, but also as a sage and an accomplished sportsman. In other words, what we have here is a heroic description of the ruler, which in itself might inspire skepticism about the king's real proficiency in reading and writing. There are also other, more conclusive types of evidence, however, such as the colophons on tablets recopied for his library of Nineveh: "Ashurbanipal, great king, strong king, king of the universe, king of Assyria, son of Asharhaddon, king of Assyria, son of Sennacherib, king of Assyria. In accordance with the content of the clay tablets and wooden polyptychs, versions of Assyria, Sumer, and Akkad, I wrote, verified, and collated this tablet in the assembly of scholars; and in order that it shall be read by my Majesty, I placed it in my palace. Whoever shall efface my inscribed name and inscribe his name, may the god Nabu, scribe of the universe, efface his name!"[12]

In addition, the letters he received from an astrologist named Nabuahhe-eriba contain many glosses. Pierre Villard revisited this case a few years ago and drew a moderate conclusion regarding Ashurbanipal's skills: "There is no reason to place in doubt his interest in the scribal disciplines; conversely, we must refrain from exaggerating the importance of the theme of the literate king in royal propaganda. The motif is, for example, totally absent from the bas-reliefs, though their programs were elaborated in accordance with the ruler's directives."[13]

Does this evidence, limited to three kings, mean that the other Mesopotamian rulers were illiterate? That is the claim of the famous Assyriologist Benno Landsberger: "In the long history of Mesopotamia only these three kings even claimed to know how to read and write. This emphasizes, I believe, both the closed character of the scribal corporation and the dependence of the palace on the specialized services that the scribes provided."[14] There are serious reasons for calling that conclusion into doubt. Let me note at this point that, in one of his inscriptions, Asharhaddon, father of Ashurbanipal, also claimed to know how to write.[15] It was he who began to assemble tablets in Nineveh; Ashurbanipal, in constituting his library, was only continuing his father's work.

Then there is the case of the neo-Babylonian king Nabonidus. In one of his inscriptions it is claimed that "the god Nabu, administrator of the universe, gave him the art of writing."[16] But in a satirical tract (the Verse Account), likely compiled by the priests of Marduk in Babylon against their king, he is made to say the opposite: "Even though I don't know how to write cuneiform, I have seen secret things."[17] It is obvious that this "confession" was aimed at discrediting the ruler and casting aspersions on his religious reforms,[18] and surely this polemical text must not be taken seriously. On one hand, then, is the topos of royal rhetoric inherited from Ashurbanipal, on the other, polemics. It is therefore impossible to know whether Nabonidus was really able to write cuneiform or not.[19] We may at least suspect that he had mastered Aramaic writing.

The second category of potential literati, apart from the scribes, was composed of the clergy. Their mastery of writing has long been placed in doubt, as attested by this categorical view, once again put forward by Landsberger: "One must castigate as false romanticism the conception of the so-called *Priesterweisheit,* still to be found in secondary handbooks. The scribes, although a great number of them were deeply religious, were completely a lay group. The priests as well as the kings (not counting some exceptions among the latter), and the governors, and the judges were illiterate."[20]

I believe I have demonstrated in my book on the clergy of Ur what an overstatement this is. In reality, epigraphic discoveries in the houses of certain priests in charge of the main local temple attest to the writing exercises they engaged in at home.[21] It is now possible to cite more recent evidence, provided by a house in Sippar-Amnānum, from which nearly a hundred school tablets have been recovered.[22] In all probability, the teacher was the scribe who often worked for Inanna-mansum, chief lamenter (*gala-mah*) of the goddess Annunitum; the pupil must have been his son and successor, Ur-Utu. That son, therefore, was given an education in literacy. But an analysis of the curriculum revealed by these tablets shows that the level of proficiency he reached was not very high. It was enough that he know the basics: how to read and write.[23]

The case of the Old Assyrian merchants is the best known. These were traders from Assur who, in the first quarter of the second millennium BCE, established trading posts in faraway Anatolia, the most important and best known being that of Kanesh, near present-day Kayseri. Landsberger believed they had used scribes: "Private use of scribes was quite limited. The only exception was the Assyrian colonies, where all the merchants had scribes."[24] But since the 1970s, a consensus has been reached that most of these businessmen were able to read and write. The first author to my knowledge to have made the claim was Johannes Renger.[25] Studying the Akkadian syllabary, Renger noted that the Old Assyrian repertoire was particularly limited, which suggests that the mastery of writing by the merchants themselves must not have raised tremendous difficulties. That point of view was elaborated by Mogens T. Larsen: "There are indications that a great many Assyrians knew how to read and write so the need for privately employed scribes may not have been so great. The system of writing was highly simplified with only a limited number of syllabic signs and quite a few logograms, and many of the outrageously hideous private documents constitute clear proof of the amateurishness of their writers. We know for certain that some of the sons of important merchants were taught scribal art in Assur . . . In spite of these observations it must be assumed that the big firms did have their own scribes."[26]

The Old Assyrian merchants were in no way an exception, as Larsen himself has shown. In particular, we know of merchants from Larsa, in southern Iraq, who in about 1780 were visiting the kingdom of Eshnunna, east of present-day Baghdad. Leemans has noted that the letters they wrote at the time all had the characteristics of the letters from Larsa, not those from Eshnunna. Hence these merchants did not make use of the services of local scribes. Leemans concluded that they had taken a scribe with them; Larsen argued, with much more likelihood, that this was proof that they themselves wrote their correspondence.[27]

1.2. A New Approach

Most Assyriologists, therefore, believe that writing in Mesopotamia was the privilege of a tiny minority, though some concede a few special cases. In a book written in 2000, Wilcke called that consensus into question.[28] His study, which deals primarily with the period from the end of the third to the beginning of the second millennium BCE, rests on three inquiries. First, he examines the archaeological data. His view is that if the residents of ancient Mesopotamia were able to read and write, traces must have been left in the settlement areas. Unfortunately, most of our documentation comes from illicit or old excavations, undertaken at a time when little care was taken to observe and record the archaeological context. Wilcke tries to collect all the cases where tablets were found in houses. He shows that in every era, the proportion of residences where tablets were preserved was large, between one quarter and one third in Assur, more than half in Ur, and so on. It seems to me that this inventory must be qualified in two ways. On one hand, the districts excavated were those inhabited by the elite. On the other, preserving one's property deeds, debt records, and so on in one's archives does not necessarily mean one could read these texts, much less write them.

Wilcke's second approach consists of identifying in the texts themselves evidence that they were written by the interested parties. He cites a few documents that use the first person in a way that he argues is revealing. He also systematically studies two expressions frequently found in letters—"*upon seeing* my present tablet" alternates with "*in listening to* my present tablet"—and argues that the permutation is significant. In the first case, we may deduce that the letter's recipient was able to read it himself without resorting to the services of a scribe.

The third part of Wilcke's study is devoted to the deviations from the norm found in the texts, deviations he considers a sign that they were written by a nonprofessional. He is especially interested in phonetic notations of Sumerian in the contracts of the Ur III period (end of the third millennium BCE).[29] His conclusion is twofold. On one hand, he maintains that the mastery of writing was not confined to professionals alone, that is, to scribes: it was also exercised by members of the social elite, both men and women.[30] But Wilcke qualifies his assertion by arguing, on the other hand, that a passive knowledge of writing (knowing how to read) was certainly more developed than an active knowledge (knowing how to write).

1.3. The Data from Mari

Up to now, the data from the royal archives of Mari have rarely been put to use in support of this matter. Yet they provide a great deal of information on the subject.[31] One of the first questions to resolve is how letters were put in writing. Were they dictated to scribes? Were the main lines of the message given to scribes, who themselves composed the text? And more generally, who was able to read and write letters?

For a long time, the prevailing view was that the upper echelons of society were fundamentally illiterate. That is the belief of Jack Sasson, an expert on the Mari archives. He writes, concerning the reading of letters, "Written statements were read aloud by scribes to illiterate officials."[32]

It is not possible, of course, to give an exhaustive list of the officials who knew how to read. But the idea that, in this kingdom on the Middle Euphrates in the eighteenth century BCE, the possessors of power depended entirely on professional scribes to have their mail read to them is manifestly inaccurate. Several texts show that high officials in Mari—administrators, members of the military, diviners, and kings—were able to read and write letters on their own.

It is becoming increasingly clear that the top administrators at the Mari palace knew how to read and write. Hence, in the era of Yahdun-Lim, in the late nineteenth century BCE, the highest palace official, Hamatil, was described as a "scribe" on his seal.[33] It is known that, a few decades later, under Zimri-Lim, Yasim-Sumu, described on his latest seal as "chief bookkeeper" (*šandabakkum*), had originally had a seal on which he bore the title of scribe (*ṭupšarrum*).[34] The steward Mukannishum, whose importance for the management of artisanal products is well known, is called "scribe" in one text,[35] "steward" (*šatammum*) in another,[36] and his was not an isolated case.[37] It is an open question, however, how far their proficiency went. No doubt an initial distinction must be made regarding the type of text: it is very probable, given the great difference in literary genres, that some people were able to read and write administrative texts but not letters. In fact, the archives of Shemshara, a city located on the Little Zab in Iraqi Kurdistan, have very clearly demonstrated the cultural cleavage existing between scribes of letters[38] and those who wrote bookkeeping documents, who were clearly less well educated.[39]

That difference can be explained by the fact that many administrative texts contain only numbers, logograms, and proper names. Yet there is a tendency to forget, in our Western culture with its alphabetic obsession, that logograms, when they are limited in number—which was the case here—are much easier to use than phonetic signs. Take the example of a letter from Bahdi-Lim regarding tribal chiefs who had come to find him for the census. The governor of Mari wrote to the king: "So I've written a tablet concerning their people, locality by locality, and have just sent it to my lord."[40] If Bahdi-Lim had made use of a scribe to write that tablet, he would have used, as he did elsewhere, the factitive form of the verb "write" (*šaṭārum*): "I had [it] written." Most likely, therefore, Bahdi-Lim personally inscribed that tablet, a mere list of proper names. This passage does not prove, however, that Bahdi-Lim could write letters, though I find that very likely.

There were a certain number of cases where an official seems to have written a letter himself—Itur-Asdu, for example, governor of several cities of the kingdom of Mari. "Thus far, I have not sent any message to my lord. [At present], I shall write the news on a tablet."[41] The use of the infinitive *šaṭārum*, ("write") normally denotes the work of a scribe; someone who makes use of a scribe's services uses the factitive (*šuṭṭurum* or *šušṭurum*). It appears, therefore, that Itur-Asdu wrote his own correspondence, at least in part. A letter sent by Iddin-Dagan to Darish-libur shows that the recipient, one of the most highly placed administrators in the Mari palace, also knew how to write.[42] His correspondent addressed him as follows: "At present, if you are truly my brother and if you love me, write me all the news you heard from the king's mouth and have it brought to me."

The same was true at a lower level. Consider, first, a letter in which the steward Enlil-ipush wrote to Zimri-Lim: "The tablet of my lord, which Ka'alalum and Hammurabi brought me, was effaced; hence I could not read it."[43] Perhaps the surface of the tablet had been damaged when it was placed in an envelope, or when the envelope was opened. In any event, it is clear that Enlil-ipush read his own mail.

A letter from Yassi-Dagan is interesting for the distinction it makes, among the governors of Qaṭṭunan, between uneducated persons and the recipient of the letter, Ilushu-naṣir, who was a scribe by training: "Previously, Akin-urubam the Bedouin was vested with the function of governor in Qaṭṭunan, then it was Iddin-Annu, a fool with no experience, who was installed there."[44] Yassi-Dagan proceeds in the letter to enumerate the misfortunes he suffered under these two governors and expresses his hope that everything will change thanks to the competence of the new arrival: "Now [it is] you, a clear-eyed scribe who, since your early childhood, were brought up at the gates of the palace."

Given the number of statements it is possible to gather,[45] the unavoidable conclusion seems to be that the administrators, both in the capital and in the rest of the kingdom of Mari, were for the most part able to read and write on their own, not only bookkeeping texts but also their correspondence.

It might appear that these cases are rather insignificant. After all, it is not surprising that an official in the administration would know how to read. It is a priori more astonishing for a member of the military, however. Yet there is proof that General Yasim-El was literate. Zimri-Lim had sent him secret tablets with the instructions: "These tablets, read them yourself and read them out to Himdiya."[46] These instructions show that, normally, Yasim-El must have had his mail read to him by a scribe. In this case, since it was a confidential matter, he was obliged to read the tablets himself and then, word for word, "have them heard by Himdiya," that is, read them aloud to him.

Yasim-El does not represent an unusual case, as is indicated by a missive from a certain Menihum regarding tablets he had received from the kingdom of Eshnunna: "And the very day I learned of them, I took them to my lord; Yassi-Dagan read them at the same time I did."[47] This statement can be explained in terms of the suspicion that always fell on an official who received mail from abroad. He was obliged by an oath to send the tablet on to the king,[48] which Menihum hastened to do. But he added that Yassi-Dagan, known from another source to be a general, read the tablets at the same time as Menihum, who therefore could not possibly be accused of complicity with the enemy.

Yasim-El and Yassi-Dagan were both generals. A third general also seems to have known how to read. Yasim-Dagan, unhappy with the king's secretary, threatened to go personally to read his tablet to the ruler. "It is sworn by the patron god of my lord: I will go have my lord listen to my present tablet!"[49] It is clear that at this point Yasim-Dagan was planning to take the place of the royal secretary. If we had only this passage, we might have some doubt about the reality of the threat; but that doubt is dissipated by the fact that we have already had two examples of generals who knew how to read.

Is it by chance that, among officials, it is particularly military men who are attested as being literate? That is possible, of course, but I cannot help thinking that, for obvious reasons of security, a general had to be able to oversee his mail personally and even read it without the services of a scribe. Similarly, a general had to possess a certain education in divination so that he could evaluate the conclusions of the diviner(s) who accompanied him.[50]

Lower-ranking heads of troops, such as Ushtashni-El, also seem to have known how to read. In fact, when Ushtashni-El declared that he was awaiting a written order from Zimri-Lim before he would obey one of the king's envoys, Ulluri, he expressed himself as follows: "So long as I have not read [literally, "seen"] the tablet of my lord, I will not leave the city of Ilan-Ṣura."[51]

One of the letters from Yamṣum, dramatic in tone, seems to indicate that that soldier was also able to read: "Before the straps were placed across the gate [that is, before nightfall], a tablet of my lord arrived. I read [literally, "saw"] it at that very moment, and in my heart darkness descended!"[52] The use of the verb "see" (*amārum*) in this context truly gives the impression that Yamṣum read on the spot the letter addressed to him. The question of who wrote the "barbarian tablets" sent from Ilan-Ṣura is consequently raised anew.[53] It is very possible that it was the head of the Mari garrison in person, Yamṣum. He could have written some of his own letters and thus, perhaps, a part of the correspondence of Princess Kirum, to whom he was very close.

Let me cite one last case, which comes not from the Mari archives themselves but from the contemporary site of Shemshara. Larsen has remarked that a good number of the letters found in the palace of that city display marks indicating that they had been recycled. He drew this conclusion: "Some of the Shemshara letters are really palimpsests, which means that a travelling political agent in the valleys of the Zagros mountains would have to write his own letters, even reusing the tablets which had been sent to him after the original message had been more or less erased."[54]

The art of the diviner and that of the scribe were both distinct and complementary, as demonstrated by a letter from Sammetar dealing with a child to be trained: "Let him learn the art of the scribe (*ṭupšarrūtum*) and that of the diviner (*bārūtum*)!"[55] This passage shows that the two disciplines were distinguished but does not allow us to say whether that of diviner presupposed the acquisition of the scribe's art. On this matter, I part ways with Sasson, who maintains that diviners were for the most part illiterate:

> Most diviners cited in the Mari archives did not know how to write. Durand (ARM 26/1, p. 61–62) thinks that Asqudum and perhaps Erib-Sin were literate. Still, it is unlikely that the same child was schooled in the scribal as well as the divinatory arts. Durand [ARM 26/1, 63n314] . . . cites a text where a child was to be trained in *ṭupšarrūtum* and/or *bārūtum,* which may prove the rarity of the coincidence. At any rate, the sheer number of diviners in any OB [Old Babylonian] court at a time when literacy was highly restricted, makes this conclusion probable. In fact, much as other officers of the realm, divin-

> ers called on scribes to share their findings with the king. But while they did not read cuneiform, diviners certainly knew how to "read" the markings on clay models of livers.[56]

In reality, the only instance I know of regarding the use of a scribe in this context concerns not a diviner but a prophet, the famous *āpilum* of the god Shamash.[57] According to Sasson, many diviners, having ceased to practice their art, subsequently "made a career" in the administration: "For the most ambitious diviners, the goal was to penetrate the king's closest circles, to become a member of his cabinet, and so be in a position to give up their trade. This hypothesis explains the curious situation in which some of Zimri-Lim's most trusted governors, military leaders, and diplomats, among which are people like Ibal-pi-El, Ilušu-naṣir, Išhi-Addu, Itur-asdu, Nur-Addu and the like, have the same names as certified diviners. They probably were the same people, at different stages of their careers."[58] I do not know whether the diviner Ilushu-naṣir and the governor of Qaṭṭunan were the same person, as Sasson thinks. But if they were, this would be one more example of a dual training as scribe and as diviner.[59] An additional case is provided by the archives of Shemshara. A series of letters sent from the city of Kunshum by different persons, including King Pishenden, was written by a certain Sin-ishmeanni, who was a diviner.[60]

The question arises whether some kings appearing in the Mari archives may have been able to read (or write) their correspondence themselves. A first parallel can be established with divination. Durand has shown that members of the elite were able to comment on an omen on their own.[61] If they could decipher the signs of the gods on a liver, it is likely that they could also read the cuneiform signs on a tablet. Note that the child who was said in a letter to be about to receive dual training as a scribe and as a diviner[62] was destined for the throne.

Consider the interesting case of Ishme-Dagan, king of Ekallatum, in the early eighteenth century BCE. After failing for a long time to write to his brother Yasmah-Addu with news of himself, Ishme-Dagan gave as an excuse the absence of a certain Limi-Addu, who had obviously served as his secretary: "Previously, you sent me a letter, but I had just returned from an expedition and had sent Limi-Addu to organize his domain. There was no one to write a complete report; hence I did not send you a response to your letter."[63]

It is unlikely that there were no other scribes at the time in Ishme-Dagan's entourage. What was lacking was a scribe who could write a *ṭēmum gamrum,* which is generally translated as "complete report" and which can here be understood to be a "detailed letter." This passage should therefore not be used as proof that Ishme-Dagan was unable to write a letter. On the contrary, Nele Ziegler, who examined in detail the many missives Ishme-Dagan sent to his brother Yasmah-Addu, king of Mari, has been able to identify a batch of tablets with very recognizable handwriting, which deal with particularly private subjects. They seem to have been written by Ishme-Dagan personally. We therefore have the sense that Ishme-Dagan could write, but that for a letter of a certain scope, what was at the time called a "complete report," he needed a particularly well-trained professional scribe.

A letter from Zimri-Lim to his steward Mukannishum might give the impression that this king of Mari knew how to read, but the interpretation of the text is not certain. In the Archives Royales de Mari XVIII 16+, Zimri-Lim is depicted choosing the inscription to be engraved on a statue for the temple of the god Addu of Aleppo. Two drafts were composed, the first by a certain Nab-Eshtar, the second by another scribe whose name has not been preserved.[64] The king wrote to Mukannishum: "Hence, as for the votive inscription [*narūm*] to have written [on the statue], quickly send me the votive inscription that [PN_1] made, as well as the one made by Nab-Eshtar, so that I may see them and have the votive inscription I have chosen taken [to you]." Note the use of the verb "see" (*amārum*): if Zimri-Lim had not wished (or been able) to read the two texts personally, he might have expressed himself differently ("so that I can have them read to me").

Finally, the gods themselves supposedly knew how to read and write. Tablets containing prayers to be answered by them were placed before their statues. The gods could on occasion send letters to kings,[65] though the ancients did not conceal the fact that the deities used intermediaries to do so.[66] Conversely, the gods themselves inscribed on the livers of sacrificed sheep the answers to the questions that the diviners asked of them. The surface of the liver was in fact sometimes explicitly compared to that of a tablet. Moreover, the deities could use a larger support, the heavens, to inscribe the signs they addressed to men. Astrologists were given the task of deciphering these signs.

2. Why Cuneiform Writing Was Not as Difficult to Master as Is Believed

If it was long believed that the knowledge of cuneiform was very limited in ancient times, that is because the art of the scribe was held to be difficult—a manner, unconscious no doubt, for Assyriologists to assert their own value. Since it appears that the practice of cuneiform, at least at a rudimentary level, in fact was fairly widespread, it must be explained how that was possible. Two different lines of argument have been advanced. Some authors have demonstrated that cuneiform writing was not as difficult to master as is currently believed. Others have emphasized that there is no connection between the objective difficulty of a writing system and the literacy rate of the population that uses it. In any event, these two ways of thinking are not mutually exclusive.

2.1. A Writing System Less Complex than It Appears

What is the source of the supposed difficulty of cuneiform writing? It lies first in the number of signs and second in the number of different values. Epigraphy manuals list about six hundred different signs,[67] and each sign could have several logographic and several phonetic values. Hence, in the Old Babylonian period, the sign UR could designate the logogram UR, "dog" (sometimes in combination with another logogram: UR.MAH, "lion") as well as the syllable *ur,* and more rarely *lik* and *taš*. The total number of possibilities was very high. But these considerations must be qualified by two remarks. Not all the values are attested in every period: the knowledge of the present-day epigraphist must not be confused with that of the person in antiquity, who needed to know only the repertoire in use in his or her own time. And above all, not all the values are attested in every kind of text. Different studies have thus dealt with particular periods and given an inventory of the real needs of readers.

The first area studied was Old Assyrian writing, attested for the most part by the archives of merchants living in Cappadocia in the nineteenth century BCE. The syllabary was very limited at the time, so it was possible to write with a minimum syllabary of sixty-eight signs.[68] Moreover, unique in the history of cuneiform writing, there were signs that served as word separators. And finally, the content of certain texts has persuaded several Assyriologists that the ability to read and write was widespread among the Old Assyrian merchants. Let me add—and to my knowledge no one has as yet noticed this—that in Old Assyrian, unlike in Old Babylonian, there was no difference between the ordinary syllabary and that used for the notation of the names of persons. That Babylonian phenomenon of conservatism represents a further difficulty from which the Old Assyrian merchants were free.

During the same period in Babylonia, however, the situation was not a great deal more complicated. It was possible for Old Babylonian scribes to write a text with a minimum syllabary of eighty-two signs, provided they did not use heavy syllables (that is, provided they wrote not *kum*, but *ku-um*). But even without that restriction, the syllabary remained fairly limited. Goetze, in publishing divinatory texts in the Yale Oriental Series (10), counted 112 syllabic signs and 57 logograms in the corpus he was editing, figures that can be taken for representative.[69]

How had the situation developed a millennium later? Simo Parpola has republished a letter dating from the apogee of the neo-Assyrian empire. A few collations and an assessment of the particular syllabary of that letter allowed him to provide a new translation: "To the king my lord: your servant Sin-na'di. Good health to the king my lord! I have no scribe where my lord has sent me. May the king order the governor of Arrapha or Assur-belu-taqqin to send me one."[70]

This was under the reign of Sargon II (721–705 BCE), and Assur-belu-taqqin was governor of Me-Turan at the time. The author of the letter was undoubtedly on a mission in the high valley of Diyala without a scribe to accompany him. He thus must have written the letter himself, which explains the peculiarities—even blunders—it contains. The analysis Parpola conducted[71] led him to conclude that the author of that letter had to have mastered 112 signs (79 syllabic signs and 33 logograms).[72] This shows that the knowledge of cuneiform in the neo-Assyrian empire was no less advanced than in Assur or Babylonia in the early second millennium BCE, contrary to what most Assyriologists believe.[73]

All in all, the knowledge of cuneiform, at least beginning in the late third millennium BCE, was never exclusive to scribes,[74] but was in part shared by members of the ruling class as well. No doubt that phenomenon was made possible by a cuneiform writing of lesser complexity than is generally indicated. But let us also not forget that there is no direct link between the supposed difficulty of learning a writing system and the percentage of the population able to use it:[75] contemporary Japan has a lower illiteracy rate than France.

2.2. Silent Reading?

In the cuneiform world, was reading aloud the only practice or is silent reading also attested? As far as I know, that question has never been the object of systematic research in Assyriology, though it has been addressed many times by specialists in classical antiquity.[76]

When someone read a tablet to another, he "had [him] listen" (*šušmūm*) to it. The one who learned of its content, whether he read it himself or had it read to him, "listened" (*šemūm*) to it. In all cases, then, the text was read aloud, as the following letter shows: "Tell Shu-nuhra-Halu: thus speaks Habdu-Malik. I did not have you take a duplicate of the tablet intended for the king, since there is never anyone but you to read aloud the news contained in a tablet addressed to the king, and no one else has ever had occasion to do it. So I had one tablet taken twice: once for the king and [once] for you. I am sending a very urgent message. Listen to this tablet. If it is appropriate, have the king listen to it."[77]

Habdu-Malik does not distinguish here between the reading that Shu-nuhra-Halu does for himself and that which he must do for the king. It is the same verb, "listen," that is used, either in the simple form (*šemūm*) or in the factitive (*šušmūm*). That conclusion is confirmed by the fact that the verb "read" (*šitassūm*) is a form of a verb whose primary meaning is "cry out, call."[78]

One text may suggest, however, that some scribes practiced silent reading. Hulalum, who was the private secretary of Samsi-Addu, wrote as follows to Yasmah-Addu: "Tell my lord: thus speaks your servant Hulalum. With the tablets that they brought for the king [Samsi-Addu] from Qaṭna, the Qatnean messengers brought the king by mistake a tablet intended for my lord [Yasmah-Addu]. Having opened it, I saw that it was written to my lord[79] and I thus did not have the king listen to it. At present, I have just brought that tablet to my lord."[80]

In this case, then, the secretary of Samsi-Addu prepared to read the mail by breaking open the envelopes of the letters and acquainting himself with their content before reading them to his master. It is interesting to observe the distinction Hulalum makes between the reading he himself practices (*amur,* "I saw") and that which he may do for the king (*ul ušešme,* "I did not have [him] listen"). We might of course surmise that in this case Hulalum chose his words in haste. Nevertheless, he could have written, "having opened the letter, I listened [*ešmēšu*] to it and I observed [*āmur*] etc.," and he did not do so. This might therefore be taken as evidence that silent reading was already being practiced by the Mesopotamian scribes.[81]

2.3. The Reading of Public Inscriptions

I shall conclude by citing the epilogue to the famous Code of Hammurabi.[82] The king of Babylon declared: "May the wronged man who faces trial come before the statue of me as king of justice, may he read my inscribed stela, may he hear my precious words, may my stela show him his case and may he see its verdict."

The traditional translation of the passage is "may he have my stela read out," but the text actually says, "may he read." The next words show that the king is imagining someone reading to himself out loud ("may he hear"). No doubt this is a vain hope: How could a mere subject of Hammurabi have been able to find his case among the some 275 laws in the code? This would have been especially difficult in that the layout for the stela provided no guidelines. Nonetheless, we must not believe that it was because the people of the kingdom were illiterate that they were unable to read that stela.

A recently published text from Mari demonstrates that this was not the case.[83] The "chief accountant" Yasim-Sumu wrote to his master, King Zimri-Lim, "I have just sent to my lord the inscription for the chariot of the god Nergal and the inscription for the palanquin of the god Itur-Mer. Should the inscription of Nergal be written on the front or on the back of the chariot? May my lord reflect on the fact that the inscription should be inscribed on the back of the chariot, where the coat of arms is located, so that whoever will [see?] and the reader can read it. Also, should the inscription on the palanquin . . . be written on the front or on the back? May my lord write me one or the other, so that before my lord's departure these inscriptions shall be engraved." That letter from Mari has the advantage of being less suspect of ideology and at the same time more realistic than the passage from the Code of Hammurabi cited above. It seems clear that, in Yasim-Sumu's mind, a portion of the people assembled on the procession route might have been able to read these inscriptions.

Conclusion

What did they read and write? In my view, that is the heart of the problem. In studying a few recent works on the Greek world, I was struck by the almost exclusive emphasis they placed on the book. There is usually not a single passage dealing with letters. The reason for that situation would seem to be twofold. It lies first in the nature of the available sources; and second, in the fact that the works in question take the traditional history of the book as their starting point, a history that the authors wanted to expand, in particular by taking readers and modes of reading into consideration. The collection edited by G. Cavallo and R. Chartier[84] seems to me very clear in that regard.

In Mesopotamia, the situation was very different: first, for reasons having to do with the available documentation; and second, because correspondence constituted one of the principal uses of writing. Writing was not so much for storing *knowledge* as for communicating *information* long-distance. The paradox is that this mass of writings on matters of short-term interest has been preserved because of the nature of the clay support, which is resistant to both fire and water, the two great enemies of written documents.

The large quantity of cuneiform texts must not conceal the truth from us: the transmission of knowledge in Mesopotamian civilization was primarily an oral affair. It is not by chance that rituals were only very rarely put in writing before the first millennium BCE. The most explicit texts, in fact, date to not before the Seleucid period. It was only then that the idea arose that these texts would thereby be rescued from the danger of oblivion. The different traditions relating to the transmission of the diviner's knowledge are illuminating in this respect. Mesopotamian ideology, which Berossus echoed in the Hellenistic period, denied human beings any discoveries. Knowledge was bequeathed to them at the dawn of time by Oannes, the sage from before the Flood. Berossus explains, "Since that time, nothing else has been discovered."[85] The problem therefore arises as to how knowledge could have been transmitted at the time of the Flood, which ought to have entailed a rupture. One text explains that the secret knowledge of divination was originally entrusted by Shamash and Adad—patron gods of the discipline—to Enmeduranki, a king of Sippar from before the Flood. He in turn transmitted these mysteries to men of Nippur, Sippar, and Babylon, who since that time bequeathed them from father to son. The master who communicates his most secret knowledge to one of his sons is thus only the last in that long chain, which ultimately goes back to the gods themselves.[86] But according to Berossus, all the tablets that had been written up until the Flood were buried in Sippar, where they were exhumed after it was over.[87] There was thus a shift from the idea of a transmission of knowledge by oral tradition to that of a written transmission of knowledge.

It may be no coincidence that this process of putting the tradition in writing occurred at a time when alphabetical writing systems were emerging and developing, at the end of the second and during the first millennium BCE. It seems to me that Mesopotamian scholars understood that cuneiform writing could not rival the alphabetical systems, particularly Aramaic. Instead of trying to simplify cuneiform, they made it even more difficult, adding more values to the signs and playing on their different readings. It is much easier to read an omen text from the Old Babylonian period than the same omen text as it was written by scholars of the first millennium BCE.[88] That process led to the notion of secret knowledge, which was supposed to be transmitted from initiate to initiate.

Prior to that time, even the writings explicitly concerned with the future did not have the aim of transmitting knowledge: hymns and commemorative inscriptions sought to preserve the name of the king.[89] Hymn B to Lipit-Eshtar, which notes the king of Isin's qualifications as a scribe, ends with this doxology: "Your praise will never disappear from the clay [tablets] of the school/So that the scribes may sing your glory/And so that they will pay you a magnificent homage./Your praise will never end at the school."[90] And this text was recopied dozens and dozens of time, since it was among the elementary texts used for training the young scribes.[91] Hence, as soon as they began to write, apprentices perpetuated praise of the sovereign.[92]

The beginning of the Epic of Gilgamesh[93] also shows how the legendary king of Uruk's vain quest for immortality finally led him to consign the account of his adventures to writing, the only means to preserve his name in the future. And he was quite right, since his epic is still read today.

CHAPTER 2

Outline for a Diplomatics of Mesopotamian Documents

When I was a student in history and was beginning to take a keen interest in ancient Mesopotamia, I was struck by this formulation by Georges Tessier: "The notion of diplomatics . . . applies at once to our laws, decrees, and edicts, to our notarized deeds, to our bills of exchange, to the tablets of Babylonian antiquity, to Greco-Roman papyri, and to medieval charters."[1] Tessier goes on to lament that many people are engaged in "diplomatics without knowing it." Such is the case for most Assyriologists, which is regrettable. The "exportation" of diplomatics into Assyriology[2] was paradoxically handicapped by the early development of what is sometimes called "legal Assyriology."[3] Documents were often published jointly by a philologist and a jurist,[4] so that diplomatic study in the strict sense was generally neglected for a long time.

In this chapter, I would like to give a few indications regarding the particular form of the documents from Mesopotamian archives, and then on the conditions of their elaboration and transmission, before noting through a few examples the contribution of diplomatics to Assyriological studies.

1. The Form of the Documents

The most ancient cuneiform tablets found thus far date to the end of the fourth millennium BCE,[5] and it is suspected that the most recent date to the third century CE.[6] It is obvious that, over such a long period of time, there would have been considerable changes in both the external and internal characteristics of the documents.[7]

A first version of this chapter was published under the title "Esquisse d'une diplomatique des documents mésopotamiens," *Bibliothèque de l'École des chartes* 160 (2002): 487–511.

1.1. The External Characteristics

We would be hard pressed to cite a manual dealing with this question. A few sporadic studies at most have appeared.[8] They are usually limited to individual experiences and take an intuitive approach.

1.1.1. THE SUPPORT. The most noteworthy originality of Mesopotamian civilization is assuredly its almost universal use of clay as a writing support. It is this material that gave rise to the appearance of cuneiform writing itself, whose signs are incised in the soft surface of the tablet with the aid of a calamus carved from a reed.[9] Clay was an inexpensive raw material, which does not mean that its preparation did not require effort. It had to be carefully refined and cleaned, so that it would not crack as it dried.[10] As a result, it is not certain that the following assertion from the king of Ashnakkum needs to be taken with a grain of salt: "My servants tired themselves out going to the leader of the nomads [*merhūm*], and I used up the clay of Ashnakkum for the tablets that I am continually sending there."[11] The use of clay had both advantages and disadvantages.[12] The first constraint was that of space: the scribe had to calculate in advance the surface area needed. We know of tablets that were fashioned but never inscribed.[13] Based on their format, it is possible in some cases to discern the nature of the text they were intended to convey.[14] Another fundamental constraint resulted from the fact that clay, once inscribed, dries rather quickly, making any later modification of the text impossible. When exposed to the sun, the tablet hardens within a few hours. By definition, a text was therefore written all at once.[15]

Contrary to an all-too-prevalent idea, tablets were not normally baked.[16] That treatment was for the most part reserved for certain library copies.[17] Often, however, documents were baked to a greater or lesser extent when the building that sheltered them was destroyed by fire.[18] That accidental baking generally led to a modification in the color of the tablet: an oxidizing atmosphere produced a predominantly red tablet, a reducing atmosphere, a predominantly black one.[19] That is also the case for the baking sometimes conducted in museums to extract the salts and thereby slow the deterioration of the tablets.

For the ancients, there was an advantage to not baking the tablets: the clay of outdated ones could be reused by moistening them again.[20] That practice is primarily attested in schools, where exercises were written on a few perpetually recycled tablets,[21] but it is also attested in administration archives.[22]

Occasionally, supports other than clay were used. When there was a desire to solemnize a text, it could be transcribed onto stone. Such was the case for royal deeds of donation or exemption dating from the second half of the second millennium BCE, which were designated by the Babylonian term *kudurru*. These stones had a two-part inscription: the first part explicitly reproduced the text of the tablet sealed by the king; the second was composed of a series of curses against anyone who did not respect the content or who damaged the monument in some way.[23] At least some of the deities invoked in the text were represented by their symbol sculpted in the stone.[24]

Stone tablets, but also gold or silver ones, have also been found in foundation deposits.[25] The Hittites engraved certain international documents in metal. We know that the cuneiform version of the famous treaty concluded between Hattusili III and pharaoh Ramses II was inscribed in silver, though only a copy in clay survives.[26] A bronze tablet of large dimensions, reproducing the text of another treaty, was found a few years ago in Hattusha.[27]

The Hittite world seems to have used wooden tablets covered with wax for its economic and administrative needs.[28] The use of wax was not unknown to the Mesopotamians[29] and seems to have served primarily as a support for the manuscripts of "literary" works: witness the catalogs[30] that list writing boards next to "classic" tablets. Sometimes the wooden tablets had only one element (these were called *daltu* in Akkadian), but sometimes they were polyptychs (*le'u*). Excavations of Nimrud have unearthed, next to fragments of wooden writing boards, a polyptych in ivory with no fewer than sixteen volets.[31]

In the first millennium BCE, parchment scrolls (*magallatu*) were used as a support for cuneiform writing, which was set down in ink. They are mentioned in a legal text[32] but also as being used to copy divinatory texts.[33]

More anecdotally, the use of human skin is attested, but in a special way: slaves were tattooed so that they could be tracked down if they ran away.[34]

1.1.2. THE WRITING SYSTEM. It was the use of the clay support that gave "cuneiform" writing its essential characteristic. The evolution from primitive drawings to a combination of wedges or spikes to form signs can be explained by the difficulties entailed in tracing curves in a clay surface.[35] That form of writing changed considerably over the three millennia during which it was used. Paradoxically, the paleography of cuneiform was underdeveloped for a long time and in large measure still remains so.[36] That is in part a result of the reproduction techniques.

The cost of photographs, and especially the technical difficulties in photographing a three-dimensional cuneiform tablet, are two factors that explain why, for a long time, Assyriologists usually published documents in the form of handwritten copies. But however faithful a copy, it inevitably involves the loss of certain information. In addition, in not-unusual cases, the copy did not respect the layout of the original or the handwriting. Let me simply cite the case of the neo-Assyrians letters published between 1892 and 1914 in which the cuneiform signs were reproduced in printed form. In the worst cases, the normalization was such that the copies were in reality disguised transcriptions.[37]

The financial problems have now been solved by digital photography, which produces files that can be integrated without surcharge into submitted electronic manuscripts, or reproduced on CD-ROMs. In addition, photographing tablets after ammonium chloride vaporization makes it possible, with adequate lighting, to accentuate artificially the contrast between the light color of the tablet surface and the darkness of the signs inscribed in it.[38] The Tell ed-Dēr expedition made video recordings of the tablets to eliminate the problem of reading the edges and corners. Attempts at three-dimensional digital photography are currently meeting with success.[39]

Paleography was a victim of the very success of cuneiform writing, whose length of use surpassed three millennia. That form of writing has often been considered in a very (even overly) general manner. In R. Labat's classic *Manuel d'épigraphie akkadienne* (Manual of Akkadian epigraphy),[40] the evolution of cuneiform writing is treated on the left-hand page in very large blocks of time:[41] the third millennium BCE, the first and then second half of the second millennium BCE (Old and Middle Assyrian, Old and Middle Babylonian), and finally, the first millennium BCE (neo-Assyrian and neo-Babylonian). If we limit ourselves to a single one of these periods, we fall into an unfathomable bibliographical void.[42] In fact, most of the studies deal more with the geographical differences perceptible at a single moment[43] than with the evolution over time in a single region. And the remarks generally have more to do with the repertoire of signs in use (the syllabary) than with their form.[44] A joint interdisciplinary project is currently under way at the University of Birmingham and the British Museum.[45]

One of the few authors who has explicitly addressed this problem is J. Finkelstein, who quite rightly points out: "Cuneiformists with more or less exposure to tablets of relatively limited provenance but spanning many centuries have usually been able to distinguish at sight, on the basis of external criteria alone, the relative age of any given tablet within that span . . . It is infinitely more difficult, however, to formulate and to express these distinctions with any *precision*."[46] I will go even further. Those who have worked for years on the Mari archives have learned to recognize scribe's "hands": that is in fact one of the things that allows them to form "joins" between tablet fragments. But it is difficult to formulate a description precise enough to allow others to benefit from that experience, which unfortunately remains largely on the order of the intransmissible.[47]

Oddly, it is primarily in the "peripheral" areas of the cuneiform world—for example, the Hittite territory—that paleography has developed the most.[48] In that case, the essential concern was not to study the archival documents but rather to succeed in dating the copies of manuscripts from the royal library.[49]

As everywhere, paleography must take into account the support and the kind of text. Inscriptions on stone always have a more archaic-looking graph than the cursive of the same period. A famous example is the Code of Hammurabi: the characters on the stela in the Louvre, engraved slightly before 1750 BCE, almost correspond to the cursive in Sumerian tablets from the twenty-fourth century BCE. In addition, in studying an archival lot from Isin in central Babylonia, I have been able to observe the considerable differences in graphs within a single era—the reign of Samsu-iluna (1749–1712 BCE)—between bookkeeping entries and "official" texts such as sales contracts.[50] If the dates of the texts were not preserved, one might easily posit an interval of a century between them. The question arises whether it was the same scribes who wrote both categories of texts, but for the moment, it is difficult to say.

Paleography has demonstrated the existence of a few "turning points" in the history of cuneiform writing. Under the obvious impetus of the political authorities, a sudden reform would be carried out. The first occurred in the empire of Akkad (twenty-fourth to twenty-third centuries BCE). The central administration imposed a uniform style across the entire empire. Local archives therefore display the coexistence of two types of bookkeeping tablets: those for internal usage, which followed the old writing habits, and those intended to be presented to the imperial inspectors, which met the new criteria. The imposed nature of the exercise is observable on one large tablet. The scribe began it in the "imperial style" then changed his mind near the middle and ended in his usual mode of writing. It has been noted that, had the tablet been broken, the two fragments would have been dated with a chronological difference of at least a generation.[51]

A second instance took place in the kingdom of Mari in the late nineteenth century BCE. The style of the tablets, improperly called "Shakkanakku," disappeared suddenly in favor of a more "modern" style that conformed to the habits of the scribes from the neighboring kingdom of Eshnunna.[52] We possess an administrative document—a rarity in the history of writing—written in accordance with the old norms, then recopied in the "modern" way.[53] A comparison between the two shows that the changes had to do with the form of the tablets, the configuration of the signs, and the syllabary all at once.

1.1.3. THE "PAGE LAYOUT." It is obviously a misuse of language to speak of a tablet's "page layout," since the term refers implicitly to a particular support, a sheet, whether of papyrus, parchment, or paper, whereas the clay tablet is characteristically in three dimensions. In order that the tablet not become too fragile, its thickness had to increase proportionate with the size of the surface. Let me cite two extremes: a tablet measuring ⅝ by ⅝ inches and ½ inch thick, and others measuring 14 ¼ by 13 inches, with a thickness varying between 1 ⅝ and 2 inches. These physical constraints did not prevent significant variations from existing: hence, the corners could be either relatively rounded or sharp. Generally, the obverse was almost flat and the reverse more curved, but other configurations are attested. Round tablets were usually for school exercises; administrative documents with a more or less oval shape can also be found. Tablets could also be nearly square. The vast majority, however, are rectangular: usually the writing runs parallel to the short side, but the opposite is also found. To move from the obverse to the reverse, one does not generally turn the tablet like a page; rather, one flips it over like a coin.[54] As a result, the scribe might use the top and bottom of the tablets, but also the left edge. A margin was sometimes set aside for seal impressions or other uses. Practices varied a great deal depending on the kind of text and the era. It was undoubtedly during the most archaic period that the most information was conveyed by the page layout.[55] A fundamental shift occurred over the course of the third millennium BCE. Whereas previously scribes had written in columns subdivided into cells, writing became linear, with the signs inscribed left to right.[56] Large tablets could be divided into columns, as before; they ran left to right on the obverse, but right to left on the reverse. There was normally no enjambment: not only did the scribe finish a word at the end of a line, but usually also even strove to justify the margin. If the line was ever too long, the scribe would use indentation, a practice now reserved for writing verse. The Syrian scribes of the second half of the second millennium BCE did not respect that convention: on their tablets, it is not unusual for the lines on the obverse to continue beyond the right edge, occupying a good part of the reverse.[57]

Letters posed a particular problem, since by definition they are texts of variable length. Depending on the time and place, they could have either a standard form or one adapted to the content. The practices of the chancellery of Rim-Sin, king of Larsa (1822–1763 BCE), represent an extreme case: the letters are all quite large, with a very elongated form. As a result, the reverse is usually anepigraphic, and sometimes the text occupies only a part of the obverse.[58] In the neo-Assyrian period as well, the size of letters was fixed: very often, not all the available space was used.[59] In the Mari archives, conversely, letters vary a great deal in size. One truly has the impression that the scribe knew the length of the message to be inscribed before fashioning the tablet.[60] The archives of the Assyrian merchants in Cappadocia have revealed a few rare cases of letters with a "second page," described as a "supplement" (*ṣibtum* in Akkadian).[61]

The existence of envelopes is well attested. Once the tablet was dried, the scribe covered it with a thin layer of clay (about ⅛ inch thick).[62] Envelopes were used for two different types of texts: letters and contracts. In the case of letters, the purpose was obviously to keep their content confidential: the envelope, on which only the name of the recipient appeared, was broken once the recipient had examined its message. The envelope also made it possible to verify the sender, who rolled his seal over the envelope.[63] For missives that were not confidential, brief notes were written, sometimes sealed directly and often without an address (*ze'pum*).[64] But for other eras, contracts are also found in envelopes. Usually, the scribe recopied the entire text on the envelope:[65] subsequently, if the envelope had been damaged or if someone suspected that the text had been falsified, judges had only to have the envelope broken to gain access to the text of the internal tablet.[66] The envelopes also provided a larger surface than the tablets: a margin was therefore set aside on the left for seal impressions. In the last part of the Old Babylonian period, scribes no longer placed contracts in envelopes but laid out the tablets as if they were envelopes.[67]

1.1.4. THE SEALS. A seal is the impression on a malleable material of an image and/or characters engraved in a hard material (called the matrix, or also the seal).[68] It was used as a personal sign of authority and ownership.[69] That definition, borrowed from a medievalist, is also valid for Mesopotamian seals, with a few modifications.[70] The chief one is that in the Middle Ages, seals, impressed in wax, were usually suspended by various means to the parchment that served as the support for the written text. By contrast, in ancient Mesopotamia, the seal was impressed on the clay tablet itself:[71] the written text and the seal impression were thus found on one and the same support. Matrices took different forms, depending on the era: cylinder seals dominated in the more ancient eras and were gradually replaced by rings and stamps.

As for the uses of these seals, everywhere they were threefold: "to close (and guarantee the integrity or secrecy of a text), to assert ownership, and to authenticate an act (by manifesting that it truly expresses the will of an individual or of a moral person)."[72] Hence a chest, jar, or door would be closed with a piece of clay that was then sealed. Letters were sent in clay envelopes bearing the name of the recipient and the impression of the sender's seal. Finally, contracts were sealed, at the very least, by the person making the pledge:[73] the seller, who renounced forever his rights to a good, or the debtor, who entered into an obligation to repay his creditor, for example. Very often, there were also the seal impressions of a certain number of witnesses, whose names were inscribed on the contract and who were in some sense guarantors of the authenticity of the act. In ancient Babylonia, as in the Western Middle Ages, some seals were *bene cognitum et famosus* (well-known and famous), as this example shows: "You have sealed [this contract] with the seal of the high priest–*šangûm* of Shamash, of the high priest–*šangûm* of Aya, and with your seals . . . If the seal of the high priest–*šangûm* of Shamash, of the high priest–*šangûm* of Aya, and your seals are contested, whose seal will be accepted?"[74] It is understandable that the loss of a seal by its owner was judged a grave matter.[75]

When a tablet includes the impression of one or several seals, the epigraphist who publishes the text often has a tendency to overlook them, at times not even indicating their presence. At best, he will be interested only in the legend, leaving it to specialists in sigillography to copy and comment on the figures. No one will deny that a division of labor is inevitable because of the skills required, but an overall approach to the document is necessary. Indeed, sigillographers for their part long had a tendency to privilege the study of matrices over that of impressions, which are infinitely more difficult to study. All the same, impressions offer the advantage of appearing on documents that usually include a date or can be precisely situated in time. Hence, a stylistic study of seals can locate very precise reference points, which have often been lacking. From that standpoint, a whole series of recent studies has made up for lost time.[76] How seals were impressed on the tablet (before or after the text was inscribed, in what place, in what order, and so on) has also begun to be studied with increasing precision.[77]

Combinations of the different possible characteristics resulted in considerable variety. Through a study of lots from particular archives, it is possible to establish typologies: in combination with analyses of the texts' content, crucial conclusions can be drawn regarding the origin and function of the texts.[78]

1.2. The Internal Characteristics

Studies of the internal characteristics of Mesopotamian documents focus both on the language used by the scribes and on the models they followed in composing the texts.

1.2.1. LANGUAGE. At several moments in the history of cuneiform writing, a gap can be observed between the written language, used for the drafting of deeds, and the language as it was commonly spoken. Without making any claim to exhaustivity, I shall analyze several particularly significant situations.[79]

Contracts from the beginning of the second millennium BCE contain many formulas in Sumerian, at a time when it had ceased to be a living language. Gradually, beginning in northern Babylonia, Akkadian took over. This phenomenon is very similar to that regarding medieval documents, where terms borrowed from the indigenous languages gradually combined with Latin. Depending on the place and time, there were many variants of that situation, which has not yet been the object of systematic investigations.[80]

Another deviation can be observed in the same era, particularly in the regions of the central and western Near East. Two languages were spoken there, Akkadian and Amorite. Amorite belongs to the northwestern branch of the Semitic language family, whereas Akkadian constitutes its eastern branch. No text written in Amorite has yet been found; that language is attested only through many proper names and a few technical terms.[81] It is clear that the weight of the Sumero-Akkadian tradition led scribes not to set down Amorite in writing. Cultural prejudices also must have played a role. Amorite was primarily the language spoken by the Bedouins, who were scorned by the settled populations of Mesopotamia.[82]

A similar gap between the language of written culture and spoken language is found in the second half of the second millennium BCE, in the archives of Nuzi, a small city that belonged to the kingdom of Arrapha (Kirkuk region in the northeastern part of present-day Iraq). Texts were composed in an Akkadian strongly contaminated by the locally spoken language, Hurrian.[83] Akkadian was also used in texts written in Alalah, at the other end of the Mitanni empire. That was the case closer to the capital as well, in Tell Brak, though a letter composed in Hurrian has also been found there.[84] In Qaṭna in central Syria, texts have recently been uncovered that display a curious mix of Akkadian and Hurrian, sometimes within the same sentence.[85]

In the first millennium BCE, the situation was complicated by the appearance of new alphabetical writing systems used to notate languages such as Aramaic. It is obvious that there was a temptation to write in Aramaic and in ink, given the cumbersomeness of traditional cuneiform writing: witness an ostracon found in Assur, which contains the text of a long letter written in Aramaic by an Assyrian official in Babylonia to a colleague from Assur. Neo-Assyrian bas-reliefs, in fact, sometimes represent side by side a scribe writing on a tablet and another whose calamus is inscribing a text on leather, the first obviously notating Akkadian, the second, Aramaic. All the same, in a missive written to an official posted in Ur (southern Babylonia), the neo-Assyrian king Sargon II refused to receive mail written "on skin [*sipru*] in Aramaic"; letters to him had to be written "in Akkadian," that is, in cuneiform on a clay tablet.[86] It is clear from this example that a link existed between the support, the writing system, and the language,[87] and that a symbolic value could be attached to the use of cuneiform. The letter from Sargon II represents a very firm assertion of political and cultural identity and is in this respect remarkable for its implicit awareness of the underlying issues. There is no doubt that such determination is an essential factor in explaining the longevity of cuneiform in the first millennium BCE.

1.2.2. COMPOSITION. Contracts were composed from models, which varied by region in a given era. Hence, in the Old Babylonian period, the manner of describing the neighbors around a piece of property that had been sold differed depending on whether they were in Sippar or in Larsa. Certain clauses were typical of certain cities and absent from contracts composed elsewhere: hence, the pestle (*bukānum*) transfer clause appears only in northern Babylonia, never in the south.[88]

It is regrettable that at this time only a few manuals systematically present the formulas used by scribes for each category of acts in a given era: one of the few is J. N. Postgate's for the neo-Assyrian period.[89] For the Old Babylonian period, there are only a few studies limited to specific kinds of texts: sales contracts[90] or loans.[91] The only systematic study of diplomatic discourse undertaken thus far deals with treaties and other "international" acts from the second half of the second millennium BCE.[92]

Although less formulaic than contracts, letters were also composed in accordance with a number of strict practices, to which correspondents occasionally alluded, as in this example: "What is this behavior? Even when I write you by the rules, you don't send me any response to my letter!"[93] The school exercises that have been found confirm the existence of models for letters used to describe various situations.[94]

2. Elaboration and Transmission of Documents: Study of the Archives

I should like to indicate here how documents were committed to writing and then preserved.

2.1. The Elaboration of Documents

Mesopotamian documents were primarily produced by professional scribes, whose status and training I shall examine.

2.1.1. THE SUCCESSION OF OPERATIONS. No rough draft of a private or public Mesopotamian act has ever been found. It seems that scribes proceeded directly to the definitive deed. That deed was validated by impressing one or several seals: that of the debtor, of the seller, or of whoever was transferring a right by means of a contract, sometimes combined with the seal(s) of one or several witnesses. The authority responsible sometimes had to be sent a tablet so that he or she could impress a seal on it. This suggests that the tablet was kept moist. A text discovered at Tell Rimah attests precisely to that practice: "The tablet on the state of the weavers when I established their accounts, I gave to my lady. May my lady seal it now with her seal, and may she have it brought to me with the weavers."[95]

Sometimes one of the individuals whose seal was required did not have it with him. He could then use someone else's seal. The scribe mentioned that fact in small characters next to the impression: "Since he is not carrying his seal, he sealed with the seal of Apilsha."[96] This is sometimes also indicated by the sender in the body of the letter: "My cylinder seal was lost in Mashkan, that is why I sealed [the envelope of this letter] with someone else's seal."[97] Or, "I met Ipqatum outside and I therefore sealed [this letter] with the seal of my brother [Ipqatum]."[98] Sometimes the impression of the fringe (*sissiktum*) of a garment is found on the tablets, or even the impression of a fingernail (*ṣuprum*); like the seal, these could be used as a stand-in for the person.[99]

On principle, the document, of which only a single copy was made, was submitted to the person who might need a written text to prove his rights: a creditor, the purchaser of a good, the winner in a lawsuit, and so on. Under special legal circumstances, several true copies were made.[100] Such was the case for exchanges, when each of the two parties was supposed to keep a written record of the agreement concluded. In cases where both copies are found in the same archive, we must assume that one of the two parties subsequently bought back the plot they had first exchanged.[101]

2.1.2. THE STATUS OF SCRIBES. A large number of contracts include, at the end of the list of witnesses, the name of the scribe who committed the text to writing. Curiously, prosopographical studies based on this type of indication have developed only recently,[102] and many remain to be done.

The status of scribes remains poorly understood. No doubt a few figures are emerging from the shadows, such as the private secretary of Zimri-Lim, king of Mari, one Shu-nuhra-Halu, who read the mail addressed to the ruler[103] and composed the missives the king sent out.[104] Even so, we do not yet know how the scribes who composed contracts for private individuals were compensated, for example.[105]

2.1.3. LOCAL TRADITIONS. Scribes were trained to compose acts by copying model contracts. Many examples have been found in the schools of Nippur for the Old Babylonian period, characteristically without witnesses or date. In place of these indications, we find "its witnesses," "its month," "its year."[106]

The weight of tradition was ultimately even stronger among schoolmasters than among "notaries." In the first millennium BCE, that resulted in a paradoxical situation: the formulas that were recopied by apprentice scribes at the time no longer corresponded to those that appeared in contracts during the same period; rather, they were the formulas that had been used in the city of Nippur in the first half of the second millennium BCE.[107]

2.2. The Constitution of Archives

It must be admitted that attention to the archives as such has been absent from Assyriology for a very long time.[108] It is true that, at its inception, archaeology resembled more a hunt for objects—tablets included—than a scientific enterprise as it has been understood in recent decades, and the archives of major sites such as Nineveh and Sippar have paid the price. In addition, museum storerooms have been constituted in great part from documents purchased on the market of antiquities, the result of fortuitous discoveries or illicit excavations; in this respect, the situation remains extremely worrying.[109] That explains why documents have usually been published typologically, without respect for the sets of objects among which the tablets were discovered, even when these were accurately recorded. The case of Ur is altogether representative in this regard.[110]

2.2.1. FAMILY ARCHIVES AND THE ARCHIVES OF LARGE ORGANIZATIONS. So-called private archives, which would more accurately have to be called family archives, often cover a period of one or two centuries, up to six generations. Among the finest examples, let me cite those of the house of Ur-Utu[111] in Sippar (eighteenth to seventeenth centuries BCE) and the archives of the Egibis[112] (seventh to fifth centuries BCE). For the most part they contain property deeds, which were transmitted across the generations alongside the property to which they refer, particularly land.[113] Texts concerning the last generation are often more abundant and varied, since, at the time the houses sheltering these archives were definitively destroyed, the obsolete had not yet been winnowed from the up-to-date.[114] Depending on the case, documents were preserved in baskets, chests, or clay jars.

A sharp contrast exists between private archives and those found in palaces, which cover only a very limited period of time. Hence, the archives exhumed in the Mari palace document the reign of the last two sovereigns, Yasmah-Addu and Zimri-Lim, that is, some twenty-five years, before the destruction that occurred in about 1760 BCE. The most recent studies of the archives of Ebla (twenty-fourth century BCE) have tended to fix the duration of these archives to about thirty years at most.[115] Those of the palace of Ugarit, in the thirteenth century BCE, cover a slightly longer interval of time, but it would seem that a portion of those archives had been discarded on the upper floor.

There were never in Mesopotamia any truly "public" or "state" archives.[116] In the palace of Ebla during the third millennium BCE,[117] as in that of Mari during the second[118] or Nineveh during the first,[119] these were royal archives in the sense of "king's archives."

In particular, the sovereign kept the correspondence he received, both from his peers and from his officials posted in the provinces or on missions abroad. The practice was all the more remarkable in that, conversely, no duplicates were ordinarily kept of the letters sent out. The archives thus provide only the passive correspondence of individuals, whatever their status.[120] Letters did not normally bear the date or the place of origin. The messenger who brought them could orally provide the desired details about the sender's location and the time the letter was composed. When, in exceptional cases, a date does appear, only the day and month are indicated, almost never the year. It seems clear, therefore, that the archiving of letters was of very little concern to the ancients. Nevertheless, the Babylonians who sorted out the archives of the chancellery in the Mari palace were able to distinguish the letters from the era of Yasmah-Addu from those belonging to that of Zimri-Lim,[121] which they could not have done unless the letters had first been organized by a filing system. That interest in preservation is particularly astonishing, given that earlier letters, which in fact never date back very far, are almost always quoted from memory and not word for word. The correspondence of the kings from the Ur III dynasty (twenty-first century BCE) is a special case: we do not know what became of the originals. We have only modernized copies produced by apprentice scribes at the beginning of the second millennium BCE. Some letters were in fact selected by schoolmasters, who had them recopied as an exercise for their students. There was apparently a political ulterior motive governing that choice: from the outset, scribes in the service of the kings of Isin had to show their apprentices the legitimacy of the secession of Ishbi-Erra, who founded a new dynasty in Isin. They did not hesitate to insert apocryphal letters into the corpus.[122]

Beginning in the mid-second millennium BCE, sovereigns also kept the text of the treaties they had concluded with foreign rulers.[123] The sites of Hattusha[124] and Ugarit[125] are yielding many examples. The palace archives also preserved internal bookkeeping accounts: lists of rations of oil or clothing distributed to the women in the harem or to visitors, expenses incurred for the king's table and for his guests, and so on. The archives found in Ebla and Mari have preserved thousands of administrative documents of this kind. Texts concerning the kingdom as a whole are rare. One exception is the large census tablets prepared in the provinces and collected in the capital.[126]

2.2.2. LIVING AND DEAD ARCHIVES. I shall use the term "living archives" for those in which the accumulation of texts continued until the last moment. Hence, the archives of King Zimri-Lim in his palace of Mari were held until Babylonian troops entered the palace in 1760 BCE. But very often, the documents that archaeologists find are dead archives, that is, texts that were discarded by the ancients themselves. Take the case of the archives of the temple of Ninurta in Nippur: hundreds of tablets written between 1875 and 1795 BCE were found during excavations of a building constructed in the Parthian era on the ruins of the temple of Inanna.[127] Obviously, in digging through the tell in search of clay for bricks, the builders had come across an archival lot more than a millennium and a half old. They decided that the clay tablets would constitute an excellent material for reinforcing the platform on which they wanted to build a fortress. Examples of this kind abound. It is not unusual for a single building to contain both living and dead archives. In the Mari palace, several dozen bookkeeping documents from the time of Yasmah-Addu, predating the destruction of the site by some fifteen or twenty years, have been discovered sunk into the clay inside a bench used to hold large clay jars. To be precise, these were memos recording oil expenditures.[128] Tablets that document the reigns of Yahdun-Lim and Sumu-Yamam, predecessors of Yasmah-Addu, have for their part been found under the floor in certain rooms. They were thrown down there when a new clay floor was made, at the time Yasmah-Addu moved into the palace. The texts that the ancients got rid of in that way had only a temporary value—memoranda, minor bookkeeping texts, and so on—and were regularly winnowed out.

2.3. Access to the Archives

The problem raised by archives in every era is that of access to information: How to find what one is looking for? The Mesopotamians had techniques that, admittedly, were still rather rudimentary. In Ebla, tablets were stored on wooden shelves, which it has been possible to reconstitute.[129] Most often, they were kept in baskets or chests, which were sealed and equipped with a label that gave some idea of their content. One of the most interesting cases is that of trials (*di-til-la* in Sumerian) in Girsu from the twenty-first century BCE. Some of the labels for tablet baskets that have been found there suggest that the trials were classified by year and by judge.[130] These texts obviously served as a record of legal decisions and had to be available for reading when required. We also know that, at the beginning of the second millennium BCE, the "judges of the cloister" of Sippar, assigned to look after the interests of the nuns dedicated to the god Shamash, kept in their houses law texts, such as a rescript of King Samsu-iluna.[131] Finally, three of the ten jars containing the archives of the offerings in the temple of Assur in the second half of the second millennium BCE (650 tablets in all) included an inscription indicating their content, such as the following: "Receptacles for the accounts of the brewers in the temple of Assur under the authority of Ezbu-leshir, chief of offerings in the temple of Assur, servant of Tiglat-pileser (I)."[132]

Old Babylonian texts were dated using a system of "year names." Every year was designated by a name that commemorated an outstanding event—military, religious, or other—from the previous year. Of course, such a system, like that of eponymy, presupposes the existence of lists establishing the order of succession for the names. But it has recently been observed that the year names for the late Old Babylonian period systematically mention at the start of the formula the sovereign's name, which is not the case for the more ancient texts. The reason for such a change is obvious: as time passed, the archives grew, and it became increasingly difficult for scribes to find their way around them. In addition, there is now proof that private archives were sorted chronologically. In the house of Ur-Utu in Sippar-Amnum (Tell ed-Dēr), no fewer than four lists of year names have been found, obviously used to organize the property deeds of Ur-Utu's father at a time when the division of his possessions gave rise to a serious quarrel among his heirs.[133]

The question arises whether administrative texts, once archived, were actually consulted. A study of texts of "king's meals" in Mari seems to show that the writers of the summations did not always take the trouble to consult the tickets composed on a daily basis and often made estimates.[134] There are contrary examples, however. Hence, King Zimri-Lim gave instructions by letter that the census tablet chests be taken from where they were archived and the summations sent to him.[135] His aim was clear: to learn what forces he could count on for his next military campaign. Some lists in fact give the breakdown, locality by locality, of the number of men who could be enlisted (information drawn from the census tablets), the number of men who actually responded to the royal summons, and finally, the deficit.[136] Similarly, Hammurabi wrote to Shamash-hazir, manager of the Crown lands of Larsa, to come join him in Sippar with all the tablets relating to the fields attributed in tenure for three years.[137] Registries of names were in fact consulted when needed: "The palace registry was examined: Ahushina, son of Etelliya, is not listed on it for a work unit; he is listed as a replacement for Shumman-lā-Shamash."[138] An even more astonishing case is a grievance from an official, who demanded that the crop field his father had held be returned to him and, as proof, cited "the old tablets from the temple of Nisaba," which he had gone to consult.[139] The king asked Shamash-hazir to listen to the testimony of the elders from the area who might be able to confirm the claims he had made on the basis of written documents. In the case of private archives, unrecovered debts were occasionally inventoried before being assigned to someone charged with making the overdue debtors pay.[140]

Periods of political rupture gave rise to the need for conquerors to take cognizance of the wealth they had acquired; hence the taking of inventories, such as those of the palace treasures of Mari after Samsi-Addu, father of Yasmah-Addu, seized hold of them.[141] But memories of individuals could sometimes fill in the gaps in written information. When Samsi-Addu, in order to equip his armies, had a sudden need for large quantities of bronze, he wanted to take objects made of that metal that were located in the tomb of Yahdum-Lim, former king of Mari. Inquiries were therefore made among officials from that time, who were able to provide the weight of these objects—which proved a disappointment to the sovereign.[142]

3. A Few Examples of Productive Diplomatic Approaches

I shall complete this overview by setting out a few concrete examples of how a diplomatic approach to the documents allows for progress to be made in Assyriological research.

3.1. The Archives of Ur

Allow me to mention, first, a personal example in which the insights of diplomatics turned out to be decisive for a historical inquiry. For my doctoral thesis, I began by studying an archival lot brought to the British Museum in the mid-nineteenth century. Although it had twice been copied, it had never been edited or thoroughly studied.[143] That group of about a hundred tablets had been discovered by William Loftus during the time he spent in what is now southern Iraq, in Tell Sifr, about nine miles from Tell Sinkereh (ancient Larsa). Two-thirds of the documents constituted a coherent set: these were the archives of two brothers who had lived in the first half of the eighteenth century BCE, under the reigns of Hammurabi and Samsuiluna. But some thirty documents were problematic. Some were related to one another, but none had any connection to the family of the two brothers. A diplomatic study, combined with a prosopographical investigation, led me to understand that these tablets in fact came from the city of Ur. The contract models and the sigillary practices[144] made it possible to establish the case beyond dispute. The history of nineteenth-century archaeological expeditions can explain what had happened: J. E. Taylor was excavating the Ur site at the same time that Loftus was exploring the region of Larsa, and the two sent their discoveries together to the British Museum. When the crates arrived in London, all the tablets were combined and (falsely) labeled as coming from Tell Sifr.

After conducting that work, I resumed studying documents from Ur dating to the Old Babylonian period (twentieth to eighteenth century BCE). The tablets from Anglo-American excavations done during the interwar period had been published, from 1928 on, in a half-chronological, half-typological manner, without the provenance of the texts being taken into account. The definitive archaeological report appeared only in 1976;[145] it finally contained the complete catalog of objects discovered, making it possible to restore every tablet to its archaeological context. The work I undertook at that time allowed me to show that the majority of the supposedly religious and literary texts consisted of collections of manuscripts found in houses, which also contained the family archives of members of the clergy from the large local temple of the moon god Nanna-Sin. The study of the complete set could be conducted on totally revised foundations.[146]

3.2. Texts from the Kingdom of Hana

The village of Tell Ashara, on the Middle Euphrates in Syria, is built over the ruins of ancient Terqa. Since the late nineteenth century, its residents have discovered several tablets during work performed under the foundations of their houses or close to them. These documents were published little by little and their chronology was very quickly agreed upon: they were dated to the late Old Babylonian period (late eighteenth and seventeenth centuries BCE). Recently, a new tablet of the same provenance was published. Since it included a seal impression, the epigraphists responsible for its publication turned to a specialist in glyptics of that era, G. Colbow. She was categorical: the seal contained characteristics typical of the Kassite period. Hence, Iggid-Lim, who sealed the tablet, must have reigned during a more recent period than had been believed up to that time. A. Podany then launched a very fruitful diplomatic study.[147] In the absence of a royal list or equivalent document, she organized chronologically that corpus, which came for the most part from illicit excavations.[148] If we attempt to understand how these Middle Babylonian tablets could have been published by very competent scholars as coming from the late Old Babylonian period, the answer is simple: purely philological criteria prevailed over a diplomatic approach.

Conclusion

One of the contributions of diplomatics—which lies at the very origin of the discipline—was the ability to detect forgeries, modern or especially ancient. Ancient forgeries are rare in Assyriology, but several do exist, and curiously, one of these long escaped the attention of specialists: the "cruciform monument of Manishtushu." This monument looks like an authentic inscription from the twenty-third century BCE. It contains the text of a royal donation to the great temple of Ebabbar in Sippar.[149] It is in reality a pastiche, perhaps produced in the early part of the reign of Nabonidus (sixth century BCE), almost surely commissioned by the clergy of Sippar to obtain the king's aid for their sanctuary.[150]

CHAPTER 3

Old Babylonian Law: Gesture, Speech, and Writing

In Old Babylonian law, a contract between two individuals was marked by symbolic gestures engaging those who performed them and by the utterance of solemn words, all in the presence of witnesses who would remember the matter concluded. Because of that ritualized practice on the conclusion of a contract, and the recourse, in case of dispute, to testimonies and oaths, or even ordeals, gesture and speech are considered constitutive of a Babylonian "prelaw."

Conversely, the care taken to preserve and transfer legal documents (certificates of purchase, adoption, inheritance, and so on) shows the importance attached to the written text. The Old Babylonian period can be distinguished from the preceding Ur III period (twenty-first century BCE) precisely by the abundance of family archives containing these kinds of written documents.

We therefore need to assess to what extent there were two contradictory mentalities, and/or whether a chronological evolution must be posited for the four centuries that form the so-called Old Babylonian period.

1. Symbolic Gestures and Solemn Words

The conclusion of contracts, whether between individuals or sovereigns, often included the performance of symbolic gestures. The complementarity between gesture and speech can be best observed in the swearing of oaths.

This chapter is a revision of the material presented in two studies: "Le geste, la parole et l'écrit dans la vie juridique en Babylonie ancienne," in *Écritures. Systèmes idéographiques et pratiques expressives*, ed. A. M. Christin (Paris: 1982), 65–73; and "'Manger un serment,'" in *Jurer et maudire: Pratiques politiques et usages juridiques du serment dans le Proche-Orient ancien*, ed. S. Lafont, *Méditerranées* 10–11 (1997), 85–96.

1.1. Symbolic Gestures upon the Conclusion of Contracts

A first example is provided by the sales of slaves and plots of land in northern Mesopotamia, which entailed a particular clause relating to the object of the transaction: "He passed in front of the pestle [*bukānum*]." The most probable interpretation has been proposed by D. O. Edzard.[1] A pestle was placed upright on the ground, forming a symbolic border, with the seller and buyer on opposite sides of it: the sold slave took leave of the seller, and, passing in front of the pestle, joined the buyer. Even as early as the third millennium BCE, that act symbolized the transfer of ownership rights over the slave. The use of such a procedure to sanction the sale of real property, characteristic of the early second millennium BCE, poses a problem, since it obviously could not have been applied literally. We may imagine that, in this case, it was a clod of dirt or a brick—*pars pro toto*—that was passed from one side to the other. Unfortunately, there are no explicit indications on this subject. Some authors draw the likely conclusion that, by that time, the formula had been emptied of its content and had "no other meaning than to assert the proper conclusion of the affair, with no reference to a ritual actually performed."[2] Similarly, the drawing of lots for shares of an inheritance, mentioned in partition documents,[3] was in reality probably not always carried out, in view of how "chance" situated the parcels of certain heirs next to the lands they already possessed.[4]

Some sales contracts dealing with pieces of land located alongside waterways attest to an odd practice. At the time the business was concluded, the buyer threw into the water a clod of dirt (*kirbānum*), which, once submerged, slowly dissolved. The symbolism of that act is not obvious and has occasioned several interpretations.[5] It appears that the buyer, in acting in that manner, recognized the uncertain nature of the line between earth and water and thereby pledged not to turn against the seller should river erosion reduce the area of the plot purchased. At the same time, he was himself protected against any eventual claim by the seller in the contrary case, should sedimentation increase the area acquired.[6]

Property transfers were not the only contracts that gave rise to such practices. For a marriage, a ceremony taking place in the fiancée's house included a certain number of symbolic gestures (at a given moment, the fiancée covered her head, for example),[7] as well as the recitation of *verba solemnia*.[8] Written marriage contracts do not provide the formula pronounced, but it seems to be echoed in a few literary texts, such as the myth of Nergal and Ereshkigal, in which the queen of the netherworld declares to the god: "You be my husband; I shall be your wife." No doubt this was a special case, since the initiative came from the goddess. Documents on magic provide what seems to be the formula normally pronounced by the husband: "You be my wife; I shall be your husband."[9] And marriage contracts often contained clauses relating to an eventual divorce, wherein one of the spouses would say to the other: "You are no longer my spouse." In some sense, that formula stands as the negation of the words of consent exchanged upon marriage. Like marriage, divorce entailed a particular ritual in addition to the utterance of the established formulas: the husband who repudiated his wife cut off a bit of fringe (*sissiktum*) from his ex-wife's garment,[10] whereas, during the wedding ritual, the fringe of the two spouses' clothing was joined together.[11]

Another change of status, and hence an occasion for a symbolic gesture, was the manumission of a slave, which included a ceremony whose elements are provided in a few rare texts. Having "lustrated" his slave through a rite, the former master turned the freedman's face toward the rising sun. This was undoubtedly to mark a kind of new birth; the west, conversely, was the direction of death, as illustrated by the example of Gilgamesh's itinerary. The emancipation contracts of Ugarit contain the formula: "[The slave] is pure of his state of servitude, just as the sun is pure."[12] Another text adds that the master anointed a female slave's head with oil.[13] Note that the symbolic scope of all these gestures is never made explicit by the documents that report their performance.[14] Modern interpretations have sometimes given rise to controversies, and certainty about them has not yet been reached in all cases.

1.2. Oaths

The complementarity between gestures and words is particularly clear in the case of oaths.[15] Usually, scribes used the expression "swear an oath" (*nīšam tamūm*), but we sometimes find the rather astonishing "eat an oath" (*nīšam akālum*). That expression can be compared to the well-known formula "eat an *asakkum*"(*asakkum* is usually translated as "taboo"). A contract from Mari provides an interesting variant; it indicates that the parties to the contract "ate herbs [SAR.MEŠ]." In another, they "swore by herbs." It was therefore possible both to "swear" and to "eat" an oath-*nīšum*, an *asakkum*, or "herbs" (SAR.MEŠ). To explain these permutations, I am inclined to believe that the utterance of the oath was accompanied by the ingestion of plants that carried a curse should the juror violate the pledge.[16] The "materialization" of the curse that the parties to a contract called down upon themselves in the event of perjury could occur through other symbolic gestures, such as eating or drinking or covering themselves in oil. These acts are attested in different contracts from Mari and Terqa: "They ate bread, drank beer, and covered themselves with oil."[17] G. Boyer comments on the example of ARM VIII, 13, unique at the time: "That meal taken in common by the parties, alone or in the company of witnesses, surely had a legal significance. It can be seen as the symbol of a life in common being established between table companions and creating a bond of brotherhood."[18] J.-M. Durand has spoken of a "little feast" to conclude a real estate transaction.[19] These festive rites,[20] however, may have had another dimension of a magical nature. The explanation for these gestures may be found in later texts. The formula proffered during an oath in the Hittite world was as follows: "[Just as] you coat yourself in oil, may these curses come to coat [you]! Just as you put on a garment, so put on these curses."[21] This very significant passage appears among the curses in fidelity oaths to the neo-Assyrian king Asharhaddon: "Just as the bread and wine penetrate your intestines, so may [the aforementioned gods] make this oath enter your intestines and those of your sons and daughters."[22] And later on, "Just as the oil enters your flesh, so may [the aforementioned gods] have this oath enter your flesh and that of your sons and daughters."[23] To confirm the interpretation being proposed, let me note that none of the contracts from Mari that insert the bread, beer, or wine and oil clause contain any clause of irrevocability or any oath: the pledge was signified by the symbolic gesture performed and its mention in the written text. The similarity between the Mari texts and the fidelity oaths to Asharhaddon can no doubt be extended even further. These fidelity oaths also contain the curse, "May the great gods of heaven and earth make water and oil your *ikkibum*."[24] As Veenhof has argued, "perhaps the meaning may be at the same time that water and oil drunk by the vassal in the oath ceremony may become his 'destruction,' may bring about his annihilation, because he infringed upon a 'tabu.'"[25] If we replace *ikkibum* by *asakkum*—and the two words are known to have been synonyms—we obtain precisely the definition of *asakkum* proposed above. The idea would therefore be that, at the time of the oath, the juror swallowed a substance (herbs, bread, beer, wine) that would be transformed into a destructive force in the event of perjury,[26] the totality being described by the term *asakkum*.[27] It cannot be ruled out that this symbolic gesture was accompanied by an imprecation of the same type as in Asharhaddon's treaties, but such a curse never seems to have been put in writing.[28] The process that makes the *asakkum*, integrated into the juror's body, become activated in the event of perjury is explicitly described in a curse from the Code of Hammurabi: "May Ninkarrak . . . make a grave illness, a bad *asakkum,* a grave ill-*simmum* arise from his members."[29]

In other cases, no food or drink was ingested. The oath was pronounced in the presence of divine symbols (sometimes also called "divine arms"). To take one example, a dispute had led military authorities to lodge a complaint against a certain Lamassani. In the absence of witnesses, a decision could be rendered in favor of one of the parties only through an oath:

> As the authorities had ordered, the symbol of Shamash that walks at the head of the E-diku-kalama, [and] the symbol of Shamash that walks at the head of the E-dikuda, were made to stand at the Shamash Gate of the E-dikuda. Warad-Kubi, the general of the troops from the countryside [*nawūm*] of Sippar; Qurrudum, the lieutenant; Ina-paleshu, the lieutenant; Ibni-Sin, the scribe; and the elders of his *arrum* did not agree to approach the net. But Lamassani, nun-*nadītum* of Shamash, declared through the net: "Abi-sum and Ṣurarum were not begotten by Shummun-libshi. It is I who reared them." That is what she declared.[30]

These divine symbols, placed at the door of a temple or chapel, had a dreaded religious power. The plaintiffs, a group of military men, did not dare pronounce the oath that the judges demanded of them. The defendant did so, thereby winning the case.

1.3. Symbolic Gestures upon the Conclusion of a Treaty

Symbolic gestures were not confined to the sphere of what is called private law. They were performed as well within the framework of diplomatic relations.[31] So it was that in Anatolia, within the context of the conclusion of an accord between Assyrian merchants and a local prince, the prince had to perform a symbolic gesture that is obscure for us (pass over a table and a chair); then the contents of a goblet were spilt while the following formula was pronounced: "If we reject your oath-*māmītum,* may our blood be spilt like [the contents of] the cup."[32]

Another example is documented in the Mari archives. King Huziri wrote to Zimri-Lim, king of Mari, to denounce the conduct of one of his vassals, named Akin-Amar: "One time, this man sat before my lord and he drank from the cup. Having elevated him, my lord counted him among the nobles, dressing him in attire and placing a wig-*huburtum* on him. But upon his return, he defecated in the cup from which he had drunk, and he became the enemy of my lord."[33] The alliance ceremony is described here as the occasion for symbolic gestures:[34] the lord gave a garment and a wig to his vassal and the vassal drank from a cup. To demonstrate the breaking of the alliance, Akin-Amar, once he had returned home, engaged in a no less symbolic gesture: he soiled the cup from which he had drunk during the ceremony, thus putting an end, metaphorically but very clearly, to the system of relations that had previously been established.[35]

Treaties were concluded by uttering oaths before the two kings' "gods." No text indicates in what form these gods were present. They were probably not statues but symbols, like the "great arms" to which an ambassador alluded in a letter to the king of Mari.[36]

2. The Composition of Texts

Some have been unable to resist the temptation to establish an opposition between the sphere of the oral, where local customs supposedly changed, and that of the written, seemingly characteristic of the central powers. Hence a few jurists have believed that paragraphs from the Code of Hammurabi express the obligation imposed by the king to fix in written form contracts (relating to marriage, herding, or tenant farming), or risk having them invalidated. That interpretation, already of long date, has now been abandoned: nowhere in Babylonian law does a contract have to be written down to be valid.[37]

2.1. The Use of Writing

The case of marriage contracts demonstrates this clearly. There is no fixed model for that type of text, and all those that are known describe more or less unusual situations (polygamy, wives who were formerly slaves, and so on). The purpose of writing down the contract was therefore to protect the rights of those who were in a particularly vulnerable condition.[38]

A historian must be attentive to the fact that this type of text often provides only what was considered essential, without reflecting reality in its entirety. From this standpoint, documents dividing an inheritance are very characteristic. In no sense do they give a complete inventory of the deceased's property. Texts dating from after the inheritance was divided may show that certain property, such as fields, had remained jointly owned[39] or that some categories of property were divided up but not put in writing, as this example demonstrates: "sealed document of tools from Idin-Eshtar, which were not placed on the partition tablet."[40] Local customs differed in that regard. It was the scribes of Nippur who provided the most exhaustive enumeration of the property divided up by heirs.[41]

The use of writing also made inroads because of the witnesses' mortality. In the case of an inheritance falling to someone who was adopted, years could go by between the act of adoption and the death of the adoptive parent; and it was precisely at that moment that the adoptee's right to the inheritance risked being contested, particularly by members of the adoptive family. The Babylonians thus had the sense that a written text had greater longevity than the witnesses. Clay tablets, after all, were sturdy, all the more so when they were protected by an envelope of the same material.[42]

Nevertheless, these tablets could themselves be the object of symbolic manipulation, as shown in the following example. Babylonian economic life was punctuated by "redress" measures (*mīšarum*) taken by the sovereign, which consisted in particular of canceling debts.[43] Upon the proclamation of such an edict, creditors were obliged to take their debt contracts before a commission, where the tablets were solemnly broken. On one such occasion, in year 13 of Hammurabi, a creditor declared that she had lost her tablet. So that she could not subsequently enforce that contract against her debtors if she happened to find it again, a clod of dirt (*kirbānum*) was broken as a substitute for the lost tablet, whose value was rendered void as a result. But at the same time, in order to better protect the debtors, a text was delivered to them describing the ceremony and specifying that if the creditor subsequently found and attempted to enforce a tablet, it would be considered counterfeit and would be broken.[44] The two practices—performance of a symbolic act and composition of a text—were thus not felt to be in any way exclusive of each other.

2.2. Written Evidence

That complementarity appears as well in judicial procedure relating to the use of evidence. A lawsuit dating from the reign of Ammi-ditana (1683–1647 BCE) may serve as an example.[45] A certain Ilsha-hegal had purchased a built-upon lot measuring 775 square feet. A few years later, she resold half of it to a woman named Belessunu for fifteen shekels of silver. The sale was the occasion for a written contract, on which the seller, Ilsha-hegal, placed her seal. Subsequently, Ilsha-hegal contested Belessunu and her husband's ownership of the plot, claiming that they had not paid her the fifteen shekels. The judges asked her to prove that she had not received that sum by producing witnesses and an acknowledgment of debt by which Belessunu had pledged to pay the rest of the price later. This, Ilsha-hegal was unable to do. The procedure did not end there, however. Belessunu's husband also brought in the sales contract. The witnesses whose names appeared on that document were then questioned, and they confirmed that the fifteen shekels had been paid, as Ilsha-hegal was then forced to admit. Because she had disavowed her own seal, a punishment was imposed on her, and she had to leave a claim relinquishment tablet. This text demonstrates perfectly that there was no opposition between written evidence and oral testimony, since the judges both "listened" to the purchase tablet brought in by Belessunu's husband and questioned the witnesses whose names appeared on the tablet. Arguments by modern jurists about whether the old French adage *lettres passent témoins* (written texts take precedence over witnesses) was valid in the Mesopotamian world are the very prototype of a false problem.[46]

That absence of opposition is even marked in the use of vocabulary; hence, we sometimes find such indications as, "Keep my tablet as testimony [*šibūtum*]." Similarly, the expressions "the tablet's mouth" (*pī ṭuppim*) and "the tablet's speech" (*awāt ṭuppim*) were both used to refer to a text's contents. Finally, official records frequently contained the annotation, "The judges heard the tablet."[47] The living word of the (unfortunately mortal) witnesses therefore cannot stand in opposition to the dead letter of the (everlasting) text. Although no one can question a tablet, at least one can listen to the unalterable spoken words that it preserves.

In the absence of both written proof and oral testimony, the law used the procedure of the probative oath. A still-unpublished text now housed at the Louvre provides a characteristic example. It involved a resident from Isin who, with his family, was forced by military events to seek refuge and who was engaged in a lawsuit with his brother.[48] The text explains that "he could not bring either tablet or witnesses," which can be explained by his status as an exile: the archives and witnesses had remained in Isin. The judges then decided to have him swear an oath by Shamash (the god of justice) and by his own city's God, Gula. In this case, the oath was clearly considered a last resort.

2.3. The Growing Importance of the Written Document

The importance attached to the preservation and transfer of property deeds shows that it was no negligible matter to be able to take advantage of written evidence, and the preoccupation with such evidence seems to have increased throughout the period under consideration.

A first case will illustrate that thesis. It involves the arrangements an individual made when a document was lost. A first attitude is documented in a lawsuit that occurred under the reign of Rim-Sin, king of Larsa.[49] A private individual, to exercise his right to an inheritance, was obliged to swear an oath at the gate of the god Nimmar: "I am truly the son of Sin-magir, because he adopted me, and my sealed document was not destroyed." The aim of that last assertion was to eliminate the possibility that the adoption had been revoked, which would have found expression in a verbal repudiation and in the breaking of the tablet. The individual in question was obviously unable to produce the tablet relating to his adoption by Sin-magir, no doubt because it was destroyed or lost. But he swore that the adoption was never invalidated: he gave his word as a substitute for the missing written text. About half a century later, there was a similar case in which an adoptee had lost his adoption tablet.[50] At that time, the municipality met and a procedure was set in place to reconstitute the lost document. This suggests that the possibility of simply resorting to an oath by the interested party and by the witnesses was now felt not to provide sufficient guarantees.

The disappearance by about 1730 BCE of the pestle (*bukānum*) clause in sales contracts can also be explained in terms of the inroads made by the written text over symbolic practices. Other explanations have been advanced, such as the influence of the formularies of southern Babylonia (where that clause did not exist) following the conquest of that region by Hammurabi.[51] Nevertheless, to consider the disappearance of that clause as a mere editorial change assumes that the formula had already been emptied of any reference to an actually performed ritual, which has not been proven. In fact, the abandonment of that symbolic gesture and the disappearance from contracts of the corresponding clause may well attest to the growing importance of the written text in legal matters in the late eighteenth and in the seventeenth centuries.

Also attesting to the growing authority of the written word was the universalization of the transfer of deeds upon the deliverance of a property, whether in an exchange, an inheritance, or a sale: those who received the goods took the previous tablets relating to them at the same time.[52] Consider the case of someone who purchased a house. He kept in his archives the document of purchase that had been remitted to him. Upon his death, the son who inherited the house received that tablet, and, if he happened to sell the house, he would transfer the previous purchase tablet to the buyer. The new owner would thus have in his archives both purchase deeds relating to the house. The aim of that practice was obviously to consolidate the rights of the new owner: in case of a lawsuit, the previous owner would be unable to make a claim based on his property deed, since he had had to surrender it. When the seller could not provide the buyer with the document(s) to the property transmitted, an official statement was drawn up stipulating that, should the tablet(s) be found, it or they would belong by rights to the new buyer. Many examples indicate the importance that Babylonians granted to written evidence. Hence, in a matter dealing with an aunt's inheritance, a nun-*nadītum* believed she had been wronged. She had received the property deeds from her aunt, but as often happened, these were kept by her father. She therefore judged it wiser to await her father's arrival before undertaking a lawsuit, which aptly illustrates the importance in her mind of the written text for establishing her rights.[53]

Conclusion

The cases presented here in their broad outlines show the degree to which crude oppositions—such as prelaw and law, or world of rite and oath on one hand, world of writing on the other—need to be qualified. The Babylonia of the twentieth to seventeenth centuries BCE partook of both aspects, inextricably mingled.

Nevertheless, a diachronic analysis allows us to highlight the increasing place occupied by the written text, along with the decline or abandonment of certain symbolic practices, such as passing in front of the *bukānum*. Such an evolution should no doubt be linked to the realm of law. Some have spoken in this respect of the reign of Hammurabi as a turning point that marks a "secularization" of justice.[54] That inaccurate term should be replaced by "professionalization": there were now appointed judges who described themselves on their seals as "servants of the king."

But an essential phenomenon, that of historical continuity, must also be taken into account. For more than three centuries, northern Babylonia was noted for a high stability in its population. Thanks to private archives, it is possible to follow certain families over three or four generations.[55] At that time, then, collective memory proved to be inadequate for guaranteeing the rights of individuals, and recourse to the written document became increasingly indispensable as time passed.[56]

CHAPTER 4

The Transfer of Property Deeds and the Constitution of Family Archives

The starting point for this inquiry was a study I did of texts discovered in Kutalla,[1] a small locality near Larsa. In analyzing the archives of Ṣilli-Eshtar, I was able to demonstrate that on five occasions, when someone purchased a piece of land, the seller also handed over the deed of property, in this case the contract attesting that the seller (or the seller's father) had purchased the plot a few—or even a few dozen—years earlier. I then sought other examples of such a practice. There were only three in 1922, when Mariano San Nicolò published his volume devoted to the final clauses of sales contracts.[2] Since then, the documentation had increased considerably, yet the subject had not attracted the attention it deserved. At the Rencontre Assyriologique in Leiden in 1983, I delivered a paper that launched new research on that theme. Since that time, as I had hoped,[3] the staff that is publishing the archives discovered in the house of Ur-Utu in Tell ed-Dēr has communicated information that has advanced our understanding.[4]

When a piece of real property changed hands, it was the custom for the new owner to receive from his predecessor the deeds, not only for a sale, but also for an exchange, an inheritance, or a dowry. Evidence of that practice allows us to better understand the process by which family archives were formed and how they evolved.

An initial study was published under the title "Transmission des titres de propriété et constitution des archives privées en Babylonie," in *CRRAI* 30, ed. K. R. Veenhof, PIHANS 57 (Leiden: 1986), 121–40. At certain points, it is presented here in abridged form, supplemented by a great deal of material published since 1986.

1. Sales

It is well known that in ancient Babylonia, the sales contract (*ṭuppi šīmātim*, literally, "purchase tablet")[5] was written from the perspective of the purchaser, to whom it was delivered, and who kept it as the deed of property. It is also possible to show that, at the time of the sale, the seller's deed of property was not destroyed but rather was delivered to the purchaser. That customary rule is never explicitly formulated,[6] and it is primarily the exceptions that have informed us of its existence. Usually, the issue of handing over property deeds arose only when the seller found himself unable to produce them. Two practices were then possible. Either a particular clause to that effect was added to the contract, or a pledge to restore the mislaid documents was made. In addition to these negative indications, there are a few documents that definitively prove that the transfer of property deeds was the rule. In examining these cases, I shall be able to demonstrate that the expression *ṭuppāt ummātim* (or *kanikāt ummātim*) designated the property deeds thus transferred.

1.1. The Addition of a Clause

Contract YOS 13, 95,[7] which dates to year 10 of Samsu-ditana (1616 BCE), reports the purchase by two brothers of a piece of land located in Kish, from two priestesses-*ugbabtum* of the god Zababa. The scribe used the usual formulary, but a special clause followed the oath: "The *kanikāt ummātim* relating to 1 ½ *sar* of that covered house, which were lost in year 28 of Samsu-iluna, whether they are seen in the tablet chest of Dan-eressa, daughter of Awil-Ea [or] of Nish-inishu, daughter of Ili-eribam, or in whatever place where they may be located, should they be produced, they will belong [therefore] to Ina-Esagil-zeri and Marduk-muballiṭ, the sons of Awil-Amurrum, who purchased the piece of land." It is clear that reference is being made to the earlier property deeds, whose loss dates back nearly a century (ninety-two years to be exact).[8]

Consider a second example. Contract BBVOT 1, 111, which dates to 1/xii/Ammi-ditana 5 (1679 BCE), records the purchase of a bare plot of land in the cloister of Sippar, sold by Awat-Aya and purchased by Beletum, both nuns-*nadītum* of Shamash. Between the relinquishment clause and the oath is a clause relating to the nontransfer of deeds of property: "Because there is no purchase tablet [*ṭuppi šīmātim*] or original property deed [*ṭuppi ummātim*], if a purchase tablet or an original property deed is produced outside, it will belong to Beletum, the nun-*nadītum* of Shamash, daughter of Ipqusha. If it is the object of a claim, Awat-Aya, nun-*nadītum* of Shamash, daughter of Warad-Sin, will be responsible."[9]

1.2. The Drafting of a Separate Document

In certain cases similar to those just studied, rather than insert a particular clause in the sales contract, the scribe drafted a separate document.[10] Texts of this type that have already been published use similar formulas.

A first document (CT 6, 6),[11] composed in Sippar in year 11 of Ammi-ṣaduqa (1636 BCE), has to do with a fifteen-arpent field, which constituted Shamash-bani's share of an inheritance and had been purchased by the nun-*nadītum* Aya-rishat in year 3 of Ammi-ditana (1681 BCE). After Aya-rishat's death, her brothers sold to the majordomo Ina-Esagil-zeri the field she had acquired. Ina-Esagil-zeri then demanded from them tablets that were described as *ṭuppāt ummātim u sirdē* (line 23). The brothers declared that these tablets had been placed in the cloister, but that when their sister died, the brothers, despite their efforts, had been unable to find the tablets.[12] The text ends as follows: "In the future, the *ṭuppāt ummātim u sirdē*[13] of the [field] that the majordomo Ina-Esagil-zeri, son of Etel-pi-Ea, <purchased> from [name of sellers], [when] they are seen and produced, will belong to Ina-Esagil-zeri, son of Etel-pi-Ea, purchaser of a fifteen-arpent field."

YOS 13, 203, is a similar document, drawn up in Kish at the beginning of the reign of Ammi-ṣaduqa.[14] The first part of the text, which is missing, must have contained the description of the field sold. That tablet was composed when a seven-arpent field was purchased by a certain Amurrum-na—— from three individuals. It seems, according to line 8 on the obverse, that these were two brothers and a cousin. The situation is similar to that described in CT 6, 6: the sellers could not provide the buyer with the original sealed documents (*kanīkāt ummātim*) relating to the field sold. A deed was therefore drawn up, ending as follows: "The day when, in the chest of Sin-ib——, in the chest of Elmeshum and of Warad-Lahmi, in the chest of their family, of their brothers and sons, and wherever they may be found, [these tablets will be seen], they will belong to Amurrum-na——, son of Nabium——, the purchaser [of this seven-arpent field]." Hence, no member of the family of sellers, in whose houses these tablets might be located, would be able to contest the ownership of the field by the purchaser, to whom that document was delivered.

Let us now examine CT 45, 102.[15] This text, whose obverse is in a poor state of preservation, deals with the purchase of a bare plot of more than eight *sar* located in Sippar-Amnānum (line 21) by two brothers, Qurdusha and Warad-Ulmashitum, porters at the temple of Annunitum. At the time of the sale, the purchasers asked the sellers for the *ṭuppāt ummātim* (line 29). The end of the text has disappeared, so it is not possible to know whether these tablets were transferred or whether they were lost. But this document allows us to prove definitively that the *ṭuppāt ummātim* were the original deeds of property that had to be provided by the sellers. After the detailed cadastral description of the sold parcels, the scribe indicates:

> [Total]: 8 *sar* 14 *gin* of bare land, in Sippar-Amnānum, that Qurdusha and Warad-Ulmashitum, porters of the temple of Annunitum, sons of Taribusha, purchased for 16 ½ shekels of silver from Warad-Ullab, son of Warad-Ulmashitum, and Warad-Ulmashitum, son of Sin-ishmeanni, his brother. [The buyers] asked [the sellers] for the *ṭuppāt ummātim:* 2 tablets [each dealing with] 3 ⅚ *sar* of bare land, [constituting] the share of inheritance of Bikkum, son of Imgur-Sin, and Ibni-Marduk, son of Shumi-irṣitim, 1 tablet [dealing] with a stretch of land of 1 ½ *sar* leading to a plot-*šikittum,* the acquisition of Bikkum, as well as his *ṭuppi šurdē.* Warad-Ullab and Warad-Ulmashitum . . .

The first part of the document is devoted to describing the plot sold, which is broken down into two unequal parts: a bare plot (A) of 7 ⅔ *sar* 4 *gin,* whose neighbors on all four sides are listed (lines 2–14); and an adjacent stretch of land (B) of ½ *sar* (about 194 square feet), whose cadastral location the scribe also indicates (lines 15–20).

The information provided by the text makes it possible to reconstitute the history of these two plots. Plot A constituted the share of inheritance of four individuals born of different fathers, probably four cousins. Following transactions whose details are not reported, two of these four heirs found themselves equal owners of the plot: 3 ⅚ *sar* and 2 *gin* went to Bikkum, the same area to Ibni-Marduk. Plot B was purchased by Bikkum. What the text does not say is how plots A and B passed from the hands of Bikkum and Ibni-Marduk to those of Warad-Ullab and Warad-Ulmashitum, the current sellers. At the time of the sale, the purchasers demanded the *ṭuppāt ummātim* from them (line 29). All the interest of the text lies in the following lines, which explicitly describe these tablets. In the first place, there were two *ṭuppāt zittim;* these were tablets listing the share of the inheritance falling to Bikkum and Ibni-Marduk respectively, each of whom had received an individual tablet, in accordance with the custom of Sippar.[16] Second, there was Bikkum's *ṭuppi šimātim,* that is, the sales contract that was delivered to Bikkum when he purchased plot B, accompanied by its *ṭuppi šurdē*. This document thus proves definitively that the *ṭuppāt ummātim* were the earlier tablets having to do with the various transfers (by sale, but also by inheritance) of which the property being resold had been the object. These tablets, which constituted Warad-Ullab's and Warad-Ulmashitum's deeds of property, had to be delivered by them to the purchasers.

Finally, let me cite YOS 13, 532.[17] The affair can be reconstituted as follows: at an unknown date, a plot was sold by the sons of Ali-talimi to Nabium-iddinam, who then resold the plot to Iddin-Nabium, in year 8 of Ammi-ditana (1676 BCE). In year 10 of Ammi-ṣaduqa (1637 BCE), that is, thirty-nine years later, Iddin-Nabium in turn sold the plot to a certain Ibni-Marduk. At issue are therefore three successive sales of a single plot. At the time of the last sale, the purchasers asked the seller for his deeds of property. Iddin-Nabium was obviously able to provide his contract (B) since the date of it is given. By contrast, the contract concerning the first sale (A) was nowhere to be found. Iddin-Nabium undoubtedly claimed he had not received it, since Nabium-iddinam had to pledge to restore the lost document. The situation may therefore be diagrammed as follows:

contract A — contract B — contract C

sons of Ali-talimi → Nabium-iddinam → Iddin-Nabium → Ibni-Marduk

1st sale — 2nd sale — 3rd sale

(Ammi-ditana 8) — (Ammi-ṣaduqa 10)

Note that texts of the same kind were drafted when a creditor could not deliver his debt tablet to a debtor who was the beneficiary of a royal remission of debts.[18] In other words, the status of debt contracts was analogous to that of property deeds: when these documents lost their original value, they were normally handed over by their former owner. If such was not the case, the purchaser or debtor could have a document drawn up stipulating that the former property deed or debt contract had not been delivered to him or had not been destroyed.

1.3. References to Earlier Transactions

The texts examined thus far were composed at the time of a sale, because the transfer of property deeds was problematic. They demonstrate—by virtue of being exceptions—that such a transfer was the rule. There are other examples, however, where the rule can be demonstrated positively, particularly when the sales contract explicitly refers to a previous transaction, as in this example:

> A plot of land of 1 ½ *sar* with uncovered construction, located in Sippar-Yahrurum, which is described as a bare plot on the previous tablet concerning it, next to the plot of Hungullum, son of Nabium-ekalli, which he purchased from the sons of the diviner Ishkur-mansum, and adjoining the street; having on the short side the main street of the Isineans, having behind it the plot of land of the scribe Warad-Ibari, son of Warad-Mamu; [a plot] that Hungullum, son of Nabium-ekalli, purchased from Ili-iqisham, son of Ali-lumur, for 5/6 shekels of silver, including the addition, in year 29 of Ammi-ditana. From Hungullum, son of Nabium-ekalli, Iltani, the *nadītum* of Shamash, daughter of Ibbi-Ilabrat, purchased [this plot] with the ring of her silver. As its total price, she paid 17 shekels of silver and invested an extra ½ shekel of silver. [Irrevocability clause, oath, witnesses, and date: 2/iii/Ammi-ṣaduqa 17+b=18 (1629).][19]

The object of that contract was the sale by Hungullum of an uncovered house to Iltani. The text indicates that the seller had himself acquired that plot a few years earlier,[20] when it had no construction on it. The details given in lines 3–4 and 13–17 suggest that the scribe had before his eyes the previous contract, which constituted Hungullum's property deed. These details might appear superfluous, but they are in fact necessary, once we realize that the previous contract was delivered to Iltani by Hungullum. In fact, the description of the plot on the two tablets does not correspond exactly; there is a bare plot in one case, a house in the other. Moreover, the neighbors on one side have changed: in the first contract, these were the sons of the diviner Ishkur-mansum. In the meantime, the plot had been purchased by Hungullum. The scribe had to indicate explicitly these differences between the two contracts to avoid any eventual dispute about the location and nature of the parcel sold.

Such an interpretation can be confirmed by the archives of a certain Alum. When he purchased a parcel from Ikun-pi-Shamash in year 6 of Samsu-iluna (1744 BCE), the contract explicitly mentioned that the plot in question had been previously acquired by the current seller's father.[21] As it happens, we have the contract corresponding to that previous transaction.[22] This is a tablet dated year 29 of Rim-Sin (1794 BCE), in which Ikun-pi-Adad, the father of Ikun-pi-Shamash, purchased the plot from Kibri-Adad. It is obvious that in year 6 of Samsu-iluna, Alum received not only the contract drawn up on that occasion but also the seller's deed of property, which was fifty years old. The case is thus exactly like those found five times in the archives of Ṣilli-Eshtar of Kutalla.[23]

1.4. A General Practice and Particular Cases

One letter confirms the generality of that practice: "Relative to the fact that the money was not brought <to> Ili-iddinam, son of Sin-bel-aplim, I reflected on the idea of writing to the representative [?] of Sin-ishmeanni. May a trusted man take 1 1/3 minas of silver, the price of the twenty-four-arpent field belonging to Ili-iddinam, may he come and find me and give the money to Ili-iddinam! I will then be able to have the sales contract taken to my father as well as the old *ṭuppāt ummātim*. Have your tablet brought to me, so that the sales contract of Captain Sin-ishmeanni can be written!"[24] According to that letter, a transaction was under way between Ili-iddinam and Sin-ishmeanni. Ili-iddinam was preparing to sell Sin-ishmeanni a field of twenty-four arpents. Since the price had not yet been paid to the seller, the sales contract had not yet been written[25] and delivered to the purchaser. The difficulty lay in the fact that the seller and the purchaser were not in the same place: the seller was close to the author of the letter, the buyer near its addressee. The procedure proposed by the author of the letter was simple. As soon as Ili-iddinam had received his money, he personally, having had the sales contract (*ṭuppi šīmātim*) drawn up, would have it taken to his correspondent with the old *ṭuppāt ummātim*, that is, the seller's deeds of property. If the seller and the buyer had been together, the drawing up of the sales contract would, to be sure, have been likewise accompanied by the transfer of these tablets, but we would have known nothing about it.

What happened when someone sold only part of a parcel she owned? Despite its mutilations, CT 48, 82 provides an answer to that question: "Given that on the *ṭuppi ummātim* 18 2/3 *sar* of drained land are recorded, and that Ahatum, daughter of Mar——lim, is to receive the *ṭuppi ummātim* from the hands of Warad-Sin and Lu-Nanna, sons of Mannum-balum-Shamash, Ahatum being the purchaser of [only] 13 2/3 *sar* of drained land, for the excess that exists it is Warad-Sin himself, as well as his brother Lu-Nanna, who will measure it in relation to the 13 2/3 *sar*; [but] they will have to hand over in all [the 13 2/3 *sar* to Ahatum]."[26] The immediate context of this document is obviously the sale to Ahatum of a plot of 13 2/3 *sar* by Warad-Sin and his brother Lu-Nanna. The two sellers had to deliver to the purchaser the *ṭuppi ummātim* relating to that piece of land (lines 4–8). But the previous transaction reported by said tablet had to do with a parcel of 18 2/3 *sar,* of which at present Ahatum had purchased only 13 ²⁄₃ *sar*. There was thus an excess of 5 *sar* (line 11), which the two brothers were authorized to themselves demarcate within the whole parcel, provided they delivered the full 13 ²⁄₃ *sar* to Ahatum. The present document was thus drawn up for a simple reason: in transferring to Ahatum the *ṭuppi ummātim,* the sellers would have lacked a deed of property for the five *sar* they were keeping. Subsequently, Ahatum or her descendants might have argued on the basis of the *ṭuppi ummātim* that mentioned 18 ²⁄₃ *sar* that the remaining five *sar* ought to be returned to them.

We have previously seen promises to restore lost *ṭuppāt ummātim* written up to guarantee the rights of the purchaser. Here, conversely, it is the sellers who need protection. This example offers proof that the transfer of *ṭuppāt ummātim* was obligatory: it would have been simpler if the sellers had kept their deed of property—but then Ahatum's rights would have been threatened.[27] The owner kept his original deed of property only if he sold merely a small part of his property: we know of one example in which an individual sold one *sar* of land and did not transfer to the purchaser his original deed of property, which covered six *sar.*[28]

One last text, the beginning of which has disappeared, illustrates the obligatory connection between the sale of a piece of land and the transfer of the property deeds:

> My servant Iluni the clerk-*šammallūm* told me this: "The judge Iddin-Irra gave the daughter of Ipiq-ilishu ¹⁄₃ mina 8 ½ shekels of silver as the price for [her] plot. [But] Shummum-libshi and Labishtum placed an oath on [her] lips and told the judge Iddin-Irra that the plot could not be sold. Nabi-Ilabrat, priest-*šangūm* of Annunitum, gave another plot to the judge Iddin-Irra [!], for a value of ¹⁄₃ mina and 8 ½ shekels of silver. He [Iddin-Irra] gave the sealed sales contracts relating to the plot to the priest-*šangūm* of Annunitum, Nabi-Ilabrat." I have just sent ¹⁄₃ mina and 8 ½ shekels of silver to you. Give that money to the priest-*šangūm* of Annunitum, Nabi-Ilabrat, and the sealed tablets . . . to . . . [the rest has disappeared].[29]

The affair can be reconstituted as follows. First, the daughter of Ipiq-ilishu sold a plot to the judge Iddin-Irra. The seller's brothers intervened, declaring the sale void. The most simple explanation is that their sister was a nun-*nadītum* and her father had not given her the right to alienate her dowry.[30] The buyer nevertheless had to be compensated. It was then that the priest-*šangūm* of Annunitum, Nabi-Ilabrat, gave Iddin-Irra a plot of a value equivalent to the one the judge had bought. One might think that in order for the cancellation of the sale to take effect, Iddin-Irra had only to destroy her *ṭuppi šimātim* in the presence of Nabi-Ilabrat. But the text indicates that he delivered to her the sale contracts relating to that plot. The use of the plural "contracts" can be understood only if, at the time of the sale, Iddin-Irra had received not only the contract but the seller's property deeds. The sale having been voided, the daughter of Ipiq-ilishu recovered her tablets so as to be able to prove her rights to the plot in question. Once again, there appears to be a very close link between the object possessed and the written documents attached to them: the voiding of a sale obliged the purchaser to return both the object sold and the deeds of property that had been delivered to him at the time of the sale.

2. Exchanges

The obligation to transfer deeds was not limited to the sale of real property, however. It was also in force for other modes of transfer, beginning with exchanges. The land exchanges that owners sometimes engaged in were usually motivated by the desire to join together their dispersed parcels to make a totality for a single holder.[31] On the occasion of such exchanges, two copies of a contract were drawn up, to be kept respectively by each of the parties. To avoid disputes from arising later, it seems that the deeds of property were exchanged at the same time as the real estate to which they related. That, at least, is the lesson of CT 45, 60. This tablet dates from the reign of Ammi-ṣaduqa and comes from Sippar. The judge, Utu-shumundib, and the farmer at the cloister, Ada-mushallim, had exchanged two fields. For some unknown reason, Utu-shumundib wanted to go back on that exchange. An agreement between the two parties was then reached before the assembly (*puhrum*) of the city. It is the text of that agreement, preceded by a reminder about the previous transaction, that the document provides.[32] In the first place, Adad-mushallim (A) and Utu-shumundib (U) had exchanged two fields equal in area. In both cases these were acquisitions, not their own properties. At the time of the exchange, A handed over to U his deeds of property, that is, his purchase tablets.[33] Note that U did not do the same, yet that did not lead A to demand them. The reason seems to be that the field purchased by U was larger, and that he took only twelve arpents from it to give to A (lines 8–9). He therefore had to keep his purchase tablet to prove his property rights over the part of the field he was keeping.[34] The procedure seems to have been perfectly regular, and that was not the object of the debate. A year later, U expressed to A his desire to go back on the exchange (even though he had taken the initiative for it). The return of the twelve-arpent field to A required that U also return the purchase tablets relating to them, which he could not do immediately. An agreement was thus concluded before the assembly, fixing the feast of Shamash as the deadline by which U had to deliver to A his tablets so that the cancellation of the exchange could take effect.

The lesson to be drawn from this case is twofold. First, the ordinary procedure for exchanges entailed the exchange of property deeds as well. Second, the return of the deeds of property governed the cancellation of the exchange: if the tablets were not returned to A, he would have remained owner of the field he had received from U. I cannot imagine a better example of the importance assumed by writing in legal matters at the end of the first Babylonian dynasty.[35]

3. Inheritances

The documents relating to the division of possessions by the heirs of someone who had died generally mention only certain categories of goods, such as plots of land, slaves, and prebends. The most exhaustive descriptions in that regard are found in the texts from Nippur. But nowhere are there indications concerning the transfer of the deceased's archives. We might assume that the eldest child inherited them; but in reality, archives were divided among the heirs such that the tablets followed a path identical to that of the goods with which they dealt.

3.1. Normal Inheritances

Very characteristic in this respect is the document previously published by Father V. Scheil[36] and republished by W. F. Leemans.[37] Its contents can be summarized as follows: Sin-muballiṭ had purchased from his brother Enlil-issu a house measuring 5/6 *sar* 4 *gin*, located in Ur. Ili-amtahar inherited that house from his father, Sin-muballiṭ, but a certain Sin-remeni contested its ownership. Ili-amtahar sought out the judges of Larsa, to whom he showed his father's purchase tablet; his ownership of that house was thereby confirmed.

All the interest in this case lies in the fact that we possess the previous deed by which the three sons of Sin-muballiṭ had divided up their father's property.[38] Each of the heirs received ½ *sar* 6 *gin* of a house located in Larsa and 18 *gin* of a house located in Ur. Leemans comments on that division as follows: "It is more likely that Sin-muballiṭ possessed one house in Larsa and another in Ur, and that his sons were given an equal share in those houses, and that no actual division took place."[39] If we add up the three shares, we in fact obtain a house of 1 5/6 *sar* 18 *gin* in Larsa, and a house of 5/6 *sar* 4 *gin* in Ur. As it happens, the latter figure is precisely the area of the house disputed with Ili-amtahar in the lawsuit examined above. It appears, therefore, that these two houses were not held jointly by the sons of Sin-muballiṭ, contrary to what Leemans suggests. An agreement must have been reached between them by which Ili-antahar received the entire house in Ur and simultaneously the tablet by which his father had purchased said house from Enlil-issu.

This case is therefore very instructive, since it shows that the purpose of transferring the previous tablet to the heir of a property was to protect him from eventual disputes: Ili-amtahar had only to show the judges his father's purchase tablet to exert his rights over Sin-remeni.

3.2. Inheritances following an Adoption

That practice was even more necessary when the heir was not a blood descendant of the deceased but someone who had been adopted and whose rights could be more easily called into question.[40] The transfer of the adoptive parent's deeds of property to her heir constituted, alongside the adoption tablet, a guarantee for the adoptee.

This is easily seen when we consider a lawsuit, AO 5429, published by F. Thureau-Dangin[41] and republished with a decisive improvement by M. Schorr.[42] The affair can be summed up as follows. Naramtani, nun-*nadītum* of the god Shamash, had been adopted by her aunt Nish-inishu, who was also a *nadītum*.[43] Part of the property that Naramtani received from her adoptive mother was a piece of land that Nish-inishu had purchased from a certain Ishum-gamil, whose son instituted legal proceedings against Naramtani. On that occasion, Naramtani had received in an envelope the tablet that constituted Nish-inishu's purchase contract. The inheritance had thus been effected through the transfer of real property and the corresponding deed.

A second, more complex example is reported in CT 47, 63. That tablet was composed in Sippar in year 14 of Samsu-iluna (1736 BCE), after a nun-*nadītum* named Amat-Mamu had lost her archives. Here is a translation of that document:

> [lines 1–35] Inheritance of Belessunu, *nadītum* of Shamash, daughter of Manium: Amat-Mamu, *nadītum* of Shamash, daughter of Sin-ili, is her heir. [A description follows of the property Amat-Mamu inherited: 4 fields,[44]

constituting a total of 43 arpents (lines 3–16), 1 house and 2 bare plots (lines 17–19), and slaves (lines 20–21), as well as 2 cooking pots (line 22)]. All her own property [and] her inheritance, her pin having been stuck into the wall[45] from the straw to the gold, that Belessunu, daughter of Manium, has or will have [is the property] of Amat-Mamu, her heir, daughter of Sin-ili. [Lines 26 to 35 are the clauses governing the situation so long as Belessunu is still alive, particularly the payments of grain, wool, and oil that Amat-Mamu must make to her].

[lines 36–50] After Belessunu had given that inheritance to Amat-Mamu, daughter of Sin-ili, and Amat-Mamu had fed her for two years, Amat-Shamash, daughter of Sin-iqisham, and Nish-inishu, daughter of Anum-pi-Shamash, the daughters of her father's brothers, brought a claim regarding the field described in that tablet. Zimri-Erah, the mayor [*rabiānum*] of Sippar, and the guild of merchants [*kārum*] of Sippar examined at the Shamash Gate the tablets of Belessunu's dowry that her father had given her, the tablets of the inheritance of Naramtum, her father's sister, which she had given her unconditionally, as well as the tablets of the daughters of her father's brothers [the two aunts of Belessunu] who lodged a complaint against her. Zimri-Erah, mayor of Sippar, and the *kārum* of Sippar examined [them] at the Shamash Gate. They confirmed the ownership of her property based on the content of her tablets, and returned it to Belessunu. As a result of the fact that Amat-Shamash and Nish-inishu had filed a complaint against her without grounds, they imposed a punishment on them and made them leave a relinquishment tablet.

[lines 51–69] After they had been made to leave a relinquishment tablet and Belessunu died, Sin-ili placed in storage, in the house of his brother Ikun-pi-Sin, the adoption tablet, the *ṭuppāt ummātim* of the fields and houses that Belessunu had given to Amat-Mamu, daughter of Sin-ili, as well as the relinquishment tablet that the daughters of her father's brothers had had to leave; these tablets were lost in the house of Ikun-pi-Sin. Sin-ili made a deposition before Sin-ishmeanni and the *kārum* of Sippar, and Ikun-pi-Sin declared to Sin-ishmeanni and to the *kārum* of Sippar that these tablets were lost. On the order of Sin-ishmeanni and the *kārum* of Sippar, the present tablet was "brought [back] to life." The inheritance tablet, the *ṭuppāt ummātim*, and the relinquishment tablet that Amat-Mamu, daughter of Sin-ili, had received from Belessunu, in the house of Ikun-pi-Sin as well as everywhere they shall be seen, is the property of Amat-Mamu, daughter of Sin-ili. In the future, according to the content of that tablet, Ikun-pi-Sin, his sons, as well as the relatives of Belessunu, men and women, however many they may be, will raise no complaint against Amat-Mamu, daughter of Sin-ili.[46]

This affair can be reconstituted in four stages. First there was the adoption of Amat-Mamu by an older *nadītum* named Belessunu. On that occasion, an adoption contract (*ṭuppi aplūtim*) was drawn up listing the property of Belessunu (immovable and movable) that Amat-Mamu was to inherit, on the condition that she provide her adoptive mother with an income during her lifetime. Two years later, two cousins of Belessunu disputed her ownership of a field. The municipality of Sippar examined the deeds of the two parties. Belessunu then brought in her own, that is, the tablets relating to the dowry she had received from her father, as well as the tablets relating to the inheritance she had from an aunt who had adopted her. She won her lawsuit, and her cousins had to leave her a relinquishment tablet (*ṭuppi lā ragāmim*). After Belessunu's death, the archives of Amat-Mamu were stored at her uncle's. These tablets included the contract for Amat-Mamu's adoption by Belessunu, the relinquishment tablet, and the *ṭuppāt ummātim* of the fields and houses that Belessunu had given to Amat-Mamu. These could only have been Belessunu's deeds of property, that is, the tablets relating to her dowry and the inheritance she had from her aunt.[47] Hence, at the time Amat-Mamu was adopted by Belessunu, she received her adoption contract, which constituted her deed of property for the inheritance. When her adoptive mother died, however, Amat-Mamu inherited not only Belessunu's property but also the deeds relating to it. All these tablets were stored at her uncle's, where they were mislaid; Amat-Mamu then found herself lacking any written deed. The lost documents were subsequently reconstituted.[48] The text of CT 47, 63 thus falls into three sections: lines 1–35 reproduce the content of the *ṭuppi aplūtim*; lines 36–50 reproduce that of the *ṭuppi la ragāmim*; and the end of the text explains the reason for the present document. Note that the *tuppāt ummātim* were not reconstituted; that was obviously not possible, since these documents dated back to Belessunu's youth, when her father gave her a dowry and her aunt adopted her. When Amat-Mamu's archives were lost, Belessunu was dead (and had been for a period of time we cannot assess), as no doubt were all the witnesses to the two contracts in question.[49]

3.3. Complex Trajectories under Samsu-ditana

Let me end this chapter by mentioning a few equally complex but later cases, dating from the reign of Samsu-ditana, the last sovereign of the first

Babylonian dynasty (1625–1595 BCE). These are sale contracts that retrace the history of the property that is the object of the transaction. The details given by the scribe suggest that he had consulted the tablets corresponding to the successive stages of the transfer of these plots of land.

The first contract, YOS 13, 90,[50] has to do with a parcel that had initially been given as a dowry (*nudunnum*) to a priestess-*ugbabtum* of the god Zababa named Nish-inishu, in year 14 of Samsu-iluna (phase A), that is, 1736 BCE. After the death of Nish-inishu's brother (?), a certain Belessunu surfaced as the owner of the plot; we may suppose that this was another *ugbabtum* adopted by Nish-inishu (phase B), but the text does not clarify this point. It simply indicates that Belessunu sold the plot to another *ugbabtum*, Nish-inishu, daughter of Ea-naṣir (phase C). The last phase (D) entailed the sale of the plot by that Nish-inishu to a certain Nanaya-ibinishu. But the contract explains that this last sale was made "in conformity with the terms of the old sealed tablet dealing with the dowry,"[51] that is, the document dating to year 14 of Samsu-iluna. That tablet, 114 years old, had thus passed from hand to hand over a series of different transactions (adoption, then sales). In addition, if the text does not explain how Belessunu entered into possession of that plot, it is because her adoption contract (*ṭuppi aplūtim*) was not transferred when she resold the property she had inherited. The situation may therefore be represented as follows:

A	B	C	D
father(?) → Nish-inishu	→ Belessunu	→ Nish-inishu	→ Nanaya-ibinishu
dowry	(adoption?)	sale	sale
(Samsu-iluna 14)			(Samsu-ditana)

A record-setting case is known thanks to YOS 13, 96. This sales contract from Kish dates from about year 10 of Samsu-ditana (1614 BCE).[52] The text begins with the cadastral description of the sold parcel, but has the peculiarity of giving the names of the neighbors three times:[53] first, based on the content of the tablet of year 20 of Sin-muballiṭ (1793 BCE); second, based on the content of the tablet of year 1 of Abi-eshuh (1711 BCE), when Utul-Eshtar purchased the plot from Marduk-naṣir; and third, in terms of the current situation, the neighbors who owned the parcel at the time being the great-grandchildren of Utul-Eshtar. Such a document obviously suggests that the scribe had the previous contracts, dating from 1793 BCE and 1711 BCE, before his eyes; however well developed collective memory may have been, it would have been difficult to identify the names of the neighbors to that plot living more than 180 years earlier. We must therefore assume that Marduk-naṣir, who probably obtained that plot through an inheritance, had received the first sales contract at the same time. In addition, he must have handed over that tablet to Utul-Eshtar along with the plot when it was sold in 1711 BCE, after which the plot and the two contracts were transferred via inheritance to the descendants of that Utul-Eshtar, from generation to generation. Here, then, is a quite extraordinary example in which we can follow the transfer of a plot and of the tablets relating to it, through the combined operations of inheritances and purchases, for almost two centuries.

A further example was recently published,[54] this one from Babylon. That tablet, which records the sale of a plot in year 11 of Samsu-ditana (1615 BCE), contains a number of interesting elements. As sometimes happened in that late period, the former neighbors (*itū labīrūtum*) are mentioned (lines 6–11), then the history of the plot is recalled: a first sale in Samsu-iluna 19, that is, 1731 BCE (lines 12–17); another in Ammi-ditana 27, that is, 1657 BCE (line 18–4'); then, in year 7 of Samsu-ditana (1619 BCE), the purchase by Ibni-Marduk of the parcel from Utlalum, after he and his brother had divided up the property of their sister, who died without heirs (line 5'–18'). After all that, the current neighbors are indicated (lines 19'–25').

Conclusion

It appears therefore that the custom of transferring deeds of property was widespread in Babylonia.[55] It is attested from Sippar to Ur, whatever the mode of transfer (dowry, sale, inheritance, or exchange). From the reign of Hammurabi on, the deeds thus transferred were designated by the expression *ṭuppāt* (or *kanīkāt*) *ummātim*,[56] the usage of which is perfectly clear, even if its etymology is less so.

Von Soden classified examples of that expression under *ummatum*, within the general category "etwa Stamm-, Heimateinheit," adding: "eine Besitzstandsurkunde?"[57] That etymology is unsatisfactory, since the usage of the term in no way refers to collective ownership. In addition, the full graph *um-ma-a-tin* in *BE* 6/2, 97[58] shows that we are probably dealing with the plural of *ummum* (literally, "mother").[59] The particular sense of *ummum* in this context would be "point of origin," like the Sumerian *ama* in the expression *ama-ar-gi$_4$*.[60] The *ṭuppāt ummātim* were thus the old deeds of property, whatever their nature (sales contract, dowry, inheritance, or exchange), insofar as they defined the "previous status" of the property transferred.[61] Handing them over at the time of a new transfer of property had two essential aims: to make it possible to verify the legality of the transaction[62] and to prevent the former owner from subsequently contesting the rights of the new owner by producing his deed.

What was the impact of that practice on the constitution of private archives? In the first place, we must avoid taking a unilateral view of family archives as entailing a gradual accumulation over the course of their history. In fact, a family whose patrimony was diminishing saw its archives dwindle to an equal degree: the sale of a field was accompanied by the loss of the corresponding tablets. In Babylonia, poor people had no archives, but neither did the bankrupt.

A second consequence is methodological in nature. We have seen that, upon the partition of property, the heirs divided up the tablets corresponding to their share of the inheritance. When the archives of an individual are discovered, we must therefore realize that the texts relating to the previous generations constitute only a portion of what existed. Consider once again the famous case of the Iddin-Lagamal family in Dilbat. It is clear that the uncovered archives correspond to the fourth generation of the family. It is thus very dangerous to attempt to reconstitute the grandfather's policy in acquiring real estate based on the texts preserved by a single branch of his descendancy.[63] From that perspective, we can also better appreciate the case of the great amasser of land Balmunamhe. In light of that example, Leemans wonders whether the practice of transferring deeds was truly generalized: "It is remarkable that in this archive none of the older records concerning the same objects are found, although these had to be delivered to the purchaser with the object."[64] Thanks to the texts recently published in YOS 12, we have the likely explanation for that apparent anomaly: the tablets that have come down to us did not constitute the archives of Balmunamhe, who lived under Warad-Sin and Rim-Sin, or even those of his children, but those of his grandchildren, active during the period when Samsu-iluna ruled Larsa.[65] These contracts can therefore be considered the deeds of property preserved by his heirs after they had divided up the patrimony constituted by their grandfather.[66]

That custom had a serious shortcoming, however: the tendency of the tablets to proliferate. The more years that elapsed, the greater the number of tablets transferred with the property. And the more numerous the tablets, the greater was the risk of mislaying them. That is no doubt why all the texts reporting the loss of *ṭuppāt ummātim* date from after the era of Hammurabi, though that phenomenon may also attest to the growing importance granted to writing in legal matters.[67]

I shall end this chapter with a regret and a hope. The regret concerns a well-known state of affairs. With a few exceptions, the private archives we have from Old Babylonia come from illicit excavations. As a result, tablets discovered at a single site have been dispersed, and, in the case of the *ṭuppāt ummātim,* the link that united them is very difficult to reestablish.[68] As for the hope, it was elicited by the discoveries of the Tell ed-Dēr expedition, which confirm the importance of the phenomenon studied here. Let me express the wish that these archives will continue to be published in the near future.

CHAPTER 5

The Status of the Code of Hammurabi

Babylonia was very different from the Greek world, where one of the foremost characteristics of democracy was to set down the laws in writing and display them in the center of the commonwealth. The desired goal was that the laws would be the same for all citizens. Despite certain resemblances, the Code of Hammurabi, a copy of which was no doubt located in each of the main temples of the kingdom of Babylon, provided nothing similar. Some punishments laid down in the code explicitly varied depending on a person's status.[1] It is therefore necessary to move beyond that surface similarity.

I have chosen the Code of Hammurabi as an exemplary case,[2] primarily because it is the most complete text and the only one with a monumental dimension.[3] But there are other, more circumstantial considerations, including a symbolic justification: it has been exactly a century since Father Scheil provided the *editio princeps* of the code, a few months after the fragments of the stela had been exhumed and assembled.[4] Such a tour de force surely merits being remembered. In addition, the stela of Susa was recently displayed at the Louvre within a new setting, which displays this monument much better than before.[5]

I shall examine two aspects of the Code of Hammurabi: the modalities of its composition and the manner in which it was used, during its author's time and subsequently.

This chapter is a revised and augmented version of a study published under the title "Le statut des 'codes de lois' des souverains babyloniens," in *Le législateur et la loi dans l'Antiquité. Hommage à Françoise Ruzé, Actes du Colloque International du CRHQ de l'Université de Caen, 15–17 mai 2003*, ed. P. Sineux (Caen: 2005), 93–108.

1. The Formation of the Code

The text of the stela found in Susa, which probably first stood in Sippar, has three parts: a prologue, about 275 "laws," and an epilogue. The uncertainty about the number of laws stems from the fact that part of the bottom of the Louvre stela's face was later obliterated. There are doubts about the number of columns that thereby disappeared (between five and seven), and hence, doubts about the number of lines and consequently of laws. The manuscripts existing on tablets do not yet allow us to restore that lacuna completely and reliably.[6] The "laws" are always formulated casuistically: instead of articulating a general principle, each law stipulates a case (expressed as a protasis), then gives the corresponding verdict (apodosis), in accordance with a type of presentation in effect in all kinds of collections (of medicine, divination, and so on) set down in writing at that time. The Babylonian word *dīnum* can designate the law in its totality but also the case or corresponding verdict separately. The Code of Hammurabi belongs to a tradition of similar, older texts, from which it borrowed a great deal. It also resulted from the king's judicial activities. "Traditional" cases and those judged by the king were systematized with the aim of giving the code the appearance of an exhaustive collection.

1.1. A Developing Tradition

The Code of Hammurabi is, in the first place, the end result of a cumulative process. It belongs to a literary genre of which it is not the first attestation: at least three other similar collections preceded it. Two were composed in Sumerian, those of Ur-Nammu, king of Ur (2111–2094 BCE)[7] and of Lipit-Eshtar, king of Isin (1936–1926 BCE).[8] The Code of Hammurabi is also not the first to have been composed in Akkadian: it was preceded by that of Dadusha, king of Eshnunna (d. 1779 BCE), known through two tablets discovered in Tell Harmal (Shaduppum), now supplemented by a fragment from Tell Haddad (Me-Turan).[9] These older codes obviously inspired that of Hammurabi,[10] whose current form dates from the end of the king's long reign (about 1755 BCE).

An example of the Code of Hammurabi's reliance on an older collection can be seen in the share of an inheritance attributed to a daughter whose father had consecrated her to a god. Usually the father gave his daughter a dowry. If he did not, the Code of Hammurabi stipulated that she would have to be included in the inheritance (section 180): "If a father has not given a dowry to his daughter, a cloistered nun-*nadītum* or a recluse-*sekertum,* after the father is deceased she will have a share of the movables of the paternal house as an heir and will have possession of them during her lifetime. Her inheritance will fall to her brothers." This provision had already appeared in the Code of Lipit-Eshtar: "If during her father's lifetime, a daughter becomes a *nin-dingir, lukur,* or *nu-gig,*[11] they [the sons] will divide up the house [in considering her] an heir."[12] A comparison between the two texts reveals the extreme concision of the old formulation, which does not explain that the provision is valid only if the father has not given his daughter a dowry. The categories of women at issue are not exactly the same. But the spirit of the two laws is clearly identical: in the absence of a dowry, a daughter has a right to a share of the inheritance.

1.2. A Collection of Case Law

The Code of Hammurabi was also the result of the king's judicial activities. A recently published letter from Hammurabi has provided a new example of them: "The son of Ipqusha the goldsmith told me this: 'Last year, thieves broke through [the wall of] my house and seized my property. In addition, they have now again broken through [the wall of] my house, but I was able to seize these thieves.' That is what he told me. At present, I have just sent you this son of Ipqusha. Tie up the thieves whom he seized, place them under strong guard, and have them brought to me. In addition, send me the witnesses of the son of Ipqusha."[13] According to that letter, Hammurabi wanted to investigate the matter personally. It is likely that section 21 of the code resulted from the sentence the king issued at the end of his inquiry: "If someone has broken through [the wall of] a house, he will be put to death in front of the hole and will be hanged there."

Another recently published document allows us to consider more thoroughly the fundamental question of how the Babylonian rulers' law codes were formed. It is a letter from the son and successor of Hammurabi, Samsu-iluna (1749–1712 BCE). He had been alerted to two matters by those responsible for the nuns-*nadītum,* celibate women dedicated to the god Shamash. The king then wrote to the authorities of Sippar:

> Tell Sin-naṣir, Nuratum, Sin-iddinam, the guild of merchants [*kārum*] of Sippar, the judges of Sippar-Amnānum, Awil-Nabium, Sin-iddinam, the priests-

> *šangum*, the judges, the temple officials, the officials for the nuns-*nadītum*, and the guards at the gate of the cloister of Sippar-Yahurum: thus [speaks] Samsu-iluna . . .[14]
>
> [*Report on the second case*:]
>
> They told me this, moreover: "The judge Awil-Sin has a claim of money owed by Mar-Shamash, a man from Sippar. Because the latter did not pay it back, he seized Mar-Shamash, saying: 'If you keep your property[15] and I receive nothing, I will seize the slave of your daughter the nun-*nadītum* of Shamash, who lives in the cloister.' That is what he said." That is what they told me.
>
> [*Royal Directive*:]
>
> A nun-*nadītum* of Shamash whose father and brothers have provided her support for her to live and for whom they wrote a tablet,[16] and who lives in the cloister, is not responsible for the debts or the service-*ilkum* of the house of her father and her brothers.[17] Her father and brothers shall perform their service-*ilkum* and . . . Any creditor who seizes a *nadītum* of Shamash for the debts or the service-*ilkum* of the house of her father and brothers, that man is an enemy of Shamash![18]

This document is altogether remarkable, both from the standpoint of its composition and from that of its legal significance. Observe, first, how the king rendered his verdict. Instead of writing, "The judge Awil-Sin does not have the right to seize the slave of the daughter-*nadītum* of Mar-Shamash," he formulated in anonymous terms a rule with a general import, which the local authorities then had to apply. Even the style of the passage is altogether similar to the verdicts (apodoses) of the Code of Hammurabi. The literary genre is different, however, since this is a letter. What we have here is what jurists call a "rescript" and what the Babylonians termed a *ṣimdat šarrim* ("king's ruling").[19] The letter was in fact preserved in the archives of the cloister of Sippar and in those of the temple of Shamash;[20] it was subsequently recopied several times, which shows that this precedent was not forgotten. In the case of Samsu-iluna, things do not advance beyond that stage. No collection of his rescripts was promulgated in a more solemn form. Not only was the Code of Hammurabi too recent for anyone to have felt the need to provide a sort of "new, updated edition" of it, but such an action was also alien to the practices of the time; its text was not to be altered. Samsu-iluna's rescript simply made it possible to supplement it with two cases that had not been considered by his father in his code. That example illustrates well that the codes had a dimension beyond the simple compilation of verdicts resulting from the king's judicial activities.[21]

1.3. Systematization

We must therefore consider another aspect of the codes: their systematic (which does not mean complete) nature. Starting from a certain number of "traditional" cases on one side, and of verdicts rendered by the king on the other, the codes could grow through a process of variation. That is, verdicts were proposed for situations that constituted so many exemplary cases, without ever exhausting the possibilities, despite the overt desire to do so.[22]

A comparison of the provisions relating to murder in the Code of Ur-Nammu and in the Code of Hammurabi is very instructive in this respect.[23] Section 1 of the Code of Ur-Nammu indicates simply: "If a man has committed murder, that man shall be killed." By contrast, we find in the Code of Hammurabi, section 1: "If someone has accused a man, imputing a murder to him, but has been unable to bring proof against him, the accuser shall be put to death." That more complex formulation reveals many elements of the judicial system. First, a private individual could formulate an accusation, which was therefore not reserved for an official or a body.[24] Second, such an accusation had to be supported by evidence. And finally, the false accuser suffered the punishment that would have been that of the guilty party, in accordance with a principle found elsewhere in the code. That punishment for the murderer is explicitly formulated only in section 1 of the Code of Hammurabi; it is merely implicit in section 1 of the Code of Ur-Nammu.

A good example of variations on a single case is provided in the Code of Hammurabi by the four laws relating to someone who has captured a fugitive slave:

> [Section 17] If someone has captured a fleeing slave, male or female, in the countryside and takes him or her back to the master, the master of the slave will have to give the person 2 shekels of silver. [Section 18] If that slave does not want to name the master, the person must bring him or her to the palace; the case will be the object of an investigation and the slave will be returned to the master. [Section 19] [But] if the person keeps that slave in his house and if, subsequently, that slave is seized in his possession, that man will be put to death. [Section 20] If the slave flees from the house of the one who had seized hold of him or her, that man will have to swear an oath to the slave's owner and will be acquitted.

The general case, then, is articulated in section 17. Section 18 stipulates the case of a slave who persists in his attitude, refusing to say to whom he belongs. Section 19 introduces another variant: the person who has taken in the fugitive slave keeps him for himself. Last case: the fugitive slave repeats the offense with the person who captured him and who was preparing to return the slave to his master. Not all cases are envisioned: for example, that of someone who, having stopped a slave in flight, allowed him to leave voluntarily. Moreover, it is clear that this set of laws concerns only the person who seized a fugitive slave. It does not deal with relations between the master and the slave: the slave's punishment will be the master's affair once the slave is returned to his house.[25]

Everyone is agreed in comparing, from a formal point of view, the casuistic method in the law codes to the method in other kinds of collections. Those devoted to divination occupy an important place. One example, drawn from a treatise on teratology, is very clear in this respect: "If a deformed newborn has teeth [at birth]: the days of the king are finished, someone else will sit upon his throne."[26] But the analogy between divinatory collections and "codes of laws" goes further.[27] In the questions (*tāwītum*) asked of the gods, the names of the consultant and of the protagonists are always given. Hence, in ARM XXVI/1, 170, the Benjaminite diviners in the service of Sumu-Dabi, then at war with Zimri-Lim, king of Mari, reproduce the question they have formulated (lines 9–15): "If Zimri-Lim with his troops approaches our lord Sumu-Dabi, must Sumu-Dabi, with troops small or large, who are all at his disposal and whom he will send off, obstruct Zimri-Lim's way? Must he wage battle with him, and will he be safe and sound, will he be victorious, will he stand in triumph?" In ARM XXVI/1, 169, the same two diviners cite and discuss the result obtained during another consultation: "The month having elapsed, the first one, we took omens for the safety of the city for a month [with] two sheep. According to the content of these omens of ours, this month, *'the enemy will not come against you with his troops and his allies. He will not besiege me. He will not install himself across from my main gate, his bronze spear will not cause any wounds.'* The ominous sign of a raid was obtained several times [which means]: *'His desires are turned to the act of raiding and he will raid my* salhum.'"

The difference is clear. The question raised, as it is reproduced in ARM XXVI/1, 170, is very precise and names the enemy—in this case, Zimri-Lim. The response, by contrast, as it is cited in ARM XXVI/1, 169, consists of quoting apodoses excerpted from collections, even though the diviners do not indicate this explicitly.[28] This is the same phenomenon as in Samsuiluna's rescript examined above. The questions that the authorities of Sippar asked of the sovereign were very precise, naming the protagonists in the two cases to be judged. The king responded in impersonal terms, prescribing a rule with a general value. It is possible to argue that, similarly, in divination the god Shamash responded in a general manner. The diviners, like the judges, had to interpret these indications and apply them in the precise case that had been submitted to them and regarding which they had formulated a request.

The similarity is also striking from a theoretical standpoint. The diviners designated the "predictions" of the Babylonian omens as, literally, the "verdicts" (*dīnum*) of the gods.[29] But to my knowledge, no one has ever compared the divinatory activity that ultimately gave rise to these collections[30] to the judicial activities that produced the codes.[31] It seems to me, however, that the parallel must be pursued to its extreme conclusion. In the case of divination, some omens corresponded to real observations, for which there was an equivalent in royal case law. But there were others that were added by the same process of variation as in the codes of laws. A comparison between the old version of the treatise of teratology, dating from the eighteenth century BCE, and the version known through manuscripts dating from a millennium later, indicates an evolution of that kind.[32]

As for the "incomplete" character of the code, which some authors have emphasized in order to denounce the inappropriateness of the modern term "code" used to designate that text,[33] judges of the time likely did not experience it as a hindrance. Having become proficient in the code, they entered into its spirit and must have been able to decide cases that were not anticipated in it. In that respect, they were acting no differently from their diviner colleagues;[34] in case of difficulty, they could always turn to the king.[35]

2. The Various Uses of a Single Text

We must now address a second question, which is simple only in appearance: What purpose did the Code of Hammurabi serve?

2.1. A Text for the Reading . . .

Ideally, the code was in some sense a way for the king to render justice everywhere and to everyone, as the epilogue indicates: "May the wronged man who faces trial come before the statue of me as king of justice, may he read my inscribed stela, may he hear my precious words, may my stela show him his case and may he see its verdict, and be reassured."[36] Most of the translations render the passage as "may he have my stela read out to him,"[37] but, word for word, the Babylonian is "may he read" (and that is how Scheil translated it). The "classic" commentary, though conceding that the verb *šitassūm* can describe an act of reading aloud to oneself, adds: "As, however, hearing has no point after reading a document to oneself, the meaning must be that the man shall have the text read to him by someone else and so hear it; this agrees with the fact that few litigants are likely to have been able to read it for themselves."[38] In reality, we now know that the ability to read and write was not as restricted at the time as was long believed and was in no way exclusive to scribes.[39] As a result, there is no doubt that the desire expressed by Hammurabi is that the plaintiff may himself read the verdict corresponding to his case.

In addition, the Louvre stela was not unique: other fragments, also found in Susa, come from several different copies.[40] There was, then, a real desire for diffusion and the possibility of consultation. Everyone was supposed to have access to the just king. Because of the vast territories conquered by Hammurabi at the end of his reign, he could no longer be accessible in person. It was then that he turned to the written word, to continue to fulfill the duty of justice that the gods had entrusted to him.[41]

Nevertheless, the limits of that desire quickly become clear. It must be admitted that the material layout of the different stelas on which the Code of Hammurabi was engraved did not favor a consultation of the text. There are no subdivisions allowing one to discern the plan presiding over the organization of the code's 275 paragraphs, and the prologue and epilogue are not separated from the laws themselves. This is in sharp contrast to the ingenious system of *axones* represented on a goblet in the Metropolitan Museum.[42] But the situation is hardly different from that of the Gortyn laws: the very layout of the text made them difficult to consult. These laws were engraved primarily for ideological reasons: to borrow a formula used recently by François Lissaragues, "that text is not made to be read, it is made to be there" (ce texte n'est pas fait pour être lu, il est fait pour être là). We could say the same thing about the Code of Hammurabi: it was not made to be read (*lu*) but to be seen (*vu*).

The difficulty in consulting the Code of Hammurabi is one of the reasons that many Assyriologists have argued it should not be considered a compilation of laws meant to be applied.[43] They have pointed out the analogies between this text and the commemorative inscriptions intended to present the monarch to the deities and to preserve his memory among future generations.[44] They rely especially on the text of the epilogue, in which Hammurabi himself addresses posterity: "May every king who exists in the country in the future, forever, respect the words of justice (*awāt mīšarim*) that I inscribed on my stela. May he not change the judgments of the country that I rendered or the verdicts of the country that I decided." In this view, the code is primarily a commemorative inscription. Instead of placing the emphasis on the king's activities at war, or on his talents as a builder, it depicts him as a judge whom every subsequent monarch will be able to take as a model—just as a future king could restore the ruins of the buildings erected by his predecessor by following the plans for them.[45] It seems to me that this point of view is valid, but it is not necessarily the only one possible.

2.2. An Applied Code?

A number of indications seem to show that the code was actually applied, or at least that it sometimes served as a guideline. The case involving the ransoming of a prisoner of war is ambiguous. The Code of Hammurabi foresees the following situation: "If a merchant ransoms a soldier-*rēdūm* or a soldier-*bā'irum* who was taken prisoner during a royal expedition and has him return to his city, if there is in [the soldier's] house the means to ransom him, it is he who should ransom himself; if there is not in his house the means to ransom him, he shall be ransomed by the temple of his city's god; if there is not the means to ransom him in the temple of his city's god, the palace shall ransom him. His field, his garden, and his house shall not be given over for his ransom."[46]

A letter from Hammurabi may illustrate the application of that provision: "Sin-ana-Damrum-lippalis, son of Maninum, whom the enemy captured—give his trader 10 shekels of silver from the temple of Sin and ransom him."[47] It is possible to imagine, of course, the opposite relationship between this letter and the code: it could have been because Hammurabi had individual cases of this kind to settle that he prescribed a general law in his code.[48]

A second example has recently been discovered.[49] This is a letter known through two manuscripts. Consequently, there is a good chance that it was a school exercise. "Tell Sin-ay-abash: thus [speaks] Shamash-naṣir. May Shamash and Marduk give you life out of regard for me! Concerning the field of Sin-magir, the soldier-*rēdūm:* Sin-magir, the soldier-*rēdūm,* fled, and his field was given to Munawwirum. Today, his sons appeared, saying: 'We want to have possession of our father's field and we will perform our father's service-*ilkum*.' The king said: 'Their field is returned to them and they will have to perform their father's service-*ilkum*.'"[50] This case is in fact stipulated in section 28 of the Code of Hammurabi: "Given a soldier-*rēdūm* or a soldier-*bā'irum* who was taken prisoner [while he was at his post] in a royal fortress: if his son is able to perform the service, he shall be given the field and the garden and he will have to perform his father's service." Hence, the heirs of a person who had one of the Crown lands as a benefice could lay claim to that land after their father had ceased, voluntarily or not, to serve the king, once they had taken upon themselves the service relating to its tenure. The letter gives the impression that the king's decision, which Shamash-naṣir was responsible for applying, was general in character: it may in fact be an allusion to section 28 of the code.

The case involving wages is even clearer. Section 273 of the code reads: "If someone has hired a wage earner, from the start of the year to the fifth month he shall give him 6 grains of silver per day; from the sixth month to the end of the year he shall give him 5 grains of silver per day." The difference can be explained as a function of the seasons: since the Babylonian year began in the spring, the first five months were those during which agricultural activity was most intense. Since the labor force was more in demand, the remuneration was higher. Such rates were not vain wishes on the part of sovereigns, but are rather occasionally referred to in archival documents. Hence, in response to a correspondent who told him of the demands of textile workers working under his orders, a certain Alammush-naṣir wrote: "The wage of a hired worker is inscribed on the stela."[51] It is likely that this is an allusion to a copy of the code, whose public character is therefore clear; its text truly served as a guideline.[52]

I must nevertheless point out that other stelas, more limited in character, may also have served as guidelines in the matter of fees. This is indicated by a brick of Atta-hushu, who reigned in Susa in about 1900 and who alludes to a monument of that kind: "Atta-hushu, shepherd of the god Inshushinak, son of Silhaha's sister, made a stela of justice. He installed it in the marketplace. Anyone who does not know the correct price,[53] may Shamash inform him of it!"[54] The Code of Hammurabi does not contain a list of prices of this kind. But the collection of Eshnunna's laws does, beginning with a list of equivalents in silver for a whole series of goods, followed by the prices for renting various objects (chariots, boats, and so on), as well as wages.

It is true that examples of explicit references to the Code of Hammurabi are rare. Nevertheless, two pieces of evidence need to be introduced. Let me remark, first, that though we do not possess any quotations from the Code of Hammurabi in legal documents, we also possess very few from any royal edicts, which we are nonetheless certain were applied.[55] In addition, the situation must be linked to divinatory practices in the age of Hammurabi.[56] When they rendered a verdict, judges never cited the code, but the diviners of the time also never explicitly cited a compendium of omens to support their predictions, contrary to what is attested for the first millennium BCE.[57]

2.3. The Secondary Uses of the Text

Finally, let me mention what I shall call the secondary uses of the Code of Hammurabi. This text was employed in the training of scribes. A certain number of copies have been found on tablets from the Old Babylonian period, which date from the time of Hammurabi's successors until the end of his dynasty in about 1600 BCE. At the same time, the text of the Code of Hammurabi also played a privileged role in safeguarding the king's memory for a longer duration.[58] We possess many copies of excerpts from his code, quoted until the Achaemenid period. Let me point out that this was a unique case: no other collection of laws, such as that of Ur-Nammu, king of Ur, or Lipit-Eshtar, king of Isin, or Dadusha, king of Eshnunna, was recopied for centuries in that way.[59] Several manuscripts of the code appeared in the famous library that King Ashurbanipal constituted in Nineveh in the seventh century, and in the library of Ebabbar of Sippar.[60] We should nevertheless not believe that the code still played a precise role in the legal life of that time:[61] it was obviously copied within the context of scribes' training, and commentary entailing explanations of a philological nature was composed. From the standpoint of the Babylonian language, that text represents a sort of "classic," playing a role comparable to the writings of Cicero for Latin. An exegetical text from the late Babylonian period contains a quotation from the code's prologue, which shows that this text was even part of the corpus used by the particularly erudite literati as a starting point for esoteric considerations.[62]

Conclusion

I have intentionally placed the emphasis on what differentiates the situation in Babylonia from that of the Greek city-states, despite the similarities of content identifiable in their respective laws. The Code of Hammurabi clearly belongs to a religious ideology of the exercise of kingship. This is indicated at the beginning of the prologue: "Therefore, the gods An and Enlil, to improve the people's well-being, pronounced my own name, Hammurabi, devout prince who reveres the gods, in order to make justice arise in the country, to eliminate the bad and the perverse, to prevent the powerful from oppressing the weak, to appear like the god Shamash over all men and to shine over the country." That comparison of the king to the sun god

Shamash is at the heart of the question, and the scene that appears on the top of the Louvre stela is very significant in that respect. The king is represented standing in front of the god Shamash, who is recognizable by the rays coming from his shoulders.[63] It is not by chance that Shamash is also the god of divination, designated the "master of judgment and decision" (*bēl dīnim u purussim*). This is not a question of inspiration but of imitation: just as Shamash judges in heaven and decides human beings' fate, so the king on earth must judge trials and render a verdict to all his subjects.[64]

CHAPTER 6

The "Restoration" Edicts of the Babylonian Kings and Their Application

If there was one fundamental theme in the kingship ideology of Mesopotamia during the three millennia of its history, it was truly that of justice. The image par excellence of the sovereign was that of "good shepherd,"[1] guide to his people. All the same, the notion of justice was embodied in two terms with rather different connotations, *kittum* and *mīšarum*. The first is derived from a root that means "to be stable": this is justice inasmuch as it guarantees the established order. Hence the king had to assure respect for ownership and the repayment of debts. *Mīšarum*, by contrast, is derived from a verb meaning "to straighten out, to set right": this is justice inasmuch as it corrects iniquitous situations. That term was used, for example, when a king decreed the abolition of debts.

That second image of the king, which portrayed him as the protector of the oppressed, was a constant. Its first attestations date back to the princes (*ensi*) of Lagash in the mid-third millennium BCE, and it was also found among the neo-Babylonian sovereigns in the sixth century BCE. The whole problem is whether that form of justice, of which the kings availed themselves in their inscriptions, was a literary "topos" or whether it corresponded to real measures.[2] Documentation from the Old Babylonian period gives us an excellent opportunity to respond to that question. In fact, several "restoration" edicts, the texts of which have come down to us, were promulgated during that time.[3] The oldest dates from the era of Hammurabi's successor, Samsu-iluna (1749–1712 BCE); unfortunately, only a few scraps of

A version of this chapter was published under the title "Les édits de 'restauration' des rois babyloniens et leur application," in *Du pouvoir dans l'antiquité: Mots et réalité,* ed. C. Nicolet (Paris: 1990), 13–24. Many points have been clarified here and supplemented with documentation that appeared after the original article was written.

it remain.[4] Another, larger fragment, cannot at present be dated with precision.[5] But we also possess the complete text of the edict dating from the ascension to the throne of King Ammi-ṣaduqa (1646–1626 BCE), which constitutes our chief point of reference.[6] The aim of the present chapter is not only to present the content of these edicts but also to assess the degree to which they were actually applied. To do so, I shall turn to legal documents, which are particularly abundant and varied for these two centuries. Many of them have been published in recent decades.[7]

The measures decreed by the sovereigns concerned, in the first place, the administration of the Crown lands. But in their desire to correct iniquitous situations, kings did not limit themselves to these lands: they also ruled on the fate of persons and property. I shall also focus on the circumstances surrounding the proclamation of these edicts and the problem of their periodicity, closely linked to that of their application and efficacy.

1. The Measures Internal to the Administration of the Crown Lands

The existence of a vast area of Crown lands was one of the fundamental economic and political characteristics of Babylonia. The "restoration" edicts included measures relating to the products of these lands and others relating to their marketing. I shall examine in detail these two series of measures, before showing how the provisions of the edict were applied.

1.1. Measures relating to Products

The first measure announced in Ammi-ṣaduqa's edicts consisted of canceling the arrears of the tributaries to the palace (section 1): "The arrears of the farmers, shepherds, knackers, people working in the summer pastures, and [other] tributaries to the palace, in order to strengthen them and treat them equitably, are cancelled: the collector must not take any legal action against a tributary's house." The details of that measure are made explicit in sections 12–18.

That cancellation can be explained in terms of the farming method employed on the Crown lands. These lands were rented out to individuals (the *nāši biltim,* literally, "royalty holders") for an annual fixed payment, partly in kind and partly in silver. The farmers (*iššakum* in Akkadian) were assigned certain lands, as well as cattle and agricultural implements. In addition, the administration pledged to provide the water necessary for irrigation, indispensable in a country where the scant rainfall made dry farming impossible. In return, the farmers had to supply a fixed quantity of silver and grain. Similarly, the shepherds responsible for vast flocks had to provide a certain level of increase every year as well as a sum of money. Knackers were responsible for recovering the carcasses of dead animals belonging to the palace's herds. For each head of livestock (cattle, sheep, or goats), they had to pay the palace a certain quantity of raw material (wool, hide, or sinew) and silver. The system was thus in great part identical for the cultivation of land (cereal fields or palm groves) and for the management of herds.

The best case currently known is that of a palm grove located south of Babylon during the reign of Samsu-iluna (1749–1712 BCE). We possess, in particular, a large tablet, dated year 3 of that sovereign, which lists the contributions of palm dates and silver made by twenty-six head gardeners and calculates the remainder to be paid. And in four cases we have the receipt for that remainder, and we see that the gardeners in question could not acquit themselves of their arrears until two or three years later.[8] Letters relating to the same issue allude to this problem of arrears and show how acute it was.[9]

1.2. Measures relating to Marketing

The second measure in the edict concerned the merchant groups (*kārum* in Akkadian) responsible for marketing the surplus production of the Crown lands. In this case as well, the arrears were canceled (section 3): "The *kārum* of Babylon, the *kārum* of the country, and the *rā'ibānum* that were assigned to a collector by the tablet of the New Year—their arrears since year 21 of Ammi-ditana [1663 BCE] until month 1 of year 1 of Ammi-ṣaduqa [1646 BCE], as a result of the king's instituting of 'restoration' for the country, are cancelled; the collector shall not take any legal action against . . ."

For both the eighteenth and seventeenth centuries BCE, many extant documents illustrate the activities performed by the members of different *kārum* on behalf of the palace. In the seventeenth century, business representatives in Babylon received wool, livestock on the hoof, and sesame; they had to sell them in their native cities and pay large quantities of silver in return.[10] The correspondence addressed to one of these intermediaries, the head merchant of Sippar, Ilshu-ibni, has been preserved. It shows that the representatives had to be persuaded when the time came to pay the palace the money resulting from the sale of the merchandise entrusted to them. A bookkeeping document also shows that the price for the merchandise received in year 27 of Ammi-ditana was repaid completely only in year

34, that is, seven years later. Here again, the arrears seem to have been considerable, to such an extent that the edict of Ammi-ṣaduqa stipulated the cancellation of arrears accumulated since the previous *mīšarum,* which had taken place seventeen years earlier.

1.3. The Application of the Edict's Provisions

Although there is a great deal of evidence regarding the size of the arrears hanging over the tributaries and merchants, at present no legal document illustrates the application of the cancellation measures stipulated by the edict. Such silence on the part of the sources may give rise to a certain skepticism. That would probably be a mistake, for several reasons.

First, let me recall that we unfortunately do not have in our possession the archives of the palace of Babylon,[11] where the lists of arrears were certainly kept up-to-date.[12] Moreover, the very nature of these measures had a negative consequence as regards the written sources: the cancellation of arrears translated into the physical destruction of the tablets on which the amount was inscribed. The only type of text we could have would be a legal action by a tributary or a merchant against a collector who tried to make him pay a sum cancelled by the king. The absence (thus far) of such a document leads us to suppose that the orders were properly respected and that collectors had no interest in being overzealous.

2. Measures Relating to the Status of Persons and Property

The provisions I have examined thus far concerned the relations between individuals and the authorities within the context of the management of the Crown lands. But when the monarch proclaimed a *mīšarum,* he also intervened in relations among his subjects in three ways: by canceling noncommercial debts, by ordering the return of individuals to their original status, and by returning alienated goods to their former owners.

2.1 The Cancellation of Noncommercial Debts

The third measure announced in the edict did not concern individuals' relations with the palace but rather constituted an intervention by the authorities in the purely "private" sphere of the economy (section 4): "Whoever has lent grain or silver to an Akkadian or an Amorite as an interest-bearing loan or as a loan-*melqētum* or . . . and has had them leave a tablet, as a result of the king's instituting 'restoration' for the country, his tablet is rendered void; he shall not be reimbursed for grain or silver in accordance with the content of that tablet." Without entering into the rather complicated details of terminology, let me say that the edict distinguishes between two sorts of debts: what individuals were reduced to borrowing as a result of poverty on one hand, and, on the other, advances on funds agreed upon by persons for purposes of commercial operations. Only the first category was the object of debt forgiveness: the sum borrowed (in grain or silver) remained the debtor's property.

In that case, the question of whether the edict was applied arises even more urgently: Did the king have the means at his disposal to see that his decision was respected? Did creditors really renounce being repaid?

That this was truly a problem of authority is shown clearly by the edict itself. In fact, section 4, which announces the cancellation of noncommercial debts, is followed by a paragraph devoted to possible violations of that rule. The stipulated punishments in case of violation by the creditor ranged from payment of compensation equal to six times the total debt to the death penalty.

The efficacy of these threats seems to have been real. In fact, there are a certain number of debt contracts drawn up shortly after the promulgation of an edict in which the creditor took care to have added to the usual formula the note, "after the king's edict," so as to avoid any later dispute: since the debt was contracted after the edict, it would have to be repaid. The cancellation of debts stipulated by the edict obviously applied only retroactively. The very frequency of that type of comment[13] proves that creditors took the edict's provisions seriously.

One royal edict is even quoted in a letter: "Tell the man that Marduk gives life: thus speaks Awil-Sin. May Shamash and Marduk give you life! The musician Pu-illi made a deposition before me in these terms: 'I rented out my field and he [the lessee] gave me 2 shekels of silver as a loan. He gathered and brought in the grain that was in my field but did not give me the rent for my field.' That is the deposition he made before me. As you know, as a function of the order of my lord, *whoever has had [a loan] repaid and has taken it must return it. He is ordered not to take any legal action against the house of a soldier, a fisherman, or any other person performing the service*-ilkum [*of the king*]. Upon seeing my tablet, return to its owner the grain that you recovered and that you took. Is that how you carry out what the edict of my lord [prescribes]? In his absence, you deprive me of grain."[14] The allusion to "the order of my lord" (*ṣimdat bēliya*) is followed by a quotation from the edict of Samsu-iluna,[15] which the author of the letter urges his correspondent to apply.

Other indications that these measures were actually applied are provided in many private archives, like those of a certain Awiliya.[16] These are primarily composed of a dozen debt contracts issued between months 7 and 11 of year 7 of Samsu-iluna. Such a concentration in time calls for an explanation. We know that, in principle, a debt contract was destroyed at the time the debt was repaid. As it happens, a restoration edict was promulgated by Samsu-iluna at the start of year 8 of his reign: since all debts were cancelled, Awiliya's debts were never collected. Many other examples of this phenomenon have been identified.[17]

Nevertheless, it seems that there were attempts on the part of certain creditors to legally evade the application of the measures. A clause was inserted into the acknowledgment of debt specifying, "If a debt cancellation is instituted, this money [i.e., the money that is the object of the loan] will not be affected by it." Hence the debtor "voluntarily" gave up the benefits of an eventual royal edict. All the same, that type of clause is currently documented only in regions located on the periphery of Babylonia (in Syria or Anatolia).[18]

Unlike loans "of necessity," which were cancelled by the edict, commercial debts had to be honored as before (section 8): "An Akkadian or Amorite who has received grain, silver [or any other] good to make a purchase for a commercial expedition or for an organization, or as an advance of funds without interest for a business trip—his tablet will not be rendered void: he will have to make payments in accordance with the content of his contract." That explains why many debt contracts specify that the money was lent to make a purchase (*ana šīmim*) or for a commercial expedition (*ana harrānim*); since this type of loan did not fall within the purview of the edict, it had to be repaid in every case. Moreover, the wording of the debt contract could not leave room for ambiguity.[19] The edict also anticipated the case of an unscrupulous creditor who might try to pass off a loan of necessity (hence forgiven) for a commercial debt (section 7):

> If someone lent grain or money with interest and required that a tablet be left, then, when in possession of the tablet, declared: "I did not lend it to you with interest or as a loan-*melqētum:* the grain or the silver I lent you, I gave as an advance for a purchase, or as an advance of funds without interest for a business trip, or for another reason," then whoever received the creditor's grain or money shall produce people to testify about the content of the tablet that the creditor misrepresented. They shall make a declaration before the deity. As a result of his [the creditor's] altering his tablet and changing the

business arrangement, he shall give six times [the total of the debtor's loan]. If he cannot fulfill his responsibility, he shall die.

Another way of circumventing the royal edicts was to lend money or grain in exchange for labor.[20] The king clearly specified in his edict that this type of loan, if it was made under constraint, was invalid (section 22): "The lieutenant [*rā'ibānum*] of the military governor [*šakkanakkum*] of the country who constrains the family of a soldier-*rēdūm* or of a soldier-*bā'irum* to accept grain, silver, or wool in exchange for [labor at the time of] the harvest or a[nother] job shall be put to death. The soldier-*rēdūm* or the soldier-*bā'irum* shall be able to take [without repayment] everything that he gave him."

2.2. The Return of Persons to Their Original Status

Among the special measures added to the end of the edict, sections 20 and 21 stipulate the case of insolvent debtors from certain regions or cities who had had to place as security, or sell into slavery, their own person or members of their families (section 20): "If an obligation weighed upon an inhabitant [of the regions] of Numhia, Emutbalum, Idamaraṣ [or of the cities] of Uruk, Kisurra, or Malgum, and he had to place his own person, his wife, or his children in servitude for debts in exchange for money, or as a security, as a result of the king's instituting redress [*mīšarum*] for the country, he is liberated: his *andurārum* will be carried out." The term *andurārum* is traditionally understood as a synonym for "liberation."[21] The edict clarifies, however, that if the same person had to alienate one of his slaves, the *andurārum* of that slave would not be carried out (section 21): the slave would therefore remain the property of his purchaser. But if we translate *andurārum* as "liberation" in this case, we misunderstand the meaning of the measure. In fact, whether the slave was liberated or remained the property of his purchaser in no way affected his former owner, to whose fate both section 20 and section 21 are devoted. We gain a better understanding if we translate *andurārum* as "return to previous status":[22] the *andurārum* of a free man who has fallen into slavery is in fact his liberation, but the *andurārum* of a slave sold by his master to a third party is the return of that slave to his former master. That interpretation of *andurārum* is confirmed by the literal meaning of the Sumerian ideogram often used to notate the term (*ama-ar-gi*$_4$), "return to the mother," that is, to the original state.[23] Note, moreover, that the edict specifies in section 21 that this slave was *wilid bītim*, "born in the house," hence, born to a slave mother:

the possibility of his *andurārum* could signify only the return to the original house, that is, to that of his former master, and not the return to a freedom he never had.

Hence, the edict stipulated, in the case of a family facing hard times, that its members who had become debt slaves would be liberated; by contrast, the slaves who had belonged to that family would not be returned to it.

2.3. The Return of Property to Its Former Owner

Of the "redress" measures affecting individuals' relations with one another, some also had to do with the return of sold property to its former owner. Unfortunately, neither the edict of Ammi-ṣaduqa nor any official text describes these provisions. It is nevertheless possible to deduce their existence in several ways.

In the first place, on certain sales contracts for fields, orchards, or houses, we find the comment that the sale took place "after the royal edict."[24] By analogy with the measures concerning debts, we can confidently draw the conclusion that the edict in question would have affected the sale if it had taken place before the edict and not, as the contract is careful to specify, after it. How so?

An altogether extraordinary document,[25] dating no doubt to year 28 of Samsu-iluna (1722 BCE),[26] clarifies matters. It is a petition addressed to the king by a resident of Sippar, who complains that he was the victim of an injustice at the time an edict was applied. To deal with that problem, the king constituted a commission in the city of Sippar, composed of a general, judges from the capital, and judges from Sippar. The aim of that commission was to "[re]view the lawsuits of the residents of Sippar, listening to the purchase tablets of fields, houses, and orchards, and canceling those having to do with a property that should be returned pursuant to the edict" (lines 7–9). Other similar examples, though less explicit, also date from the reign of Samsu-iluna.[27]

I have been able to gather together the elements of an analogous case from a few decades earlier, concerning the kingdom of Larsa. During the last month of year 35 of King Rim-Sin (1788 BCE), a commission made up of judges from Larsa and Ur sat in Ur and similarly reviewed the property deeds. In the archives of two families of priests from that city,[28] we find that certain lands had to be returned to their former owner; in other cases, the land was divided between the former owner and the new one.[29]

That retrocession was sometimes also described by the term *andurārum*, as in this example: "In addition, as for the house [valued at] one mina of silver, the king established the *andurārum* of the house and returned it to us."[30] Just as we saw regarding persons, here too *andurārum* signifies "return to the previous status." We do not know what percentage of sales was thus affected by the measures of the edict. It appears that the sale of property that individuals had been obliged to alienate by necessity, particularly when they could not pay back a debt, was primarily at issue.[31] The "restoration" in this case had the effect of counterbalancing the tendency toward a decrease in the patrimony of the poorest people and the accumulation of large fortunes in land.[32]

As might be imagined, such a measure did not fail to provoke a reaction on the part of the buyers thereby obliged to retrocede the land they had acquired. A certain number of lawsuits illustrate such resistance but also demonstrate as a result that the restoration edict was not a vain wish on the ruler's part: people do not attempt to avoid a measure that is not being implemented.

The king's intervention in economic relations among individuals was thus intended to attenuate the effects of impoverishment at three different stages. The cancellation of sales allowed people who had been forced by financial troubles to alienate their patrimony to reclaim possession of it. Those who had been impelled to borrow out of need were granted relief by having their debts cancelled. Those who had borrowed but who, having been unable to repay their creditor, had become debt slaves, were liberated. These three measures, in their complementarity, attest to a resolute will to "rectify" intolerable economic situations.[33]

3. Circumstances Surrounding the Proclamations of These Edicts and Their Periodicity

3.1. Accession to the Throne

Beginning with Hammurabi for certain, it was the custom for a king to proclaim a *mīšarum* the year he acceded to the throne. According to the dating system prevailing at the time, that event gave its name to the following year. It is therefore possible to identify as "year names":

- Hammurabi 2 (1791 BCE): "The king instituted redress in his country"
- Samsu-iluna 2 (1749 BCE): "He instituted the *andurārum* of Sumer and of Akkad"
- Abi-eshuh 2 (1710 BCE): "Year when King Abi-eshuh, the beloved shepherd that the gods An and Enlil faithfully watched in the country of Sumer and

Akkad, straightened out the people and in which he instituted forever [?] in the country peace and good words; in which he brought into existence law [*kittum*] and restoration [*mīšarum*], and in which he delighted his country."

- Ammi-ditana 2 (1685 BCE): "The shepherd, beloved of the god Enlil . . ."
- Ammi-ṣaduqa 1 (1646 BCE): "The submissive shepherd, who obeys the gods An and Enlil, rose like the sun over his country and instituted the redress for the entire people."[34]

The proclamation of a *mīšarum* thus appears clearly to be the exercise of a duty toward justice that the gods themselves expected from the new king; it took the form of a ceremony during which the king brandished a gold torch. The torch was obviously a solar symbol, the king being explicitly compared to the rising sun. This is particularly significant given that the sun god, Shamash, was at the same time the god of justice. A recently published letter connects that ceremony to the end of the mourning period observed after the death of the previous king:[35] "The king promulgated the 'restoration' [*mīšarum*] of the country: he lifted the gold torch for the country and put an end to the country's mourning."[36]

In practical terms, how was such a decision brought to the knowledge of the interested parties? As it happens, we possess a letter written to a governor by King Samsu-iluna, at the time he acceded to the throne:

> Tell Etel-pi-Marduk: thus [speaks] Samsu-iluna. The king my father is ill and I have just ascended to the ancestral throne to redress the country. And in order to strengthen those who must pay a tribute, I have cancelled the arrears of the [shepherds], farmers, and kna[ckers]. I have cancelled the debt acknowledgment of the soldier-*rēdûm*, of the soldier-*bā'irum*, and of the simple subject [*muškēnum*]. I have instituted redress in the country. In the country . . . no one must use coercive measures against the house of a soldier-*rēdûm*, a soldier-*bā'irum*, or a simple subject. As soon as you see my tablet, you and the elders of the country that you administer, come up, so as to have an interview with me.[37]

In light of this document, it seems that not only the governors but also all the "municipalities" of the kingdom were summoned to Babylon. We may suppose that a tablet including the text of the edict was delivered to them,[38] which would explain why several copies of Ammi-ṣaduqa's edicts exist. The application of a redress edict entailed holding special commissions composed of judges from the capital and local judges.

3.2. The Periodicity of the Edicts

The promulgation of a redress edict was not restricted to the year the sovereign acceded to the throne. Hence, over the forty-three years of Hammurabi's reign, the *mīšarum* was proclaimed at least four times; under his four successors, it was proclaimed at least twice per reign.[39] It is possible that the scope of these *mīšarum* was not always the same, whether in terms of the catalog of measures or of the regions where they were supposed to be put into effect.

Some have wondered whether there was not a certain regularity to the dates at which the redress edicts were proclaimed. The question arose in 1965,[40] when F. R. Kraus discovered that under the reign of Samsu-iluna, the accession *mīšarum* (year 1) was followed by a second in year 8: the interval of seven years obviously brings to mind the biblical institution of the sabbatical year.[41] Nevertheless, it appears methodologically unsound, in discussing the Babylonian edicts of the eighteenth and seventeenth centuries, to rely on much later biblical texts whose real application many have placed in doubt.[42] In addition, the existence of a regular seven-year cycle marking the redress edicts would have run the risk of compromising the smooth application of the stipulated measures: at the approach of a new *mīšarum,* creditors would have declined to issue loans.[43] As a result, economic and social life would have been paralyzed every seven years. As it happens, we possess a letter attesting to the anxiety of a creditor who wished to be repaid before the sovereign decreed a cancellation of debts, at an obviously unpredictable time:

> Tell Warad-Sibitti: thus [speaks] Sin-eresh. Relating to 1 mina of silver, part of the silver I delivered to Ili-wekedu: yesterday, I, you, and Urim-sheme sat down and we closed the accounts before the god Shamash. After everything I had received was deducted, I still had a debt of 10 shekels of silver for him, about which I seized on him in these terms: "Until you return my money to me, you and I will not let go of each other. The king will cancel the debts, a great deal of time will elapse—therefore bring me my money [immediately]!" He replied to me: "I swore by the king! I will return your money to you in five days." I received from Paridum the guarantee that the money would be paid in five days. Pursue Paridum's pledge therefore, so that I obtain the money. Please don't be negligent.[44]

Finally, it has now been proven that the seven-year interval that existed between the first and second *mīšarum* of Samsu-iluna was not the general rule. The third *mīšarum* took place in year 17, and the fourth in year 28. Upon Abi-eshuh's accession to the throne, eleven years had elapsed since the last *mīšarum* of Samsu-iluna. Note as well that the *mīšarum* of Samsu-iluna's accession followed by eleven years the last known by Hammurabi, promulgated in year 32. Over half a century, then, we have the pattern 11–7–9–11–11. In other words, during that period, the interval between two *mīšarum* was 9±2 years (the average value being 9.8 years, the modal value 11). In addition, the edict of Ammi-ṣaduqa, promulgated in year 1 of his reign, stipulated the cancellation of arrears since year 21 of his predecessor. That date obviously corresponds to the last redress edict and, in that case, the interval was 17 years. It seems certain, therefore, that the edicts were not promulgated at regular and predictable intervals, if only because no one knew when the sovereign would die and his successor would accede to the throne.

3.3. Repeated Ineffective Measures?

We cannot fail to be struck by the multiplicity of edicts. There is no need to automatically conclude from that repetition that the edicts were not applied, as medievalists have done, for example, regarding the Carolingian capitularies. In fact, these were not reform edicts but exceptional measures; hence, the edict cancelled debts not yet repaid, but interest rates did not change. In other words, the cards were reshuffled, but the rules of the game remained the same. Inevitably, the same causes produced the same effects: hardly had a cancellation been proclaimed when the factors that had produced the accumulation of arrears and debts once again began to come into play, until the king judged the situation intolerable and decided on a new *mīšarum*. Perhaps, in certain instances, popular pressure hastened the promulgation of a new edict.[45] In several cases, a famine was followed by the proclamation of an edict canceling debts: fleeing residents often seem to have preoccupied the sovereigns. That situation is documented in the kingdom of Mari by letter *ARM* IV, 16 (LAPO 18, 1049), within the context of a famine in the region of Suhum. Yasmah-Addu decided to make a decree (*šipṭum*) by which he cancelled loans of grain, including the interest; he thereby hoped that those residents of Suhum who had fled would return. This is clearly an example of insolvent debtors taking flight.[46]

3.4. An Edict by Hammurabi?

The first edict known is that of Ammi-ṣaduqa,[47] which to this day remains the only one of which we have nearly a complete text. In 1965, Kraus published the vestiges of an edict of Samsu-iluna,[48] whose content seems to have been identical to that of Ammi-ṣaduqa. Given that the text of the edict does not appear to have changed between Samsu-iluna and Ammi-ṣaduqa (except for some additions), the question arises how far the prototype for the edicts of the kings of Babylon dates back. I have proposed to situate it in the last third of the reign of Hammurabi, for two essential reasons.[49] First, let us consider the cities listed in the edict. Section 10 is devoted to the relief that the king agreed to provide, on the occasion of the *mīšarum*, to the merchants groups (*kārū*) in eleven cities, eight of which are known to us: Babylon, Borsipa, Isin, Larsa, [Kazal]uk,[50] Malgum, [Mankis]um, and Shitullum. Kraus concluded that, in this context, *kār* GN designates the merchants organization from a city belonging to the kingdom of Babylon: that is clear for Babylon and Borsipa, and by analogy must be the case for the other cities as well. It is not comprehensible why the king would grant a favor to these *kārū* if their members were not his subjects. But we know that some of the cities no longer belonged to the kingdom of Ammi-ṣaduqa and had not for a long time. That was the case for Larsa, lost in year 12 of Samsu-iluna (1738 BCE). Isin was held until year 29 of the same king (1721 BCE); after that, there is only silence. Refugees from Malgum are attested in northern Babylonia from year 4 of Samsu-iluna (1746 BCE) onward, probably following the deportation instigated by Hammurabi.[51] Of the eight cities mentioned on the list of the *kārū* in section 10 whose names have been preserved, only Babylon and Borsipa still belonged to Babylonia at the beginning of Ammi-ṣaduqa's reign (1646 BCE), and it is certain that Isin, Larsa, and Malgum had no longer been part of it for a long time. Nevertheless, the content of this paragraph implies that these cities belonged to the kingdom of Babylon. To escape that aporia, there is only one solution: concede that the text reflects a situation that was no longer current.[52] That is altogether possible, since it appears that the *mīšarum* edicts all followed the same model. It must have become customary, with each proclamation of a *mīšarum*, to recopy the previous edict word for word.[53] That view of things radically shifts the particulars of the problem. It becomes necessary—and possible—to situate chronologically the period during which the edict that subsequently served as a model was composed: it was a time when the kingdom of Babylon included all the cities cited in section 10 of Ammi-ṣaduqa's edict. The most narrow interval of time is provided by Larsa, conquered by Hammurabi in year 30 of his reign (1763 BCE) and lost by Samsu-iluna in year 11 (1739 BCE): it was thus during that quarter century that the first of the edicts was written. It is not certain that Hammurabi was its author, but it is rather likely.

That conclusion can be confirmed by analyzing the economic realities described in Ammi-ṣaduqa's edict. Hence, the "palace commerce" system that emerges from section 11 applies better to the reality of the Hammurabi/Samsu-iluna period than to that known during the Ammi-ditana/Ammi-ṣaduqa period.[54] Some aspects of the terminology were also "archaic-sounding" in the Ammi-ṣaduqa era.[55]

Conclusion

The "restoration" edicts promulgated by Hammurabi and his successors thus seem to have been fairly well applied. We do not know how they were received by the population, but we may suppose that they were the occasion for festivities, if "fête" is defined as a momentary inversion of certain social practices. In this case, debts were no longer repaid, sales were cancelled, and debt slaves were liberated. In fact, we know of an example of an insolvent debtor who had fled Sippar to escape his creditors and who returned to his city following a *mīšarum* edict.[56]

Conversely, we may be dubious about the effectiveness of these measures over a relatively lengthy period of time, when compared to the goal officially proclaimed by the sovereign, "to strengthen the people who pay a tax" or even to act in such a way that the "strong do not crush the weak." After each cancellation, the debts and arrears began once more to accumulate.

In fact, the underlying ideology of these measures of justice was the opposite of reformism. It stemmed from a desire to return to the origin, sensed to be the point of social equilibrium whose restoration had to be attempted. The Babylonians did not envision the ideal society as a future but rather as a past with which connections had to be reestablished. It is therefore not possible to speak of a spirit of "reform" in reference to these measures, except in the very special sense that one speaks of the "reform" of a monastic order—aimed at reestablishing observance of the Rule in its original purity—or of the sixteenth-century Reformation. The notion of "social progress" was totally absent from these *mīšarum* edicts.

CHAPTER 7

Hammurabi and International Law

When the question of law arises with respect to Hammurabi, one immediately thinks, of course, of that ruler's "code," but it deals in practical terms only with private law.[1] In this chapter, I should like to discuss a different aspect of Hammurabi's legal activities: those that belong to "international law." As we shall see, however, that notion is somewhat anachronistic in the case of the Near East at the start of the second millennium BCE.

The sources available for treating the subject are abundant, even though, paradoxically, none were discovered in Hammurabi's capital. From 1907 on, the excavations of the Deutsche Orient-Gesellschaft in Babylon took advantage of an accidental drop in the phreatic nappe to explore the Old Babylonian layers in the region called "Merkes." The soundings reached those strata only for very small areas, since they were located about thirty-nine feet deep. These were a few houses in a sector called *ālum eššum ṣīt Šamši,* "the new eastern city."[2] A copy of two royal inscriptions was discovered in one of these buildings. Falkenstein has noted that these inscriptions could be signs that this was a building larger than a mere house, but that it could not have been the royal palace, since the walls measured only 31 ½ inches thick.[3] But in fact, two letters were also discovered in that building, as well as a cash loan contract dated year 25 of Samsu-iluna. It is therefore clear that this was a private home, as in the rest of the sector, where the exhumed archives published by Horst Klengel date for the most part to the last kings of the first dynasty, particularly Samsu-ditana.[4] I sense in Falkenstein's

This chapter repeats elements from my "Hammu-rabi de Babylone et Mari: Nouvelles sources, nouvelles perspectives," in *Babylon: Focus mesopotamischer Geschichte, Wiege früher Gelehrsamkeit, Mythos in der Moderne,* ed. J. Renger, *Colloquien der Deutschen Orient-Gesellschaft* 2 (Sarrebruck: 1999), 111–30. The most notable addition is data that were the object of a lecture, still unpublished, at the Institut de Droit Romain on January 19, 2001.

remark a certain disappointment that Hammurabi's palace was not located. Nevertheless, it is not certain that, if it had been found, the discoveries there would have been as spectacular as we might at first imagine. Indeed, that palace, built by Sumu-la-El (1880–1845 BCE),[5] founder of the dynasty, was abandoned by Samsu-iluna, who, in the name of his twentieth year of reign (1730 BCE), commemorated the construction of a new royal palace. The old palace continued to be in use, but we do not know what its exact purpose was. It is thus very possible that the tablets from Hammurabi's time were no longer kept there.[6]

By contrast, we have a small portion of the correspondence Hammurabi wrote, and in particular, the hundreds of letters he sent to Sin-iddinam and Shamash-hazir, who were posted in the ancient kingdom of Larsa after the Babylonian conquest. Although they deal primarily with administrative questions, a few data can be found in them relating to international law. But most of our information is provided by the archives of the Mari palace. Paradoxically, it is in that building, destroyed by Hammurabi himself in the thirty-fourth year of his reign (1759 BCE), that we find the most evidence about him. Among the thousands of letters addressed to King Zimri-Lim and discovered in his palace, several dozen were written by his envoys to Babylonia.

The period for which the information is most dense is fairly limited: it covers the years 28–30 of Hammurabi (1765 to 1763 BCE). It was at this time that the Elamites attacked Mesopotamia from Iran, provoking an outbreak in most of the Amorite kingdoms, which decided to set aside their traditional rivalries and unite against the invader. After the victory of the coalition, another conflict erupted between Babylon and Larsa: aided by his allies, Hammurabi succeeded in defeating Rim-Sin and annexing his kingdom in 1763 BCE.

I shall not attempt to be exhaustive here.[7] I would like, with the aid of documents that have recently been published or are still in the process of being deciphered, to address three themes: the reception of foreign messengers, the law of war, and the conclusion of treaties.

1. The Reception of Foreign Messengers

The Amorite period had no permanent ambassadors: messengers were therefore the essential instrument in diplomatic relations.[8] I shall show what access they had to the palace of Babylon and how audiences ordinarily unfolded, and shall examine the meals and presents the king offered messengers. I shall conclude by analyzing the composition of the king's council and the secret audiences he granted at times to certain foreign emissaries.

1.1. Access to the Palace

Not everyone who wished to enter the palace was allowed to do so. Visitors were carefully screened by guards, as Ibal-pi-El indicates: "It was early morning when we arrived at the palace gate. The guards let a messenger from the king of Kurda enter."[9]

Visitors did not necessarily obtain an audience immediately, as an envoy of Zimri-Lim complained: "Since I arrived in Babylon, I have not been able to have an interview with Hammurabi or to set before him what I had to say to him. Hence I could not send my lord my complete report of how he might have answered me. Therefore, my lord must not be angry."[10]

Those who were not allowed to enter generally became annoyed. Some noisily demonstrated their indignation, like the Elamite messengers described by Yarim-Addu: "These messengers did not cease to shout at the palace gate. They tore their clothes with their own hands, saying: 'We came to [transmit] words of peace: why can we not . . . or enter and have an interview with the king?' They said that and many other things at the palace gate, but no one replied and they went away again."[11] As diplomatic tensions with Elam increased, Hammurabi had these messengers confined to their residence: "The Elamite messengers arrived but could not approach the palace gate. The king's guards kept them in their lodgings."[12] Ultimately, these messengers were treated like prisoners: "The Elamite messengers were put in irons. Their servants, donkeys, and belongings have just been taken for the palace. May my lord know."[13] It was only at the end of the war that they recovered their freedom: "The Elamite messengers who were imprisoned long ago, at present he [Hammurabi] has liberated them. He has *placed* them in lodgings and has *reestablished* their former provender."[14]

1.2. Ordinary Audiences

During the war against Elam, when Zimri-Lim wanted to transmit a letter to Hammurabi, he sent out two copies. The first contained the message addressed to the king of Babylon; the second was a copy for Ibal-pi-El, head of the Mariot expeditionary corps, so that he would know in advance the content of the message to be read. The tablet for Hammurabi, meanwhile, was to remain in its sealed envelope until the audience. At the same time, Ibal-pi-El received orally the salutation formulas to be given to Hammurabi—which at that time were not put in writing—and also recommendations. One day, upon leaving his lodgings, he went to the palace. It was there that he noticed a messenger from Kurda: "He entered with us, but I managed to keep the messenger from the king of Kurda separate from the retinue of La'um, Etel-pi-Shamash, and all the [other] servants of my lord."[15] The rule at the time was that all the messengers present in a capital attended the audiences. A letter[16] even notes the embarrassment on the part of Ishme-Dagan's messengers, who were forced by Hammurabi to carry out their mission in the presence of Zimri-Lim's envoys, even though their master was complaining about the king of Mari. Since they did not want to say anything, Hammurabi ordered them to express themselves with an energetic *qibē qibē* ("Speak! Speak!"). The public nature of the situation did not prevent asides: Mut-Hadqim, the Ekallatean general, was occasionally seen whispering something in Hammurabi's ear. Ibal-pi-El's ears were apparently sharp enough to catch the words he was not supposed to hear, and of course he reported them to the king of Mari.[17]

Certain etiquette problems arose because messengers from various places were received at the same audience. The first matter was the order in which the foreign delegations would enter, and thus in what order greetings would be exchanged. A letter from a Mariot envoy reports an incident that pitted a group of messengers sent to Babylon by the king of Mari against another from Qaṭna in western Syria. The matter was judged serious enough by Hammurabi's "minister of foreign affairs," one Sin-bel-aplim, for him to ask for the sovereign's instructions. The Mariot delegate reported the event as follows: "We have protested before Sin-bel-aplim, and the Qatnean messengers have quarreled with us. They have declared: 'One must first ask [news of our lord] and [only] then news of your lord.' Sin-bel-aplim reported the affair to the palace [then told us]: 'My lord [Hammurabi] said: "I shall first ask news of Amud-pi-El [that is, the king of Qaṭna], [then] I shall ask news of your lord [Zimri-Lim]."' That is what he told us [and we entered]."[18] The king of Babylon, then, gave precedence to the envoys of the king of Qaṭna, which amounted to showing publicly that he held that king to be more powerful than the king of Mari. Another incident of the same type is reported by Itur-Asdu, which shows that these quarrels about priority were common and had a political significance obvious to all.[19]

1.3. Meals and Presents

Once their mission was accomplished, the messengers were invited to a meal in the palace and on that occasion received a gratification. The Mariot

La'um describes one very famous scene in which he quarreled with Hammurabi's minister of foreign affairs. This time, the problem concerned the hierarchy between the envoys of the king of Aleppo and those of the king of Mari:

> We entered for the meal in front of Hammurabi. We entered the palace courtyard. Then Zimri-Addu, myself, and Yarim-Addu, only the three of us, were dressed in garments, and all the Yamhadeans [i.e., the messengers of the king of Aleppo] who entered with us were so dressed. Since he had dressed all the Yamhadeans, whereas he had not done so for the secretaries, servants of my lord, I said to Sin-bel-aplim regarding them: "Why that segregation of us on your part, as if we were the sons of swine? Whose servants are we therefore, and the secretaries, whose [are they]? All of us are servants [of a high-ranking king]. Why do you make the right a stranger to the left?" That is what I sharply told Sin-bel-aplim. I myself got into a quarrel with Sin-bel-aplim; and the secretaries, servants of my lord, got angry and left the palace court. The matter was reported to Hammurabi and subsequently they were dressed in garments. Once they were dressed, Ṭab-eli-matim and Sin-bel-aplim reproached me and spoke to me as follows: "This is what Hammurabi is telling [you]: 'since this morning, you have not stopped picking a fight with me. Is it your job, then, to censure my palace on the subject of clothing? I dress whom I like and do not dress whom I like. I shall not again dress [mere] messengers on the occasion of a meal.'" That is what Hammurabi said: my lord is informed of it![20]

The hierarchical positions of foreign envoys was also indicated by the place they occupied during the meal offered them. A fundamental distinction existed between those who had the right to a seat (*wāšib kussim*) and those who had to remain squatting (*muppalsihum*).[21] But the location of the seat counted as well. This was reported by Zimri-Lim's "prime minister" on a mission to the region of Jebel Sinjar: "Having left Andarig, I entered Kurda. At nightfall, I was called for the meal and I went there. None among the auxiliary forces had a place seated before him [i.e., the king of Kurda], except me. And Yashub-Dagan, servant of my lord, was with me, but he remained apart, on a seat to the side."[22] On another occasion, Itur-Asdu, sent by Zimri-Lim to Babylon, guaranteed his colleague, sent by the king of Kurda, that he would not seek to have him "declassed" despite the diplomatic tensions existing between their masters.[23] A few years later, Ibal-pi-El, sent in turn to Hammurabi by Zimri-Lim, exerted pressure to prevent another envoy of the king of Kurda from having the right to a seat during a meal. He ended his letter as follows: "I said to myself, fearfully: 'My lord must not, with the servants of the emperor, his father, being there and having a seated place, hold it against me. On one hand, I have scruples about not giving a seat; but on the other, I am afraid to do something reprehensible in giving a seat.' At present, my lord must communicate to him his decision concerning that man's place at the table. And my lord must now fix the place of each messenger who comes here, saying: 'He will sit at a place higher than this one and lower than that one,' so that I can now assign him a place and we can conform to the etiquette fixed by our lord."[24]

When foreign troops arrived, Hammurabi left his palace to welcome them: for example, a thousand soldiers from Kazallu were set up in a palm grove in Babylon upon their arrival and were offered a meal and presents.[25] That was also the case for the thousand Bedouins brought by Bahdi-Addu from Mari, whom Hammurabi welcomed into a garden for a meal, and who held a sort of military parade in front of him.[26] It seems that the reception of allied troops by the king in person was in some sense an obligation of his office, since unpublished letters contain further examples, such as the welcome of troops coming from Yamhad to aid Hammurabi in his struggle against Elam.[27]

1.4. The King's Secret Council

The public audiences granted by Hammurabi constituted only a portion of the king's political activities in his Babylon palace. He sometimes deliberated with the members of his council and could on occasion have a private interview with a foreign ambassador.

As seems to have been the custom at the time, Hammurabi was surrounded by a council called *pirištum*, literally, "the secret."[28] In wartime, the leaders of the allied troops were normally part of that council. But during the war against Elam, the troops sent by Zimri-Lim were so numerous that not all their leaders were admitted, which led to a diplomatic problem: "When the instructions of my lord [Hammurabi] [*were listened to*], Sakiran the Suhean and Addu-naṣir were expelled upon delivery of the instructions. They became angry, saying: 'Why have you excluded us from the secret council of our lord [Hammurabi]?' My lord [Zimri-Lim] must have a list of those of his servants who have a right to attend the secret council of my lord [Hammurabi] drawn up on a tablet."[29]

It was primarily within the framework of that council that diviners gave the gods' responses to oracular questions.[30] How scandalized Ibal-pi-El must have been, therefore, when he learned that generals from Ekallatum were participating in Hammurabi's *pirištum* and as a result heard the report given by the Mariot diviners: "The servants of Ishme-Dagan—Ishar-Lim, Mutu-Hadqim, and Rim-Addu—have expelled the lords from the country and have themselves become the lords on Hammurabi's council. He abides by their advice. When Hali-Hadun and Inib-Shamash [the Mariot diviners] had taken oracles once or twice, and when they reported the oracles, Ishar-Lim, Mutu-Hadqim, and Rim-Addu did not move aside; being present, they heard the content of the oracles each time. What is more secret than the diviners' report? Even though his own servants did not hear the diviners' sẹcret reports, they do hear them!"[31] And Ibal-pi-El ends his letter to the king of Mari with a warning: "These men and Ishme-Dagan will cause a rift between Hammurabi and my lord."[32]

That letter dates from the time when Ishme-Dagan and his generals were in Babylonia to fight against the Elamite invasion, in year 29 of Hammurabi (1764 BCE).[33] And if Ishme-Dagan did not participate in person in the *pirištum* of the king of Babylon, it was because, having been wounded, he remained in the residence assigned to him.[34] Only once do we see him come out, carried in a litter, to enter Hammurabi's palace.[35]

1.5. *"Private Audiences"*

Audiences were generally open to all foreign messengers present in a capital, but there were exceptions. Such was the case described in another letter from Ibal-pi-El. He was very upset by a matter of secret tablets relating to Ishar-Lim. It seems that, in them, Zimri-Lim had cast doubt on the integrity of Ishme-Dagan's general, who was supposed to be participating in the common struggle against Elam. Having arrived in Babylon, Ibal-pi-El, as usual, attended the audience at which two Babylonian messengers, Ikun-pi-Sin and Belum-kima-ilim, received their instructions about the mission to the king of Mari that they would have to carry out.[36] Ibal-pi-El went on, "The next day, we entered and he [Hammurabi] gave further instructions to Ikun-pi-Sin. After he had given these instructions, we wanted to leave; we were held back and made to return, me, Ikun-pi-Sin, and Belum-kima-ilim. I said to myself: 'For what reason are all three of us given special treatment and why do they have us come back? It is surely because he [Hammurabi] wants to speak of the Ishar-Lim affair.' That is what I imagined."[37]

Ibal-pi-El, fearing an indiscretion on Hammurabi's part, then turned to the minister of foreign affairs, Sin-bel-aplim: "'My lord [Hammurabi] should not speak before his own servants of the tablets that have arrived from my lord [Zimri-Lim].' That is what I told Sin-bel-aplim. He told me:

'My lord will say nothing of the affair of the tablets. Another affair is at issue, which is secret. Once he has spoken of [that] secret affair to Ikun-pi-Sin and Belum-kima-ilim, my lord will speak to you alone of the affair of the tablets.' That is what he replied to me." Sin-bel-aplim thus promised Ibal-pi-El two successive interviews with Hammurabi. The first was to be a restricted audience, since only two Babylonian messengers, Ikun-pi-Sin and Belum-kima-ilim, and the Mariot general, Ibal-pi-El, would be present before Hammurabi. The rest of the letter indicates that his minister Sin-bel-aplim as well as his private secretary were in fact also in attendance. The second interview was to be a private interview. Ibal-pi-El's account continued as follows: "We [therefore] came back: he [Hammurabi] gave instructions to Ikun-pi-Sin and Belum-kima-ilim. After he had completed his instructions, I was kept back: he and I—neither his minister nor his private secretary was present—he and I, and a deaf servant stood by to serve him. Having approached him, I engaged him in these terms." The rest describes the personal interview that Ibal-pi-El had with Hammurabi.[38] Unfortunately, it is precisely from that point on that the tablet is seriously damaged.

2. The Law of War

The second aspect of international law that I shall examine is the law of war. I shall consider two points in turn: war declarations and the annexation of conquered kingdoms.

2.1. War Declarations

The Hague Convention of 1907 CE required that its members not start a war without a preliminary warning, in the form either of a declaration of war, accompanied by the reasons for that declaration, or of an ultimatum with a conditional declaration of war.[39] Such measure are known to have been taken as early as the eighteenth century BCE.[40]

We have the actual ultimatum that the Elamite emperor addressed to Hammurabi after his victory over Eshnunna.[41] That sovereign was accustomed to taking such actions, since, at almost the same moment, he sent a warning to the king of Kurda, namesake of the sovereign of Babylon. The affair is known through a representative of the king of Mari, who wrote to his master:

> So I am sending to my lord, on my present tablet, the copy of a tablet from the emperor of Elam, which he sent to Hammurabi [of Kurda]: "Thus

> [speaks] the emperor to Hammurabi. Atamrum, a servant of mine, took you in vassalage. At present, I hear it said everywhere that you are constantly sending your tablets to Babylon and Mari. Do not send your tablets to Babylon or Mari anymore! If you again send your tablets to Babylon or Mari, I *will rage like a storm* over you."
>
> Such is the message that the emperor of the Elamites sent to Hammurabi. I personally heard the tablet.[42]

The king of Kurda, therefore, immediately had to break off diplomatic relations with Babylon and Mari, which were then at war with the Elamite emperor; otherwise, that emperor would have considered him his enemy and would have attacked him.

Another fine example of a "declaration of war" is constituted by the letter from Yarim-Lim to Yashub-Yahad, king of Der. Yarim-Lim, after reminding the king of Der of the aid he had previously given him and his neighbor from Diniktum, swore to go personally to the site and annihilate the country of Der and its sovereign: "Assuredly, Sin-gamil, king of Diniktum, like you repays me with only hostility and obstructions. But there are five hundred vessels that I moored at the quay of Diniktum, and for twelve years I have not failed to do good for his country and himself. Today you, like him, repay me with only hostility and obstructions. I swear to you by Addu, god of my city, and Sin, god of my head: [may I be cursed] if I return home before having annihilated your country and yourself! At present, I shall arrive at the very beginning of spring and [*I shall stay in front of your city's gate*], I shall make you see the powerful weapons of the god Addu and of Yarim-Lim."[43] The historicity of that letter has been disputed,[44] but in any event, it shows that the literary genre of the war declaration was current in that era and that the gods were an integral part of the conflicts.[45]

Shortly after his victory over Elam, Hammurabi launched a war against his southern neighbor, the king of Larsa.[46] Because of the alliance uniting Mari and Babylon, Zimri-Lim found himself, very much against his will, dragged into that distant conflict: Hammurabi thus had to justify his conduct. A Mariot on a mission to Babylon reported to Zimri-Lim the deterioration in relations between the two sovereigns:

> On the subject of Rim-Sin, king of Larsa, as my lord has learned, his previous inclinations have absolutely not changed: he is hostile toward Hammurabi. His detachments ceaselessly make incursions into the country of Hammurabi; they engage in plunder and deportation. And each time they have infiltrated it, they carry away [something] of it. The messengers of Rim-Sin have

> been put in irons [and taken] to the palace and they are prevented from leaving. Hammurabi ceaselessly sets out his grievances to me . . . now remain . . . no longer arrives. No messenger of Rim-Sin goes to Babylon anymore and there is no longer any messenger of Hammurabi in Mashkan-shapir.[47]

The king of Larsa is thus presented as the aggressor. The first retaliatory measure taken by the king of Babylon was to imprison the Larsan messengers. A break in diplomatic relations between the two kingdoms followed, Mashkan-shapir being the chief northern city of the kingdom of Larsa.[48]

Interestingly, we possess the retranscription of a speech in which Hammurabi justifies the war he subsequently waged on Rim-Sin: "Now the Larsan displeased my country by plundering. Ever since the great gods [wrested] this country from the Elamite's influence, I had many presents taken to the Larsan, but he did not repay me with a benefit. Hence I complained to the gods Shamash and Marduk and they ceaselessly replied yes: I did not carry out that attack without [the agreement] of the deity."[49] This mix of political and religious considerations constitutes a sort of *pro domo* plea that Hammurabi pronounces before "his troops," which included many allied contingents. This speech, which repeats the theme of ingratitude, can be decoded as follows. The king of Larsa had not participated in the coalition against the Elamites, yet Hammurabi continued to send him presents. Despite the diplomatic practices in force, the king of Larsa did not send him any gifts in return;[50] even worse, his armies plundered Babylonian territory. Hammurabi then questioned the gods through diviners. The question asked of Shamash and Marduk must have been something on the order of: "Must Hammurabi go to war against Larsa?" The result of that oracular consultation was obviously favorable. The text of that consultation has not survived but we do have a few others, particularly regarding the campaign Hammurabi had conducted shortly before against the city of Kazallu. They have been preserved on a tablet from the neo-Assyrian period held at the library of the temple of Nabu in Kalhu.[51]

2.2. The Annexation of Conquered Kingdoms

The right of the victor is nowhere defined, and its elements must be reconstituted on the basis of the legal documents.

The victor did not confiscate lands that were private property. Following his victory over Larsa, Hammurabi seized only the Crown lands of Rim-Sin, as shown by the archives of several families for the period preceding and following the Babylonian conquest.[52]

What was the status of the former kingdom of Larsa after Rim-Sin's defeat?[53] In the prologue to his "code," Hammurabi presents himself as "the one who spared Larsa"; in fact, he did not destroy the city but was content to take down its walls. Rim-Sin, his entourage, and his possessions were transferred to Babylon, and Hammurabi installed himself in Larsa, where he was acknowledged as "king of Sumer and Akkad." He took a new title: "king who brings peace to the four regions." Initially, he instituted a sort of personal union between the two kingdoms of Babylon and Larsa. His desire for unity was expressed in several ways. Although texts ought to have been immediately dated using the Babylonian "year names," Hammurabi instead established a new way of computing his years of reign in the recently subjugated kingdom, taking the conquest of Larsa as the starting point. In addition, like every sovereign acceding to the throne, Hammurabi proclaimed a *mīšarum,* whose scope seems to have been limited to the former kingdom of Larsa. But the fiction did not last: it was truly an annexation. The demolition of the ramparts of Larsa shortly after the city was taken left its residents with few illusions. Fairly soon, the Babylonian year names prevailed.

Letter *AbB* XIII, 10 seems to attest to the reception of Babylonian law in the former kingdom of Larsa.[54] At issue were deserters whom Hammurabi sent back to Sin-iddinam, his former secretary, whom he had appointed governor of the new province, which was called Emutbalum. This governor had to "render justice to them according to the laws that are now in force in Emutbalum." Obviously, these deserters had left the kingdom of Larsa during the war and had taken refuge in the kingdom of Babylon, hence Hammurabi's insistence that the law to be applied to them was Babylonian law, now valid in the former kingdom of Larsa.

3. The Conclusion of Treaties

In the Amorite world, two modes of conduct coexisted.[55] On one hand, the sovereigns could come together and meet. They would begin by reaching an agreement about their reciprocal commitments. The alliance ritual entailed the solemn words of an oath sworn by the interested parties, and a symbolic gesture, namely, the immolation of an animal.[56] On the other hand, treaties could be concluded long-distance. In that case, the text of each king's pledge was communicated to him by his partner. The alliance came about through a solemn oath, accompanied by another symbolic gesture: "touching the throat" (*lipit napištim*). Durand has recently interpreted that expression as describing an anointing in blood.[57] In the case of Hammurabi of Babylon, only the second action is attested. Two alliances are particularly well known: the one that united Zimri-Lim of Mari and Hammurabi of Babylon against the Elamite sovereign; and the one concluded between Hammurabi of Babylon and Ṣilli-Sin, king of Eshnunna, to put an end to several years of war between their kingdoms.

3.1. The Treaty between Hammurabi and Zimri-Lim against Elam

The alliance between Mari and Babylon against Elam represents an altogether privileged case, since we have knowledge not only of the preliminary negotiations but also of the procedure,[58] and even possess the text of the pledge to which the king of Babylon subscribed.

The king of Babylon was reluctant to conclude an alliance with Zimri-Lin, as Ibal-pi-El indicates in several letters: "Regarding the tablet of alliance (*lipit napištim*) that came here several times and [for which] Hammurabi did not want to 'strike his throat,' at present, Hammurabi listened to that tablet and immediately replied to me . . ."[59] To overcome the king of Babylon's reluctance, wrote Ibal-pi-El, "I stood up, and before him I took the god Shamash as a witness, saying: 'My lord [Zimri-Lim] is not allied with the lord of Elam. He raised his hand toward Shamash for you by the flour-*maṣhatum* and by the flour-*saskūm,* and also my lord swore in these terms: "I swear that I shall not make peace with the lord of Elam." That is what my lord swore. At present, what is your pretext for not swearing at the same time as he?'"[60] Here is the text of the oath that Zimri-Lim wanted to have Hammurabi swear: "From this day forward, so long as I live, I will be at war with Ṣiwapalarhuhpak. I will not have my servants take to the road as messengers with his servants and will not dispatch them to him! I will not make peace with Ṣiwapalarhuhpak separately from Zimri-Lim, king of Mari and the Bedouin country. If I propose to make peace with Ṣiwapalarhuhpak, I will deliberate on it with Zimri-Lim, king of Mari and of the Bedouin country, and if there is no *obstacle,* together we will make peace with Ṣiwapalarhuhpak!"[61]

The chief article of the king of Babylon's pledge was that he would not conclude a separate peace with the enemy. As Ibal-pi-El's letter indicates, the oath that Zimri-Lim had uttered was identical.[62] To avoid any possible temptations, the two kings exchanged troops, who in some sense served as a guarantee of their sincerity.

3.2. The Treaty between Hammurabi and Ṣilli-Sin

Another alliance is also well known, the one Hammurabi concluded a few months after his victory over the Elamites with Ṣilli-Sin, the new king of Eshnunna. A letter from Yarim-Addu describes very precisely the procedure that was observed at the time:

> When Hammurabi [went?] to Borsipa, messengers of the lord of Eshnunna joined him [there] [*but had no interview*] with him. The next day, they sat before him. Having made them wait one night, in response to their news he answered them. He gave instructions to [Sin——], son of Kakkaruqqum, and to Mar[duk-mushallim, son of . . .] and he sent them to Eshnunna. They took in their hands the little tablet. They will have the lord of Eshnunna pledge [literally, "touch his throat"] by that tablet; [PN] will go and here Hammurabi will pledge [literally, "will touch his throat"]. After they have pledged by the little tablet, Hammurabi will have a large tablet, a treaty tablet, taken to the lord of Eshnunna, and he will have the lord of Eshnunna swear an oath. The lord of Eshnunna will send the large tablet, the treaty tablet, back to Hammurabi . . . and they will thereby establish an alliance between them. The alliance between Hammurabi and the man of Eshnunna is concluded, or at least imminent, that is certain.[63]

The "little tablet" included only the clauses to which each king proposed that the other subscribe. Letters were exchanged on this subject. Hence Samsi-Addu had written a few years earlier: "The lord of Eshnunna wrote me regarding the pledge (*lipit napištim*): there is one thing that I removed from the treaty tablet and I wrote [of this] to Eshnunna, but the lord of Eshnunna is obstructing matters."[64] In the case of the treaty between Hammurabi and Ṣilli-Sin, negotiations dragged on and on, foundering on a territorial dispute: Babylon from the Euphrates Valley and Eshnunna from the Diyala Valley were fighting for control of the banks of the Tigris, from Mankisum to below Opis. That is indicated, notably, in another unpublished letter from Ibal-pi-El, which reproduces a declaration of Hammurabi's: "The lord of Eshnunna abides by his previous proposals. If he abandons Mankisum, Opis, Shahaduni, and the banks of the Tigris over a distance of some three miles downstream from Opis, my marches, as established by my grandfather Apil-Sin, then I truly want to make peace with him [the king of Eshnunna]. Or, if I must abandon Mankisum, let him reimburse me for the expenses I incurred against the emperor of Elam in order to have Mankisum, and let him then seize Mankisum; and I [will keep] Opis, Shahaduni, and the banks of the Tigris over a distance of some three miles downstream from Opis."[65]

There was a continuity in the territorial interests that the king of Babylon was defending: it was over that same region, judged strategically essential, that he had already clashed with Elam. He thus did not want to hand it over to the new king of Eshnunna, even if that meant preventing the treaty from being concluded. The only concession he was ready to make concerned Mankisum, but it was very theoretical: the cost of the war with Elam must have been considerable, and no figure was put forward by Hammurabi.

Once an agreement was reached on the content of the clauses, the kings had to exchange a "large tablet." The treaty tablet between Hammurabi and Ṣilli-Sin has not come down to us, but we know of several others, all of which follow the same pattern.[66] They begin with a list of deities serving as guarantors of the agreement, proceed to the clauses of the treaty, and end with curses in the event of perjury. Not only the clauses but also the list of deities could be the object of discussions. Consider this message sent by Atamrum, king of Andarig, to Hammurabi, who had submitted a draft treaty to him: "On the subject of the treaty tablet that my father sent to me, [there is not in that tablet] any excessive gods or clauses [and I do not desire] anything more as regards the gods or [any] supplementary clauses. Here is what is written on this tablet: 'Be hostile [against my enemies and on good terms] with my friends.' That is what my father [Hammurabi] wrote me."[67] Not only were the gods witnesses to the pledges made by the kings, they also had to punish any eventual perjury. A recently published text shows that the curses themselves could be a subject of debate before a treaty was concluded. In a letter in which he gives an account of his mission to Babylon, Itur-Asdu indicates to the king of Mari: "Hammurabi listened to the curses of the treaty tablet [*ṭuppi nīš ilī*] and he said: 'The curses of that tablet are very constraining! This is not to be [*meditated on internally*] or to be heard verbally! Of course, there have been treaty tablets since the time of Sumul-la-El, since the time of my father Sin-muballiṭ, and since I myself ascended the throne of the paternal house—and I swore an oath to Samsi-Addu and to many kings! Yes, these tablets exist, but they are not constraining like this treaty tablet!'"[68]

The interest of this passage is manifold. As in his commemorative inscriptions, Hammurabi associates himself here with the true founder of the dynasty, Sumu-la-El, and not with Sumu-abum.[69] And the figure of Samsi-Addu, even years after his death, continued to serve as a reference point. Unfortunately, Hammurabi does not give the number of treaty tablets that had existed since the beginning of his reign or since that of his dynasty:

Are we to suppose that they were archived somewhere in his palace?[70] Finally, the text of the treaty proposal communicated by Itur-Asdu has not come down to us, so we cannot judge what provoked the king of Babylon's agitation.

3.3. *The Nature of the Treaty Texts*

In the cases just examined, if the two kings did not meet but concluded the alliance long-distance, it was because, each time, they were in a very strained military situation, which required each sovereign's presence at the head of his troops. To my knowledge, Hammurabi and Zimri-Lim never met. But that is not so surprising: over the thirteen years of Zimri-Lim's reign, distrust and even tension prevailed more often than good relations.[71] By contrast, at least once during his reign, Zimri-Lim met his father-in-law, Yarim-Lim, king of Aleppo, to whom he was much closer politically.[72]

Such behavior had several consequences that made the texts of treaties from the Amorite period essentially different from those beginning with the era of El Amarna in the second half of the second millennium BCE.[73] In the first place, treaties were always composed unilaterally: every king sent his partner in the alliance the text of the pledges he wished him to make. Second, the text of the treaty had no value in itself. Some "little tablets" of treaties were exchanged but ultimately not ratified. It is clear, then, that the status of these texts was entirely different from that of contracts committing individuals, and it is understandable why the treaties of that era were not authenticated by the contracting parties' seal impressions.[74] Finally, these treaties committed only the person who swore the oath. When a king died, they had to be renewed with his successor.

Two texts, however, might give the illusion that they were treaties concluded "for eternity." The first case is a letter sent to Zimri-Lim by his emissary to Ibal-pi-El, king of Eshnunna, which recalls the object of the mission as follows: "At present, my lord sent to his father his gods, the large 'arms' [*kakkī rabûtim*],[75] and us his servants, in order to take the pledge [*lipit napištim*] and to tie together the fringe [*sissiktum*][76] of the father and of the son forever [*ana darētim*]."[77]

A similar expression was used by Hammurabi himself, when he addressed Zimri-Lim through his envoy and envisioned the conclusion of an alliance: "A fringe will be tied together between us forever."[78] But the expression "forever" (*ana darētim*) must not be taken out of context: "between us," says Hammurabi. This was a perpetual commitment, of course, but one limited to the lifetimes of the kings making the pledge. Its scope therefore did not differ from that of the expression, "from this day forward, so long as I live," which begins the text of the oath in certain treaties.[79]

It was not rare for the new king to cite the example of his predecessor in calling for the conclusion of a treaty, but this was only the evocation of a precedent: there was nothing legally binding about it.[80] At most there was a kind of moral obligation. By contrast, from the era of El Amarna on, treaties committed not only the kings who concluded them but also their descendancy: their temporal value was no longer limited to the contracting parties' lifespan. That difference is apparent in the solemnization of the document itself, which was sometimes recopied onto a bronze or even silver tablet[81] and placed in a temple. Some texts include a clause outlining the obligation to reread its content on a regular basis.[82]

3.4. International Arbitration?

Was there any recourse in the disputes kings had with one another?[83] One possibility was to ask a more powerful king for his arbitration, and his verdict was supposed to be recognized by both parties. In the conflict between Hammurabi and Zimri-Lim concerning the delimitation of the border along the Euphrates between their two kingdoms, the emperor of Elam attempted a reconciliation in the year 1770 BCE. That did not settle the matter, however.[84] Five years later, at the time of the Elamite invasion, Hammurabi declared he was ready to accept the judgment of a sort of "international tribunal" composed of kings of the same rank as the king of Mari and himself: "When the aim is achieved [i.e., when the Elamites are defeated], may the kings our brothers then sit and deliver a judgment for us: I will submit to the judgment they will pronounce."[85] Since the "father" recognized by them all until that time—the emperor of Elam—had become an enemy, it was to the judgment of his "brothers" that Hammurabi declared he wanted to submit. This was merely a delaying tactic, however, and we know of no genuine example of such a procedure.

Conclusion

In concluding this chapter, let me point to two paradoxes. The first is that, in the very rich correspondence found in the archives of the chancellery of Mari, only four letters in all sent by Hammurabi to Zimri-Lim have been found,[86] whereas we possess thirty, for example, sent by a king of lesser importance, Ibal-Addu of Ashlakka. We might suppose that most of the messages from the king of Babylon to his counterpart in Mari were transmitted orally by his messengers, but that would have been a departure from the general custom of the time. Moreover, we have proof that we are not in possession of some of the letters Hammurabi sent to Zimri-Lim. One of them is quoted by Yarim-Addu: "Hammurabi sent to my lord his son Mutu-Numaha. In addition, he wrote to my lord as follows: 'I previously sent you [my] eldest son and he remains with you. At present, I have just sent you his brother [damaged passage]. Otherwise, send this child either to Yamhad or to Qaṭna, wherever you judge right.' That is what Hammurabi wrote to my lord."[87] That letter is known only through this quotation, and the original does not appear in the Mari archives. The conclusion is therefore simple: the letters sent by Hammurabi were among the tablets taken to Babylon when Babylonian scribes winnowed the archives of the Mariot chancellery after the taking of Mari.[88] And it is not by chance that, of the four letters from Hammurabi known to us, three are minuscule fragments: these tablets must have been broken in antiquity, and hence were judged not worthy of interest.

The second paradox is that, through the Mari archives, Hammurabi's personality is ultimately much better known than Zimri-Lim's. We get an idea of the king of Babylon's character, when, for example, he forcefully summons his interlocutors to speak, whether these are Ekallatum's messengers[89] or the Mariot diviners who would have liked to let the Babylonian diviners speak first.[90] In another case, he sharply silences a troublesome person with an equally peremptory *qūl qūl* ("Shut up! Shut up!").[91] He could be tough in negotiations—for example, he refused to yield the city of Hit to Zimri-Lim—to such a degree that Asqudum was not afraid to call him a liar.[92] But when the king of Mari asked for the return of his troops, Hammurabi simply put him off: "'Yes, today, yes, right away,' then, 'In five days.'"[93] We need to realize that, amid that profusion of detail, we possess only a single description of an audience given by Zimri-Lim.[94] For what we know of the Mari palace, we are primarily beholden to the administrative texts and to a few letters that describe to the king what was happening in his absence. These provide very important information on his harem, for example.[95] But diplomatic life in the palace is not described in any letter. In a diametrically opposed manner, the letters from Mari do not reveal anything about Hammurabi's private life.[96] By contrast, the king of Babylon's foreign relations are known to us in great detail, though within a very limited interval of time, since Zimri-Lim's envoys stayed continuously in Babylonia for only three years. Most of the correspondence from the Mariot envoys to Babylon (Ibal-pi-El, Zimri-Addu, Yarim-Addu, La'um, Sharrum-andulli, and others) dates to years 10–12 of Zimri-Lim (1765–1763 BCE). In fact, it was a misinterpretation to maintain that relations between Zimri-Lim and Hammurabi were good until the king of Babylon's final about-face. Over the thirteen years of Zimri-Lim's reign, there were only two brief periods of alliance: in years 3–4 of Zimri-Lim (1772–1771 BCE), when Babylonians came to the aid of Zimri-Lim against Eshnunna; and especially in years 10–12 of Zimri-Lim (1765–1763 BCE), when Mari aided Babylon, first against Elam and then against Larsa. But it is clear that, in year 10 (1765 BCE), considerable rancor existed between Mari and Babylon: the Hit affair had poisoned relations between the two sovereigns. The friendly words spoken by Hammurabi himself[97] should not fool us—Asqudum may not have been wrong to call him a liar.

CHAPTER 8

Controlling Cross-Border Traffic

It is generally believed that the Old Babylonian period was dominated by the figure of Hammurabi. This is in great part an illusion: that sovereign imposed hegemony over Babylon only in the last third of a forty-three-year reign. Before that, from a political standpoint, the Near East as a whole was characterized by extreme fragmentation. About a hundred kingdoms[1] were grouped around six major poles: the capitals of Larsa, Babylon, and Eshnunna in southern and central Iraq, Aleppo and Qaṭna in northern and central Syria, and of course Mari in eastern Syria, not far from the present-day border with Iraq. One of Zimri-Lim's intimates declared to allies of the king of Mari: "There is no king who is really strong on his own: ten or fifteen kings follow Hammurabi of Babylon, the same number Rim-Sin of Larsa, Ibal-pi-El of Eshnunna, and Amud-pi-El of Qaṭna; twenty kings follow Yarim-Lim of Yamhad [Aleppo]."[2]

Borders were everywhere, then. From a historical perspective, we have the impression, first, that this was an era of intense exchanges, at the political but also at the commercial and cultural levels,[3] and second, that constraints on freedom of movement were nevertheless very great.

1. A World without Borders?

Did the borders within the Amorite Near East have the importance that we would automatically be tempted to attribute to them? Might not the kings

This chapter is a reworked version of "La circulation des commerçants, des nomades et des messagers dans le Proche-Orient amorrite (XVIIIe siècle av. J.-C.)," in *La mobilité des personnes en Méditerranée de l'Antiquité à l'époque moderne. Procédures de contrôle et documents d'identification*, ed. C. Moatti, Collection de l'École française de Rome 341 (Rome: 2004), 51–69.

have been more interested in controlling men than in controlling territories? These questions have recently been raised[4] and deserve our attention.

1.1. The Notion of Border

The term "border" (*pāṭum*) was commonly used in the documents of the Amorite period.[5] Its use was not restricted to borders between kingdoms; the word could also designate the boundaries of a field,[6] and the Code of Hammurabi employed it to designate the limits of a communal territory as well.[7] Such an absence of specificity is not restricted to the term *pāṭum*: it is also found in the territorial notion of *halṣum*, a word too often translated exclusively as "province," whereas it is more generally a "zone of responsibility."[8]

Some Assyriologists have long warned against an anachronistically linear view of borders.[9] But that is in great part because of the physical configuration of the Near East, with its large desert zones, such as the area between the kingdoms of Mari and Qaṭna.[10] If we consider, for example, the Middle Euphrates, it is clear that the delimitation of kingdoms along the course of that river was very clear, as is demonstrated by the heated discussions between Zimri-Lim of Mari and his neighbors, the king of Eshnunna and then the king of Babylon, about fixing the southern boundary of Zimri-Lim's kingdom.[11] Similarly, in Samsi-Addu's kingdom to the east, the conquest of Shusharra, located along the Little Zab, transformed it into a "border city."[12] And when King Dadusha of Eshnunna wanted to strengthen his presence along the Tigris, he set up a fortress, giving it his name and presenting it as "Dur-Dadusha, my border city."[13]

1.2. Borders and the Restrictions on Movement

It is clear that political borders played a role in restricting movement. Hence the escorts given to foreign messengers stopped at the kingdom's border: "Tell Yasmah-Addu: thus speaks Ili-asu, your servant. Belshunu will be going to Qaṭna. My lord must give him seven porters, who will go to Qaṭna, and an escort as far as the border."[14] Belshunu, dignitary to the kingdom of Qaṭna on a mission to Mari, was about to return home: the Mariot porters would accompany him to the end of his journey, but the escort would stop at the border between the kingdoms of Mari and Qaṭna.

Another example is provided by the boat traffic on the Euphrates.[15] Atamrum, king of Andarig, had gone to the kingdom of Babylon. Hammurabi made small boats available to him for his return. These boats went up the Euphrates to Hit, which constituted the border between the kingdoms of Babylon and Mari, then went back downriver to Rapiqum.

When a foreign messenger arrived in the kingdom of Mari without an escort, the governor of the border province provided him with one, as indicated in this letter from Yaqqim-Addu: "Halu-rabi, messenger of Haya-Sumu, is bearing tablets intended for my lord. Having observed that this man was journeying all alone, I assigned guards to him and then had him taken to my lord."[16]

1.3. Customs

Inasmuch as the circulation of merchandise was taxed,[17] checkpoints existed at the borders, targeting not the merchants themselves but the goods they were transporting. The Mari archives have thus yielded a few dozen notes issued by what was called the "customs service." These were short form letters, which informed Iddiyatum, the chief merchant, that the cargo of a boat had been inspected and the tax-*miksum* levied.[18]

That institution also existed in the kingdom of Babylon, but as it happens, only a single letter attesting to it has been preserved in the sources. It was written from a "customs" official on the Euphrates, installed on the northern border of the kingdom of Babylon: "As my master knows, since the 'brick' of Baṣṣu was placed under Hammurabi [that is, since the foundation of that city], we have remained posted in Baṣṣu. For a boat traveling up or down [the river], we examine [every] merchant carrying a tablet from the king and we let him pass. But we send back to Babylon [any] merchant who is not carrying a tablet from the king."[19] The rest of the letter concerns an incident that occurred when the official had to absent himself.

The control of trade targeted not only marketed goods but also diplomatic gifts, as illustrated by a letter from a Mariot governor. Yaqqim-Addu, having stopped someone who was conveying four slaves to Karkemish, told him: "Without the permission of my lord, a present-*šābultum* cannot pass through into a foreign country. Why are you not carrying a tablet from my lord?"[20] In all these cases, then, the traveler had to carry a written text allowing him to pass through the checkpoints.

The correspondence of Assyrian merchants indicates that the proliferation of pay stations (for tolls or taxes) along the route leading to Anatolia led them to cheat.[21] They might conceal the merchandise at a stopover city, or a caravan might take a "byway," that is, they might deviate from the normal route—and accept all the risks relating to that "detour"—to avoid the collection points. The texts from Mari also occasionally describe people who took "shortcuts" through the steppe so as to bypass the string of checkpoints in the valleys. That is attested in this excerpt from a letter to Yasmah-Addu, sent by his minister La'um: "Last year the sheikh of Harrâdum and his brother suborned a cook from Taribum. They had him cross at Iddissum, then passed without letting themselves be seen in Ṭabtum, and arrived in Harruyatum. They sold him to the son of the Babylonian Hammanum.[22] He was seen in Hit. The sheikh and his brother were then brought to me."[23]

1.4. The Requirement that Private Individuals Carry a Pass

Many texts indicate that individuals could not move about unless they were in possession of a pass in good order. After a major invasion of locusts struck the district of Qaṭṭunam, in the northern part of the kingdom of Mari, the local governor quoted the order he had received from the sovereign: "Any private individual [*muškēnum*] who wants to leave without your permission for the land of Subartum, stop him and have him brought to me."[24] The governor, fearing that the day laborers would leave the kingdom to bring in the harvest elsewhere, was afraid that the king would write him as follows: "Give firm orders that the roads be guarded, and do not be negligent about those passing!" He knew that it would be impossible to halt the flight of people without resources.

A group of foreigners from the kingdom of Aleppo, coming for an ordeal in the city of Hit, were supposed to have been provided with a pass from the king of Mari, whose territory they had crossed. The matter was reported by the local authority, Meptum: "A band of Yamhadeans came down toward me. That band was accompanying a little girl, a young boy, and a woman to submit to the ordeal. *I inquired* about a royal authorization. Since they were not carrying a tablet from my lord, I stopped that band and questioned them. [An account of the ordeal follows. Meptum concludes:] At present, I have just written that news to my lord. When a group that is to dive [into the river, i.e., for an ordeal] comes to me again, it must not come without a tablet from my lord."[25]

Formal procedures thus had to be carried out at the border before people could cross. But some enjoyed a privileged status that allowed them to pass through more easily.

2. Privileged Statuses

Because of the nature of their work, messengers and nomads tended to cross borders frequently. A few documents are particularly interesting, however, for the reference they make to merchants as symbols of freedom of movement.[26]

2.1. Merchants and Bedouins

In a letter to Zimri-Lim, king of Mari, the Bensim'alite chief of the nomads, Ibal-El, transmitted the contradictory rumors he had heard regarding the death of one of his enemies, King Zuzu of Apum: "My lord knows that I command the Bedouins and that, just as a merchant goes through war and peace, the Bedouins go through war and peace [in collecting] grain-*šepātum*, learning in the course of their travels what the country is talking about. A Bedouin came up to me and told me: [etc.]."[27] Ibal-El begins by explaining himself in a way that may surprise us: he compares the status of nomads to that of merchants, whereas we would have a tendency to do the reverse. These two categories of people, by virtue of their status, were not involved in local conflicts and thus could cross borders not only in peacetime but also when a conflict was raging. That did not mean total freedom of movement, however.

In concrete terms, the Bensim'alites, members of Zimri-Lim's tribe, recognized his authority wherever they happened to be: not only throughout the territory of the kingdom of Mari (*namlakatum*), where a portion of them had settled, but also in the steppe (*nawûm*) extending beyond the borders. Such a duality was characteristic of the exercise of power in the Bedouin monarchies of the central Near East.[28]

2.2. Merchants and Messengers

Another text indicates that the status of messengers and that of merchants may have been comparable. This is a letter sent to the king of Mari from the king of Qaṭna, who was worried about the bad news he had learned, corroborated by the fact that Mariot messengers had not come to him for a long time: "Even before, when the Turukkeans engaged in hostile acts inside the country, your messengers and mine you kept with you. You did not even let the merchants come up here."[29] The context shows clearly that the author of the letter was alluding to a situation felt to be the exception: to keep the news of the rebellion that was shaking the kingdom from spreading outside, not only messengers but even merchants were no longer authorized to cross borders. A treaty concluded between the Assyrian authorities and an Anatolian prince actually guaranteed the prince a "minimum income" should the war interrupt the passage of Assyrian caravans over his territory.[30]

For merchants, that immunity carried certain obligations with it. The Code of Hammurabi provides an illustration in section 32, which required that merchants ransom their compatriots who were prisoners of war. This means that Babylonian merchants could circulate in enemy territory.[31] Several letters from Mari allude to such acts of ransoming. The merchants' immunity explains why they were normally exempted from "military service": it took extraordinary circumstances for them to be subject to conscription like other persons.[32]

The merchants' freedom of movement had some restrictions, however, as attested by this letter from Yasmah-Addu to his father, Samsi-Addu: "The inhabitants of the *kārum* of Mari met and came looking for me to say: 'Our lord must make peace with the lord of Babylon. Why does our lord not let the convoys coming from upstream go to Babylon, and why does he not let us levy the tax-*miksum* [on commerce] downstream and upstream?'"[33] This text confirms that the imposition of the tax-*miksum* was entrusted to the heads of the "merchants guild" (*kārum*).[34]

2.3. Announcing the Arrival of Foreigners

Merchants were obliged to announce their passage in advance, through a letter designated by the term *tabrītum*.[35] When that obligation was not fulfilled, the caravan could be stopped. This occurred in Andarig with a caravan of merchants coming from Assur via Karana, which was supposed to continue on its way toward Kurda:[36]

> Tell my lord: thus speaks Yasim-El, your servant. Regarding the matter of the Assyrians who are detained at the gates, I previously wrote to my lord about it. At present, Asqur-Addu wrote to the queen, wife of Atamrum, telling her to let those people go: "Why did you detain people in caravans who were passing through toward Kurda? Let those people go! It is on my order that they passed through to the interior of the country." That is what he wrote her. She, here, responded as follows to her messenger: "When the announcement [*tabrītum*] of their passage came to you from the city of Assur, and those people passed into the interior of your country, why did not the official announcement of it come to me as well? Or why did you yourself not inform me in writing of their passage up there, so that I would know? At present Atamrum, the king of this country, is not here; he is staying in Babylonia. Now this country is dependent on Zimri-Lim, my lord. The day I detained those people, I wrote to Zimri-Lim, my lord. Would it be seemly that, without the

> agreement of my lord Zimri-Lim, I should let those people go? Until a decision about those people comes to me from my lord, those men shall not pass through the gates!" That is what she responded to his messenger, and she has just sent him away. Now, concerning the matter of these people, may my lord write whether they must be let go or not.[37]

Such an obligation was also in place for the passage of an army corps: "Tell my lord: thus speaks Yasim-Sumu, your servant. There came to me from Babylon an announcement [*tabrītum*] from Abimekin: 'The troops of the man of Babylon have come up.'"[38]

When a particularly important messenger returned from a mission abroad, the governor of the border province was charged with alerting the king of the diplomat's arrival: "The arrival of Hammi-shagish was announced to me and I installed guards on the bank of the river: they watched over the river. The day I sent that tablet to my lord, Hammi-shagish's retinue arrived in Sahru. My servants announced the arrival of these people to me and I wrote to my lord. I had that letter taken to my lord on the 21st."[39]

In a letter to the secretary of King Zimri-Lim, the governor of Saggaratum announced the imminent arrival in Mari of an embassy from the kingdom of Aleppo (Yamhad). The governor asked him to alert the king, while he himself alerted the "prime minister," Habdu-Malik: "Tell Shu-nuhra-halu: thus speaks Yaqqim-Addu, your friend. The day I sent that tablet to you, there arrived in Dur-Yahdun-Lim [the caravan] of donkeys of the messenger from Yamhad. His servants will arrive tomorrow or the day after tomorrow. So long as the messenger had not come to me, I did not write to the king. Alert the king; I wrote to Habdu-Malik to alert him."[40]

2.4. Messengers' Documents of Accreditation

Messengers carried letters of accreditation, such as this one, sent to the ruler of Mari by an otherwise unknown king: "Tell my father Zimri-Lim: thus [speaks] Ishkur-andulli, your son. Here I have given instructions to Yashub-Addu in response to your message and I have just sent it to my father."[41] A tablet of that kind served simply to identify the message sent to the king of Mari by one of his "vassals."

Conversely, it seems to me that the interpretation of a tablet that has been described as the oldest example of a "diplomatic passport" needs to be abandoned.[42]

3. Controlled Freedom of Movement

The existence of these privileged statuses did not prevent controls from being set in place.

3.1. Merchants Abusing Their Immunity

The political authorities obviously feared that, in a period of conflict, the immunity enjoyed by merchants would be used by the enemy to send messages secretly. They therefore did not hesitate to establish controls without prior warning.[43] Meptum, head of the region of Suhum, downstream from Mari, thus indicated he had turned away a caravan heading for Mari from Eshnunna. It was transporting tin, which the palace of Mari needed at the time. He added: "I searched them for tablets, telling myself: 'Perhaps they're passing tablets somewhere.'"[44]

Samsi-Addu himself gave very strict orders when he feared that the members of the tribe of Ya'ilanum would make contact with the king of Eshnunna: "The Ya'ilanum will not fail to write to the lord of Eshnunna. Form a blockade! Do it [both] by the border of the steppe [and] by Mount Ebih! Set up patrols. Seize and put in the ergastula messengers who would move about without asking [for authorization] or merchants who would move about without asking [for authorization]!"[45]

In another case, an Assyrian merchant was accused by an Anatolian king of colluding with his enemy, the sovereign of Tawiniya: the charge against him consisted precisely of having transported a tablet.[46]

3.2. Controlling the Circulation of Messengers

The circulation of messengers was also controlled: they had to be prevented from abusing their privileges. Moreover, the status of political relations sometimes had consequences for the circulation of messengers. Those who were judged undesirable were taken back to the border or even thrown in prison.

In a letter addressed to the governor of Shaduppum (present-day Tell Harmal, on the periphery of Baghdad), the king of Eshnunna announced the measures he had taken to keep couriers from abusing their freedom of movement:

> Tell Tutub-magir, thus [speaks] your lord. There are many fugitives among the couriers-*rakbū*.[47] I therefore reflected as follows: "As a matter of fact, fu-

> gitives have become too numerous. A courier-*rakbum* who wants to go to his village will not be able to go there unless he carries a document sealed by me." That is what I decided and which, as a result, I write to you. From now on, a courier-*rakbum* who shows you a document sealed by me, will be able to set himself up in his village. Let him have possession of his house and his field, and, so long as he remains, let a house be truly established! Before his departure, have a trusted person take him to the palace and have him bring the document sealed by me as his identification. Anyone not carrying a document sealed by me and who would go to you, do not allow him to stay. Have him brought to me.[48]

The explanation for this document obviously lies in the status of the couriers-*rakbū*.[49] This was a particular category of dependents of the Crown, who were charged with delivering the mail. The freedom of movement they enjoyed led to abuses: many of them, instead of continuing their work, returned home. The governor then had to control them. Henceforth the king would supply the couriers-*rakbū* with documents sealed by him, which would leave no doubt in the minds of local leaders as to the status of the people coming to settle in their district. Unfortunately, we have not yet found any documents sealed by the king that would make it possible to identify couriers. There is no trace of any application of that royal order; we know only that it was received by a provincial governor.

When a king refused to listen to the messengers sent by a foreign sovereign, he arranged to have them accompanied back to the border (*pāṭum*). This is indicated explicitly in remarks made by Zimri-Lim, king of Mari, shortly after he ascended to the throne: "[The king of] Eshnunna constantly sends me messages in view of an alliance treaty. A first time, he sent me a messenger; I sent him all the way back to the border. He sent me one a second time, I sent him all the way back to the border. And subsequently, a dignitary came, and I sent him all the way back to the border, saying: 'How, without the consent of Yarim-Lim, could there be a peace alliance with Eshnunna?'"[50]

Yarim-Lim, king of Aleppo, had played an important role in Zimri-Lim's ascension to the throne: therefore, Zimri-Lim could not conclude an alliance with another major regional power without his agreement. Note as well the three successive refusals, which in the Eastern world marked a radical break, a memory of which is preserved in Western culture in the three denials of Christ by Saint Peter.

Another example dates from a time when relations between the kingdoms of Mari and Babylon on one hand, and Larsa on the other, had become poisoned. The king of Babylon recounted a recent diplomatic incident to the envoy of his ally, the king of Mari: "[On the subject of the] messenger of my lord [Zimri-Lim] [who] was sent on a mission to Larsa, Hammurabi told me this: 'The messengers of my brother [Zimri-Lim] and my own messengers were not allowed to cross in order to go [join] my servant Mutu-hadqim. They were detained at the ford of Mashkan-shapir[51] and sent back to my border [*pāṭum*] and were told this: "Go on! Keep the tablets of Hammurabi until an order from our lord [Rim-Sin, king of Larsa] is sent."'"[52]

Messengers from Zimri-Lim and Hammurabi had wanted to go to Larsa to join the Babylonian Mutu-Hadqim, who was already there. But they were stopped at Mashkan-shapir, the most northern city of the kingdom of Larsa,[53] and conducted back to the border.

Another example of halting undesirable messengers dates from the time when Elamites invaded Mesopotamia from the Iranian plateau. The kings of Babylon, Mari, and Aleppo formed a coalition against the invader, whereas the king of Qaṭna was leaning toward an alliance with Elam. An envoy of the king of Mari to Aleppo informed his sovereign:

> Tell my lord: thus speaks Hammi-shagish, your servant. When the Elamite messenger passed in the direction of Aleppo, he sent three of his servants from Imar to Qaṭna. When Hammurabi [the king of Aleppo] learned of it, he sent [guards] to his border, and they seized these people on their return. They were questioned, and here is what they said: "The lord of Qaṭna sent us with the following message: 'The country is delivered to you, come up to me! If you come up, you will not be taken by surprise.'" These people are being held in isolation in a village. Yet currently, the lord of Qaṭna has just sent [the emperor][54] two messengers to him, some . . . having taken their head. My lord must give strict orders, and must write to the lord of Babylon, so that these men cannot leave.[55]

The road that the messengers—sent by the king of Qaṭna—were to take to Elam could not avoid the kingdoms of Mari and Babylon: orders therefore had to be given for them to be stopped before crossing the border. Some messengers tried to thwart surveillance by taking roundabout routes. Their ruse was sometimes denounced to the authorities.[56]

Conclusion

It is clear, therefore, that different logics faced off in the vast space constituted by the Near East during the Amorite period. No doubt some sovereigns were motivated by a logic of territorial expansion. Royal epithets emphasize the fact that a sovereign "enlarged" his kingdom, that he extended its borders. Nevertheless, the surveillance of roads obviously played a crucial role, making it possible to control the movements of those who, by vocation, ignored borders: traders, nomads, and messengers. Sovereigns had a vital need for them but, at the same time, feared the freedom of movement that was the very condition for the success of their work. Writing played an essential role in controlling these movements, whether as a pass provided by the interested parties, instructions given to the officials at checkpoints, or reports from said officials addressed to their sovereigns.

Conclusion: A Civilization with Two Faces

We can now fully appreciate the paradoxical character of Mesopotamian civilization at the beginning of the second millennium BCE. It constantly made use of the written text, something that, in certain respects, might appear very modern;[1] but alongside it, legal life resorted to magical practices inherited from the past that, conversely, we might be tempted to call archaic.

Scribes were responsible for recording everything in writing on behalf of their clients: they noted down the arrival and departure of goods, not only in large entities such as the palaces and temples, but also in the grand houses belonging to members of the elite. Hundreds of tablets of "king's meals" are in the Mari archives, and the archives of individuals also hold masses of similar documents, labeled "the man's meals."[2] The so-called administrative documentation counts in the tens of thousands of tablets and is still far from having been studied thoroughly. The reconstitution of series is an indispensable preliminary, and this thankless labor often surpasses an individual's capacity. But it is clear that, thanks to these texts, many aspects of economic and social life are becoming better known. Scribes were employed to put contracts in writing, as well. These contracts could involve the definitive transfer of rights, as in the case of sales, exchanges, or divisions of inheritances; and they were equally irrevocable on principle when a change of personal status was at issue, as for marriages, adoptions, or emancipations. But there were also short-term contracts for loans, employment, or rentals. Increasingly, it was judged necessary to fix in clay these different types of transaction so as to avoid future disputes. When goods changed hands, the earlier property deeds were transferred when possible, and the exceptions duly noted. Finally, writing played a larger and larger role in long-distance communication. Let me recall how, according to legend, cuneiform writing first made its appearance: its invention is attributed to Enmerkar, king of Uruk, whose message to the lord of Aratta was too long, so that the messenger was unable to repeat it correctly.[3] Although we now hold a different view of the origins of writing, it is essential to point out that, for scribes at the beginning of the second millennium BCE, it was within the framework of long-distance diplomatic relations that writing came into being, making correspondence possible. During the Old Babylonian period, however, correspondence was not restricted to sovereigns, whether to exchange messages or to communicate with their officials. The head of a household, absent from home for some time, could continue to give his daily orders to his steward and to receive news from home.[4] The following example attests to how commonplace the use of writing had become: "In addition, on the sealed voucher for 300 l[iters] of grain, you took 120 l. of grain belonging to Tubaliya. He sent his tablet to me in Babylon concerning the 120 l. of grain, but it was not given to me. At present, I am having you take that tablet. Alert him and have him deliver the 180 l. of grain [remaining]; thus will you be concerned for me."[5] Hence, transactions dealing with a minimal quantity of grain (300 liters) were the occasion for two receipts (one for the 300 liters, the other for 120, a fraction of the total) and a letter. Writing had deeply penetrated into the ruling social class, whose members were themselves able to read and, when necessary, to write. It seems clear to me that the degree of literacy among the elite at that time was much higher than during most of the Middle Ages in the West. The low cost of the clay writing support surely played a role in that phenomenon, in contrast to the high price of parchment, which restricted its use.

The Old Babylonian period is no doubt the era of Mesopotamian history when writing covered the broadest range of reality. Compared to its use in the third millennium BCE, the diversity of types of contracts was considerable. Letters were clearly more abundant and their content much more varied and vivid. In the first millennium, the competition of alphabetical writing systems, with Aramaic in the lead, was increasingly keen. The perishable nature of the support in that case means that a large portion of the documentation has disappeared forever. Moreover, the prospects for growth in documentation of the Old Babylonian period are great. The file drawers in the major museums or in collections of more modest size still hold thousands of unpublished tablets from ancient excavations or acquisitions. Many discoveries made during more or less recent excavations are far from being published in full. In Syria, the archives of Mari and those of Tell Leilan still have a great deal to teach us. In Iraq, most of the archives discovered in Tell Harmal and in the many other sites of the Diyala Valley remain unpublished; the same is true for the house of Ur-Utu in Tell ed-Dēr (Sippar-Amnānum). The texts discovered in Larsa and Isin have often been the object only of catalog entries. There is no dearth of more recent discoveries. A few years ago, in a building of Tell Abu Habbah (Sippar-Yahrurm), an archival lot was uncovered that numbers about nine hundred tablets from the era of Ammi-ditana, including several dozen letters sent by the king himself.[6] And let me also note the Iraqi excavations of Tell Abu Antiq, identified as Bikasi: that little city, located some thirty-one miles south of Babylon, yielded nearly two thousand tablets, dating for the most part from the reign of Samsu-iluna. We know that, since 1991, illicit excavations have ravaged many sites, putting thousands of tablets on the market of antiquities—deprived of their context, unfortunately, but which we will really have to resolve to publish in the end.

Yet such a profusion of tablets, published or forthcoming, must not make us forget that, in these very texts, the share of the implicit remains very great.[7] Whole swaths of Mesopotamian civilization are hardly touched on in writing. In the matter of law, the Code of Hammurabi was in no wise the result of the king's will to systematically put in writing the customs of his kingdom, even less to unify them. In addition, after the code was composed, different local customs remained, in matters of succession, for example. If we do nevertheless manage to apprehend certain customary behaviors, it is usually because of a chance letter. Hence, a missive addressed to the king of Mari allows us to reconstitute the traditional rules governing the exercise of the right to revenge.[8] Another letter indicates that an individual who already had sons did not have the right to adopt a slave.[9]

In Babylonian civilization, moreover, people remained very attached to meeting with one another directly. When Samsu-iluna decreed a *mīšarum* upon his accession to the throne, he sent a letter to his governors in which he gave the main lines of the measures;[10] but he ended his missive by asking that they come to Babylon, accompanied by the elders of their province, to have an interview with him. In certain circumstances, a desire was expressed not to resort to writing, but rather, explicitly, to have a face-to-face discussion. Hence, the Eshnunnian general Shallurum asked Meptum to join him: "Come, let us speak face to face [literally, 'mouth to mouth']!"[11] In that respect, correspondence was perceived only as a makeshift solution, though it was sometimes a source of ebullience. Letter *ShA* 1, 65, is a fine example of the sense of proximity the ancients felt by virtue of correspondence, which was a novelty in the region of Zagros at that time: "Bullattal brought me your news and I was very glad: I had the impression that you and I had met and embraced! And myself, I am well: be glad!"[12] The point of reference remained the personal encounter, here evoked by the gestures that distance made impossible, even though the courier could give the illusion of proximity. And in the context of certain lawsuits, preference continued to be given to the oral over the written: "Even if a sealed document is available, may an oral declaration [literally, "a mouth"] be made."[13]

Finally, the transmission of knowledge remained largely within the sphere of the oral, writing having for the most part preserved information whose interest was limited in duration. During the Old Babylonian period, there were as yet no true libraries as they became known subsequently; we possess only manuscript collections, linked less to the discipline of the specialist who owned them than to the writing lessons he dispensed at his residence.[14]

The constant recourse to the written text, particularly in the realm of law, did not eradicate behaviors stemming from what jurists have sometimes called "prelaw" and which were directly linked to magic. Oaths played an essential role, whether in contracts between individuals or alliances between sovereigns. They were accompanied by imprecations pronounced against oneself and symbolic gestures signifying the absoluteness of the pledge made by the juror. In tying together the fringe of their garments, a man and a woman visibly signified for everyone the bond of marriage that henceforth united them; kings did the same when they concluded an alliance. In anointing himself with oil, the juror, by analogy, had the malediction of the gods penetrate his body; it would not fail to seize hold of him in the event of perjury. For us, such behaviors may appear to be in contradiction with the recourse to written proof during a trial, which is very well attested. But the ancients felt no such contradiction. In addition, they considered tablets not inscribed pieces of clay but *living beings,* in a civilization where the line between the living and the inanimate was not conceived in the same way as it is in ours. We saw in chapter 4 that, in two cases at least, when tablets were lost and then reconstituted, it was said that they were being brought (back) to life: the verb *bulluṭum* was the same as that employed when someone asked a deity to bring back the dead. It is not surprising that tablets could be "killed."[15] Tablets had a "mouth" (*pûm*), which is why one could listen to them.[16] Tablets could lie,[17] like mouths.[18] The opposition between oral and written was not felt as strongly at the time as it is in our own culture.

It is clear, therefore, that our relationship to Mesopotamian civilization is itself twofold. On one hand, we identify traits in it that are clearly the basis for our own. With the significant development of the use of writing, we at times have the sense that we are witnessing the birth of an "information society." But on the other hand, there are behaviors that are altogether alien to us, such as the act of swallowing a substance that is supposed to incorporate a curse to reinforce the validity of an oath. If Mesopotamian civilization were radically other, we would be unable to understand it.[19] Nevertheless, there is little interest in placing the emphasis exclusively on the continuities and concluding that "there's nothing new under the sun": it is in the tension between the identification of our roots and the analysis of differences that the historian's labor is situated.

NOTES

ACKNOWLEDGMENTS

1. In the interest of legibility, I have omitted the macrons over proper names. By contrast, I have retained the conventional notation of the special consonants ṣ (ts), š (sh), and ṭ. [Translator's note:] Spelling of proper names in English follows *Webster's New Biographical Dictionary* or *Webster's New Geographical Dictionary*, which generally use "sh" in place of "š."

INTRODUCTION

1. For a general approach, see the excellent collection edited by J. M. Sasson et al., *Civilizations of the Ancient Near East* (New York: 1995). For the French-speaking reader, let me point out the recent *Dictionnaire de la civilisation mésopotamienne*, ed. F. Joannès, coll. Bouquins (Paris: 2001).
2. I shall confine myself here to citing the fundamental works of R. McC. Adams, esp. *Heartland of Cities: Surveys of Ancient Settlement and Land Use on the Central Floodplain of the Euphrates* (Chicago: 1981).
3. See, for example, J. L. Huot, ed., *Larsa. Travaux de 1987 et 1989*, BAH 165 (Beirut: 2003); and E. Stone and P. Zimansky, eds., *The Anatomy of a Mesopotamian City: Survey and Soundings at Mashkan-shapir* (Winona Lake, IN: 2004), along with my remarks in "Comptes rendus," *RA* 97 (2003): 188–90.
4. See B. Lyonnet, "Le nomadisme et l'archéologie: Problèmes d'identification. Le cas de la partie occidentale de la Djéziré au 3e et début du 2e millénaire avant notre ère," CRRAI 46, ed. C. Nicolle (Paris: 2004), 25–50.
5. Cf. my observations in D. Charpin, D. O. Edzard, and M. Stol, OBO 160/4 (Fribourg: 2004): 273–77 (and note 12 of this chapter), along with my remarks on the recently published stela of Dadusha ("Données nouvelles sur la région du Petit Zab au XVIIIe siècle av. J.-C," *RA* 98 [2004]: 151–78).
6. I tried to show this in *Le clergé d'Ur au siècle d'Hammurabi (XIXe–XVIIIe siècles av. J.-C.)*, HEO 22 (Geneva: 1986). Other approaches of the same kind have subsequently been attempted, especially by R. Zettler on the temple of Inanna in Nippur, E. Stone on a district in the same city, and C. Reichel on the palace of Eshnunna, not to mention the team of Tell ed-Dēr epigraphists for the house of Ur-Utu. On this theme, see R. L. Zettler, "Written Documents as Excavated Artifacts and the Holistic Interpreta-

tion of the Mesopotamian Archaeological Record," in *Mém. Albright,* ed. J. S. Cooper and G. M. Schwartz (Winona Lake, IN: 1996), 81–101.

7. See D. Charpin, "Le déchiffrement des tablettes cunéiformes," *L'archéologue-Archéologie nouvelle* (1995): 35–40.
8. In the most difficult cases, I have opted for an approximation, followed by the Babylonian term, for example, "nun-*nadītum.*"
9. See, for example, M. Civil's caveat in "Les limites de l'information textuelle," in *L'archéologie de l'Iraq,* ed. M. T. Barrelet (Paris: 1980), 225–32, and the response of W. W. Hallo, "The Limits of Skepticism," *JAOS* 110 (1990): 187–99.
10. FM II, ed. D. Charpin and J.-M. Durand, Mémoires de NABU 3 (Paris: 1994), 45, versus all the correspondence of Hammurabi to Shamash-hazir; see esp. F. R. Kraus, *Briefe aus dem Archive des Šamaš-ḫāzir in Paris und Oxford (TCL 7 und OECT 3),* AbB IV (Leiden: 1968); and M. Stol, *Letters from Yale,* AbB IX (Leiden: 1981).
11. The dates used in this book (all BCE) are those of the so-called middle chronology, according to which the reign of Hammurabi of Babylon ran from 1792 BCE to 1750 BCE.
12. For a recent survey, see Charpin, Edzard, and Stol, OBO 160/4 . That book is composed of three essays: D. Charpin, "Histoire politique du Proche-Orient amorrite (2002–1595)," 25–480; D. O. Edzard, "Altbabylonische Literatur und Religion," 481–640; and M. Stol, "Wirtschaft und Gesellschaft in Altbabylonischer Zeit," 641–975. More accessible is my *Hammu-rabi de Babylone* (Paris: 2003; English translation forthcoming).
13. See the texts collected and commented on by J.-M. Durand, LAPO 17 (Paris: 1998), 332–53.
14. A letter from Samsi-Addu is very clear in that respect (ARM I, 16 [Durand, LAPO 17, 641]); on this subject, see chapter 3.
15. See P. Villard, "Le déplacement des trésors royaux d'après les archives royales de Mari," in CRRAI 38, ed. D. Charpin and F. Joannès (Paris: 1992), 195–205; and M. Guichard, *La vaisselle de luxe dans le palais de Mari,* ARM XXXI (Paris: 2005).
16. D. Charpin, "Un inventaire général des trésors du palais de Mari," *MARI* 2 (1983): 211–14.
17. See, for example, P. Marello, "Esclaves et reines," in *FM* II, 115–29; and N. Ziegler, "Le harem du vaincu," *RA* 93 (1999): 1–26. See also B. Lion, "Les enfants des familles déportées de Mésopotamie du nord à Mari en ZL 11,'" *Ktèma* 22 (1997): 109–18; and B. Lion, "Les familles royales et les artisans déportés à Mari en ZL 12,'" in CRRAI 46, 217–24.
18. J.-P. Vernant, *Entre mythe et politique* (Paris: 1996), 52–53.

CHAPTER 1

1. See the essays by D. Charpin, J.-M. Durand, and M. Guichard in *The History of Writing from Ideograms to Multimedia,* ed. A. M. Christin (Paris: 2002); F. Joannès, ed., *Dictionnaire de la civilisation mésopotamienne,* coll. Bouquins (Paris: 2001); and C. B. F. Walker, *Cuneiform, Reading the Past* (London: 1987).
2. For more details, see chapter 2.
3. J. Sasson, ed., *Civilizations of the Ancient Near East* (New York: 1995).
4. Ibid., 2265.
5. Ibid., 2279.
6. Ibid., 2188.

7. J. N. Postgate, *Early Mesopotamia: Society and Economy at the Dawn of History* (London: 1992), 69.
8. See J. Klein, *Three Šulgi Hymns: Sumerian Royal Hymns Glorifying King Šulgi of Ur* (Bar-Ilan: 1981), 188–89, line 19.
9. Quotation and commentary of lines 13–20 in N. Veldhuis, *Elementary Education at Nippur* (Groningen: 1997), 24–25.
10. H. L. J. Vanstiphout, "Lipit-Eštar's Praise in Edubba," *JCS* 30 (1978): 33–61 (36–37, lines 18–22).
11. Asb. L[4]i 10–18 (M. Streck, *Assurbanipal und die letzten assyrischen Könige bis zum Untergange Niniveh's* [Leipzig: 1916], 254–55); and R. Borger, *Beiträge zum Inschriftenwerk Assurbanipals* (Wiesbaden: 1996), 187–88.
12. H. Hunger, *Babylonische und assyrische Kolophone,* AOAT 2 (Neukirchen-Vluyn: 1968), 97, no. 318.
13. P. Villard, "L'éducation d'Assurbanipal," *Ktèma* 22 (1997): 135–49 (148–49). See also J. Fincke, "The Babylonian Texts of Nineveh: Report on the British Museum's Ashurbanipal Library Project," *AfO* 50 (2003–4): 111–49 (119–22).
14. Benno Landsberger, "Scribal Concepts of Education," in *City Invincible,* ed. C. H. Kraeling and R. M. Adams (Chicago: 1960), 94–123 (111).
15. G. Frame and A. R. George, "The Royal Libraries of Nineveh: New Evidence for King Ashurbanipal's Tablet Collecting," in CRRAI 49, ed. D. Collon and A. George (*Iraq* 67/1) (London: 2005), 265–84 (279).
16. P. A. Beaulieu, *The Reign of Nabonidus King of Babylon 556–539 B.C.,* YNER 10 (New Haven, CT: 1989), 79.
17. Ibid., 79n10, 217.
18. Consider this comment by P. A. Beaulieu: "In short, the author of the Verse Account accuses Nabonidus of having imposed a 'knowledge' and 'wisdom' alien to Babylonian culture, and of having claimed that they were superior to the oldest and most sacred writings of Mesopotamia" (ibid., 218). Let me add that the author of the Verse Account denies Nabonidus not the art of the scribe in general (*ṭupšarrūtu*) but, precisely, "the art of writing in cuneiform [literally, "striking of the stylus," *mihiṣ qān ṭuppī*]." In the neo-Babylonian period, in fact, Aramaic writing was very widespread in Mesopotamia, but the scholarly texts continued to be written in cuneiform. To admit that one had not mastered that writing system amounted to admitting one did not have direct access to the Mesopotamian religious tradition.
19. By contrast, a different tradition, favorable to Nabonidus, credits him with that knowledge: see P. Machinist and H. Tadmor, "Heavenly Wisdom," in *The Tablet and the Scroll: Near Eastern Studies in Honor of William W. Hallo,* ed. M. Cohen, D. Snell, and D. B. Weisberg (Bethesda, MD: 1993) , 146–51 (esp. 149b).
20. Landsberger, "Scribal Conceptions of Education," 98.
21. See chapter 6 of my *Le clergé d'Ur au siècle d'Hammurabi (XIXe–XVIIIe siècles av. J. C.),* HEO 22 (Geneva: 1986).
22. M. Tanret, *Per aspera ad astra. L'apprentissage du cunéiforme à Sippar-Amnānum pendant la période paléobabylonienne tardive,* MHET I/2 (Ghent: 2002).
23. Let me flesh out M. Tanret's comments by saying that the trade of *gala-mah* must have been taught to Ur-Utu orally by his father. That no doubt explains one of the disappointments of the excavation: the almost complete absence of texts of a religious nature.
24. Landsberger, "Scribal Conceptions of Education," 119.

25. J. Renger, "Überlegungen zum akkadischen Syllabar," *ZA* 61 (1971): 23–43 (33).
26. M. T. Larsen, *The Old-Assyrian City-State and Its Colonies,* Mesopotamia 4 (Copenhagen: 1976), 305. See also "What They Wrote on Clay," in *Literacy and Society,* ed. K. Schousboe and M. T. Larsen (Copenhagen: 1989), 133; and A. M. Ulshöfer, *Die altassyrischen Privaturkunden,* FAOS Beihefte: Altassyrische Texte und Untersuchungen 4 (Stuttgart: 1995), 35.
27. "A final example from the world of the Old Babylonian traders: Larsan merchants staying at Eshnunna set up their own documents in the style of their home city, and there seems to be no good reason to think that they brought professional scribes with them from Larsa as suggested by W. F. Leemans, *Foreign Trade in the Old Babylonian Period* (Leiden, 1960), pp. 73–74" (M. T. Larsen, "The Babylonian Lukewarm Mind: Reflections on Science, Divination and Literacy," in *Mél. Reiner,* ed. F. Rochberg-Halton [New Haven, CT: 1987] , 203–26 [esp. 220n51]).
28. C. Wilcke, *Wer las und schrieb in Babylonien und Assyrien. Überlegungen zur Literalität im Alten Zweistromland,* Bayerische Akademie der Wissenschaften Philologisch-Historische Klasse 6 (Munich: 2000).
29. For the case of the letters from Mari that deviate from the norm, see note 53 in this chapter.
30. Note in particular his analysis of the case of the nuns-*nadītum* in the city of Sippar in the Old Babylonian period (Wilcke, *Wer las und schrieb in Babylonien und Assyrien,*32). Since his study, new material has become available. M. Tanret has distinguished, among the school tablets from the house of Ur-Utu (see note 22 in this chapter), a small group of exercises that are obviously of an earlier date. They must have belonged to the nun-*nadītum* who lived in that house before Ur-Utu's father moved in. This is the first evidence we have of the scribal apprenticeship of a woman of that status. For the question of female scribes at the time, see B. Lion, "Dame Inanna-ama-mu, scribe à Sippar," *RA* 95 (2001): 7–32; and B. Lion and E. Robson, "Quelques textes scolaires paléo-babyloniens rédigés par des femmes," *JCS* 57 (2005): 37–54.
31. See D. Charpin, *La correspondance à l'époque amorrite. Écriture, acheminement et lecture des lettres d'après les archives royales de Mari* (forthcoming). An English summation has appeared under the title "The Writing, Sending, and Reading of Letters in the Amorite World," in *Babylonian World,* ed. G. Leick (New York: 2007).
32. J. Sasson, "Water beneath Straw: Adventures of a Prophetic Phrase in the Mari Archives," in *Solving Riddles and Untying Knots: Biblical, Epigraphic, and Semitic Studies in Honor of Jonas C. Greenfield,* ed. Z. Zevit, S. Gitin, and M. Sokoloff (Winona Lake, IN: 1995), 599–608 (607n21).
33. "Hamatil, scribe, servant (of King) Yahdun-Lim"; legend of a seal published by D. Charpin, "Hamanu ou Hamatil?" *MARI* 3 (1984): 257. See in general D. Charpin, "Noms de personnes et légendes des sceaux en Babylonie ancienne," in *L'écriture du nom propre,* ed. A. M. Christin (Paris: 1998), 43–55.
34. D. Charpin and D. Beyer, "Les sceaux de Yasîm-sûmû," *MARI* 6 (1990): 619–24. And this was not a unique case. I was able to see, on a yet-unpublished tablet from Isin, dating to year I of Zambiya, a seal that gives another example: "Ur-Shulpaë, /scribe of the king,/son of Lu-Amar-Sin,/*šandabakkum* of the king" (ur-^{d}sul-pa-è/dub-sar lugal/dumu lú-^{d}amar-/^{d}su'en/GÁ-dub-ba lugal). The fourth line was obviously added when that "royal scribe" was promoted to *šandabakkum.*
35. Dumu é *ṭup-pí,* in M. 13021, text quoted in J.-M. Durand, "Trois études sur Mari," *MARI* 3 (1984): 127–180 (127n14).

36. ARM XXI, 398:1 (*šà-tam*).
37. A certain Mebisum also bore both the title *mār bīt ṭuppī* and *šatammum:* see S. Maul, *FM* II, ed. D. Charpin and J.-M. Durand, Mémoires de NABU 3 (Paris: 1994), 47n. c.
38. Of uneven quality, to be sure, as J. R. Kupper has shown in *NABU* (1992/105).
39. See J. Eidem, *The Shemshāra Archives 2. The Administrative Texts,* Historikfilsofiske Skrifter 15 (Copenhagen: 1992); and my review of that book in *Syria* 71 (1994): 456–60.
40. ARM III, 21 (J.-M. Durand, LAPO 17 [Paris: 1998], 741).
41. A. 2463:10–11 (unpublished text). I thank M. Guichard for bringing this source to my attention.
42. J.-M. Durand has informed me that the letters of Darish-libur that he published (*FM* VIII, Mémoires de NABU 8 [Paris: 2002]) are recognizable at a glance by their very particular handwriting and page layout. They may therefore be in the hand of the high official himself on a mission to the kingdom of Aleppo, though we cannot rule out the possibility that he had the use of a local scribe.
43. *FM* VIII 47: 18'–21'.
44. A. 2671+A. 4006. Text quoted in J.-M. Durand, "Administrateurs de Qaṭṭunân," FM *II*, 83–114 (91n. 20).
45. The examples cited (above and below) represent only a selection; I give a complete presentation of the data in *La correspondance à l'époque amorrite.*
46. ARM XXVI/2, 429:7–9; the editor's translation of line 8 ("[you], have them read to you") should be modified and note c eliminated as unnecessary.
47. Unpublished text A. 1231.
48. See the oath of Sumuhadu (J.-M. Durand, LAPO 16 [Paris: 1997], 51).
49. A. 4215 (Durand, LAPO 16, 65:27–28).
50. See the comments of J.-M. Durand, ARM XXVI/1, 62–63.
51. ARM XXVI/2, 344.
52. ARM XXVI/2, 333:3–6.
53. These letters are in a fairly crude style and deviate from the norm in many respects (syllabary, word order, etc.). See my "L'akkadien des lettres d'Ilan-ṣura," in *Reflets des deux fleuves, volume de mélanges offerts à André Finet,* ed. M. Lebeau and P. Talon, Akkadica Supplementum 6 (Leuven: 1989), 31–40 (esp. 38–39). There, I had not considered that hypothesis.
54. M. T. Larsen, "The Babylonian Lukewarm Mind: Reflections on Science, Divination and Literacy,"220n51.
55. A. 2583; quoted by J.-M. Durand, ARM XXVI/1, 63n314.
56. J. M. Sasson, "About 'Mari and the Bible,'" *RA* 92 (1998): 117–18n82.
57. On that matter, see note 66 in this chapter.
58. Sasson, "About 'Mari and the Bible,'" 117.
59. See A. 2671+A. 4006.
60. For more details, see my "Données nouvelles sur la région du Petit Zab au XVIIIe siècle av. J.-C.," *RA* 98 (2004): 151–78 (177).
61. See Durand, *ARM* XXVI/1, 53–54, 62–63. Note as well Sasson's evaluation of King Zimri-Lim's mother: "Addu-duri, it is clear from her correspondence, knew how to read the omens apparently without consulting the professionals" (*FM* II, 304).
62. A. 2583.
63. A. 3611+ (unpublished text, 5–10).
64. ARM XVIII 16+:43–48 (see Durand, LAPO 16, 92).
65. See R. Borger, "Gottesbrief," in RlA 3 (Berlin: 1957–71), 575–76; and B. Pongratz-

Leitsen, *Herrschaftswissen in Mesopotamien. Formen der Kommunikation zwischen Gott und König im 2. und 1. Jahrtausend v.Chr,* SAAS 10 (Helsinki: 1999).

66. See the case of the letter from the god Shamash to King Zimri-Lim of Mari (ARM XXVI/1, 194), which was dictated to a scribe by a prophet; cf. my "Prophètes et rois dans le Proche-Orient amorrite: Nouvelles données, nouvelles perspectives," in FM VI, ed. D. Charpin and J.-M. Durand, Mémoires de NABU 7 (Paris: 2002), 7–38 (esp. 14).
67. See R. Borger, *Mesopotamisches Zeichenlexikon,* AOAT 305 (Munster: 2003).
68. D. O. Edzard, "Keilschrift," in RlA 5 (Berlin and New York, 1976–80), 544–68 (561b).
69. A. Goetze, *Old Babylonian Omen Texts,*YOS 10 (New Haven, CT: 1947).
70. S. Parpola, "The Man without a Scribe and the Question of Literacy in the Assyrian Empire," In *Ana šadi Labnāni lū allik. Beiträge zu altorientalischen und mittlemeerischen Kulturen. Festschrift für Wolfgang Röllig,* ed. B. Pongratz-Leisten, H. Kühne, and P. Xella, AOAT 247 (Neukirchen-Vluyn: 1997), 315–24. The letter had been published in ABL 151; it has since been reprinted as SAA XV, 17.
71. Ibid., 321n17.
72. By way of comparison, during the same period, the correspondence of a highly skilled scribe such as Mar-Issar contained a repertoire of 225 signs (170 syllabic signs and 55 logograms).
73. "I submit that the alleged 'drastic' second-millennium change in Mesopotamian literacy actually never took place, and that the level of literacy in first millennium Mesopotamia was at least as high (if not higher) as in earlier times" (Parpola, "The Man without a Scribe," 321–22). It is nonetheless surprising that nowhere in his article does Parpola allude to the "competition" that cuneiform writing faced at the time with the alphabetical writing system of Aramaic. Note that King Sargon II refused to receive mail written "on skin [*sipru*] in Aramaic"; people had to write to him "in Akkadian," that is, in cuneiform on a clay tablet (SAA XVII, 2). But beginning with the reign of his grandson Asharhaddon, most of the official correspondence must have been in Aramaic (cf. M. Luukko and G. Van Buylaere, *The Political Correspondence of Esarhaddon,* SAA 16 [Helsinki: 2002], xvii). Note, however, the care Asharhaddon took to give scribal training to the sons of Babylonian dignitaries whom he kept as hostages in Nineveh; see J. Fincke, "The Babylonian Texts of Nineveh," *AfO* 50 (2003–4): 118.
74. For the situation in the third millennium BCE, see G. Visicato, *The Power and the Writing: The Early Scribes of Mesopotamia* (Bethesda, MD: 2000).
75. I am in agreement here with the conclusions of J. S. Cooper, who indicates: "It has long been a scholarly cliché that cuneiform literacy was a craft literacy confined to the very few, although the basis of this judgment seems to be little more than the difficulty we moderns have in learning cuneiform." He adds, "In fact, literacy is a social phenomenon the extent of which is not governed by the difficulty of the writing system, as attested by the example of highly literate modern Japan, with its several thousand *kanji* characters and two types of *khana,* and predominantly illiterate medieval Europe, with its very simple alphabet"("Babbling on: Recovering Mesopotamian Orality," in *Mesopotamian Epic Literature: Oral or Aural?* ed. M. E. Vogelzang and H. L. J. Vanstiphout [Lewiston, NY: 1992], 103–22 [110]). Clearly, that argument takes the opposite tack of the one I examined above regarding the Assyrian merchants.
76. See the state of the question and the bibliography in G. Cavallo and R. Chartier, eds.,

Histoire de la lecture dans le monde occidental (Paris: 1997), in particular, J. Svenbro's "La Grèce archaïque et classique: L'invention de la lecture silencieuse," 47–77; see also A. K. Gavrilov, "Techniques of Reading in Classical Antiquity," *Classical Quarterly* 47 (1997): 56–73, which contains a vigorous argument for the view that silent reading existed well before Saint Augustine's time. The only Assyriological study on the subject is A. K. Grayson, "Murmuring in Mesopotamia," in *Wisdom, Gods and Literature: Studies in Assyriology in Honour of W. G. Lambert,* ed. A. R. George and I. L. Finkel (Winona Lake, IN: 2000), 301–8.

77. ARM XXVI/2, 396.
78. See S. M. Maul, *FM* II, 50, no. 18n. h.
79. This passage seems to prove that in certain cases, the envelope in which the letter was enclosed did not bear an address or was addressed simply "to my lord," without indicating his name.
80. A. 2701, published in my "'Lies natürlich . . .' A propos des erreurs des scribes dans les lettres de Mari," in *Mél. von Soden,* ed. M. Dietrich and O. Loretz (Neukirchen-Vluyn: 1995), 2:43–56 (48–50).
81. For many Old Babylonian references to *amārum* in the sense of "to read," see CAD A/II, 18.
82. For more details, see chapter 5.
83. FM *II,* 17. On that text, see the commentary of Wilcke, *Wer las und schrieb in Babylonien und Assyrien,* 24.
84. Cavallo and Chartier, *Histoire de la lecture.*
85. S. M. Burstein, *The Babyloniaca of Berossus,* SANE 1/5 (Malibu, CA: 1978), 10.
86. W. G. Lambert, "Enmeduranki and Related Matters," *JCS* 21 (1967): 126–38.
87. Burstein, *The Babyloniaca of Berossus,* 20.
88. It is the syllabic equivalents in the Old Babylonian texts that have made it possible to establish how to read many logograms in the recent divinatory texts; from this standpoint, the texts published by A. Goetze in YOS 10 have been very important.
89. For that theme, see G. Jonker, *The Topography of Remembrance: The Dead, Tradition, and Collective Memory in Mesopotamia,* Studies in the History of Religion 68 (Leiden: 1995).
90. H. L. J. Vanstiphout, "Lipit-Eštar's Praise in Edubba," *JCS* 30 (1978): 33–61 (39).
91. H. L. J. Vanstiphout, "How Did They Learn Sumerian?" *JCS* 31 (1978): 118–26; and more recently, S. Tinney, "On the Curricular Setting of Sumerian Literature," *Iraq* 61 (1999): 159–72.
92. This practice is comparable to the way that nurses for the royal families were named. They bore function names such as *Abi-bashti* ("My father is my pride") or *Abi-ludari,* ("May my father have eternal life!"). Hence, as soon as the royal children began speaking, when they called their nurse, they praised the sovereign or formulated a wish concerning him. See N. Ziegler, "Les enfants du palais," *Ktèma* 22 (1997): 45–57 (esp. 52).
93. See A. R. George, *The Babylonian Gilgamesh Epic: Introduction, Critical Edition and Cuneiform Texts* (Oxford: 2003), 538–39.

CHAPTER 2

1. G. Tessier, *La diplomatique,* 3rd ed., coll. Que Sais-je? (Paris: 1966), 14.
2. Assyriology can be defined, narrowly, as limited to Sumerian and Akkadian writings (with Akkadian divided between Assyrian in the north and Babylonian in the south), or more broadly, to cover all the languages that were notated in cuneiform

writing (also including Hittite, Hurrian, Elamite, and others). In this chapter, I shall usually embrace the more restricted definition, which corresponds to my own area of competence, but shall not hesitate to cite neighboring cases here and there.

3. See S. Démare-Lafont, *Conférence d'ouverture de la direction d'études "Droits comparés du Proche-Orient ancien,"* Conférences d'ouverture de la Section des sciences historiques et philologiques, École Pratique des Hautes Études (Paris: 2002).
4. I am thinking here of the major collections of Old Babylonian documents, such as J. Kohler and A. Ungnad, *Ḫammurabis Gesetz* III–V (Leipzig: 1909), supplemented by a final volume, P. Koschaker and A. Ungnad, *Ḫammurabis Gesetz* VI (Leipzig: 1923); or of Middle- and neo-Assyrian documents, such as J. Kohler and A. Ungnad, *Assyrische Rechtsurkunden* (Leipzig: 1913).
5. See the overview of H. J. Nissen, P. Damerow, and R. K. Englund, *Archaic Bookkeeping: Writing and Techniques of Economic Administration in the Ancient Near East* (Chicago: 1993). See also P. Talon and K. Van Lerberghe, eds., *En Syrie aux origines de l'écriture* (Turnhout: 1998); and finally, R. K. Englund, "Texts from the Late Uruk Period," in J. Bauer, R. K. Englund, and M. Krebernik, *Mesopotamien. Späturuk-Zeit und Frühdynastische Zeit*, ed. P. Attinger and M. Wäfler, *Annäherungen* 1, OBO 160/1 (Fribourg: 1998), 15–233.
6. M. J. Geller, "The Last Wedge," *ZA* 87 (1997): 43–95.
7. An overview is provided in the catalog for an exhibition held at the Grand Palais in 1982: B. André and C. Ziegler, eds., *Naissance de l'écriture* (Paris: 1982).
8. See esp. the exemplary studies of J. N. Postgate, "Middle Assyrian Tablets: The Instruments of Bureaucracy," *AoF* 13 (1986): 10–39 (without any illustrations, unfortunately); and K. Radner, "The Relation between Format and Content of Neo-Assyrian Texts," in *Nineveh 612 BC: The Glory and Fall of the Assyrian Empire*, ed. R. Mattila (Helsinki: 1995), 63–77.
9. Many dubious hypotheses have been made regarding the calamus. See the state of the question set forth in G. R. Driver, *Semitic Writing*, 3rd ed. (London: 1976), 23–26. More recently, see esp. H. W. F. Saggs, "The Reed Stylus," *Sumer* 37 (1981): 127–28; and M. Powell, "Three Problems in the History of Cuneiform Writing: Origins, Direction of Script, Literacy," *Visible Language* 15/4 (1981): 419–40 (figs. 1–11). Gold or silver calami are mentioned in literary texts. Were these "deluxe" models or simply metaphorical? See E. Bleibtreu, "Bemerkungen zum Griffel des Tontafelschreibers," in *Mél. Kienast*, ed. G. Selz (Munster: 2003), 1–5.
10. A work station for preparing tablets has been excavated in Hammam et-Turkman in the Balih Valley. See D. J. W. Meijer, "A Scribal Quarter?" in *Assyria and Beyond: Studies Presented to Mogens Trolle Larsen*, ed. J. G. Dercksen, PIHANS 100 (2004), 387–93.
11. ARM XXVIII, 105:9–10.
12. Here I am summarizing my "Corrections, ratures, annulations: La pratique des scribes mésopotamiens," in *Le texte et son inscription*, ed. Roger Laufer (Paris: 1989), 57–62.
13. See, for example, F. N. H. Al-Rawi and S. Dalley, *Old Babylonian Texts from Private Houses at Abu Habbah Ancient Sippir Baghdad University Excavations*, Edubba 7 (London: 2000), nos. 3 (lot of several), 49, and 50. We may wonder, in fact, whether in all cases it was the scribe himself who fashioned the tablet before inscribing it: assistants may be supposed to have played a role. In that case, it would be misguided to examine fingerprints on the surface of the tablets in the aim of identifying the scribe; see D. Bonneterre, "Pour une étude des dermatoglyphes digitaux sur des tablettes cunéiformes," *Akkadica* 59 (1998): 26–29.

14. An example of this type is illustrated in my "The Mesopotamian Scribes," in *The History of Writing from Ideograms to Multimedia*, ed. A. M. Christin (Paris: 2002), 39 (fig. 4).
15. On the large tablets, however, the appearance of the writing sometimes changes near the end of the text. That transformation is a consequence of the clay hardening.
16. It was believed that a kiln had been found in a courtyard of the palace of Ugarit (thirteenth century BCE) in which various tablets, including letters (*received* by the king!) were placed to be baked. This was an error in interpretation, as J. Margueron has demonstrated in "Notes d'archéologie et d'architectures orientales 7.—Feu le four à tablettes de l'ex 'cour V' du palais d'Ugarit," *Syria* 72 (1995): 55–69.
17. Some tablets include what are generally interpreted to be firing holes, intended to promote evaporation of the water deep inside the tablet. On the problem of the baking of tablets in antiquity, see the references collected in K. R. Veenhof, *Cuneiform Archives: An Introduction*, in CRRAI 30, ed. K. R. Veenhof (Leiden: 1986), 1–36 (line 2); and J. Fincke, "The Babylonian Texts of Nineveh: Report on the British Museum's Ashurbanipal Library Project," *AfO* 50 (2003–4): 111–49 (esp. 126).
18. J. Reade even argues that the tablets of the famous "library of Ashurbanipal" were baked only when a fire destroyed Nineveh in 612 BCE: "On the whole it seems likely that the 'library' texts, unlike many of the Middle Assyrian ones and of course all the foundation documents, were not baked originally. The same applied to the royal letters, many state documents, and the private archives; these generally are made of any one of a wide range of inferior clay, only baked if at all in 612" (J. Reade, "Archaeology and the Kuyunjik Archives," in CRRAI 30, 219).
19. Some publications, on the pretext of a "scientific" approach, indicate the tint of the tablets through the use of color scales; that detail is clearly pointless.
20. X. Faivre, "Le recyclage des tablettes cunéiformes," *RA* 89 (1995): 57–66.
21. See E. Robson, "The Tablet House: A Scribal School in Old Babylonian Nippur," *RA* 95 (2001): 39–66.
22. A photo of such a tablet from the Mari archives was published in my "The Mesopotamian Scribes," 39 (fig. 6).
23. See K. E. Slanski, *The Babylonian Entitlement* narûs (kudurrus): *A Study in Their Form and Function*, ASOR Book 9 (Boston: 2003); and D. Charpin, "La commémoration d'actes juridiques: A propos des *kudurrus* babyloniens," *RA* 96 (2002): 169–91.
24. See K. E. Slanski, "Representation of the Divine on the Babylonian Entitlement Monuments (*kudurrus*): Part I: Divine Symbols," *AfO* 50 (2003–4): 308–23.
25. R. S. Ellis, *Foundation Deposits in Ancient Mesopotamia*, YNER 2 (New Haven, CT: 1968).
26. E. Edel, *Der Vertrag zwischen Ramses II. von Ägypten un Ḫattušili III. von Ḫatti*, WVDOG 95 (Berlin: 1997).
27. A photo of it can be found, for example, in P. Neve, *Ḫattuša: Stadt der Götter und Tempel; Neue Ausgrabungen in der Hauptstadt der Hethiter* (Mainz: 1993), figs. 38, 39, 45, and 46. This is a treaty between the Hittite king Tudhaliya IV and Kurunta of Tarhuntassa; English translation by G. Beckman, *Hittite Diplomatic Texts*, WAW 7 (Atlanta: 1996), 108–17 (no. 18C) (with bibliography).
28. This could be the reason why that type of text has been so little attested in Hittite documentation—though lucky finds are not to be ruled out. This raises the question of what writing system and what language were notated on the diptych with vestiges of wax discovered in the famous shipwreck of Ulu Burun off the coast of Turkey; see the series of articles published in *AnSt* 41 (1992).

29. See M. Stol, "Einige kurze Wortstudien," in *Mél. Borger*, ed. S. Maul (Groningen: 1998), 343–52 (esp. 343–44).
30. S. Parpola, "Assyrian Library Record," *JNES* 42 (1983): 1–29.
31. See D. J. Wiseman, "Assyrian Writing-Boards," *Iraq* 17 (1955): 3–13; and M. Howard, "Technical Description of the Ivory Writing-Boards from Nimrud," *Iraq* 17 (1955): 14–20.
32. V. Donbaz and M. W. Stolper, *Istanbul Murašû Texts*, PIHANS 79 (Leiden: 1997), 101, no. 27: 8 (eight parchments were part of a loan that included clay, water, and animals).
33. Under "M" in the CAD, there is only one reference for *magallatu;* but there are others, indicated in a brief note from the CAD in person (!), in *RA* 72 (1978): 96.
34. See esp. the example cited in the CAD 17-II, 231, sec. D. Cf. E. Reiner, "Runaway—Seize Him," in *Assyria and Beyond: Studies Presented to Mogens Trolle Larsen*, ed. J. G. Dercksen, PIHANS 100 (Leiden: 2004), 475–82.
35. A well-illustrated overview can be found in C. B. F. Walker, *Cuneiform: Reading the Past* (London: 1987). More technical, but excellent, is D. O. Edzard, "Keilschrift," in RlA 5 (Berlin: 1976–80), 544–68.
36. Comments on paleography generally begin, at best, only with the most ancient Semitic alphabetical writings. As Alphonse Dain has aptly observed, "A scholar who studies the Sumerian cylinders will not be said to be a paleographer. Therein lies an unfortunate restriction, sanctified by custom." And, he adds, "In fact, only three areas of paleography have been constituted into an autonomous science: the Greek, the Roman and Latin, and the medieval West and Renaissance." *Introduction à la paléographie*, in *L'Histoire et ses méthodes*, ed. C. Samaran (Paris: 1961), 530.
37. That situation is well known, for example, in the case of the tablets from the Ur III period published by N. Schneider or the collection of neo-Assyrian acts in C. H. Johns, *Assyrian Deeds and Documents*, 4 vols. (Cambridge: 1898–1913).
38. D. Owen propagated that technique, which has been used for years by the staff of *Archives royales de Mari*.
39. For the project "Digital Hammurabi," go to http://www.jhu.edu/digitalhammurabi. A very promising system has been elaborated by the University of Leuven.
40. R. Labat, *Manuel d'épigraphie akkadienne (signes, syllabaires, idéogrammes)* (1948; 5th rev. ed. corrected by F. Malbran-Labat, Paris: 1976). This work relies in part on C. Fossey, *Manuel d'assyriologie, tome deuxième. Évolution des cunéiformes* (Paris: 1926).
41. The same is true for M. J. Steve's *Syllabaire élamite. Histoire et paléographie, Civilisations du Proche-Orient Série II Philologie* 1 (Neuchâtel-Paris: 1992); all the usefulness of this volume lies in the fact that it confines itself to one geographically and culturally well-delimited region.
42. See P. T. Daniels, "Cuneiform Calligraphy," in Mattila, *Nineveh 612* BC, 81–90.
43. See the pioneering study by R. D. Biggs: "On Regional Cuneiform Handwritings in Third Millennium Mesopotamia," *OR* 42 (1973): 39–45; and more recently, W. Sallaberger, "Die Entwicklung der Keilschrift in Ebla," in *Mél. Orthmann*, ed. J.-W. Meyer, M. Novák, and A. Pruß (Frankfurt: 2001), 436–45.
44. For the Old Babylonian period, see A. Goetze's introduction in *Old Babylonian Omen Texts*, YOS 10 (New Haven, CT: 1947). This study has not yet been superseded, despite inaccuracies that would now have to be corrected.
45. Visit http://www.cdp.bham.ac.uk for information on this project.
46. J. Finkelstein, "The Hammurapi Law Tablet BE XXXI 22," *RA* 63 (1969): 11–27 (21–22n2). The rest of that note gives a few suggestions for defining these developments

over the three-century duration of the first Babylonian dynasty (nineteenth to seventeenth centuries BCE).

47. I have nonetheless made an attempt in my "L'akkadien des lettres d'Ilân-ṣurâ," in *Mél. Finet,* ed. M. Lebeau and P. Talon (Leuven: 1989), 31–40.
48. See the following standard works: C. Rüster, *Hethitische Keilschrift-Paläographie,* StBoT 20 (Wiesbaden: 1972); and C. Rüster and E. Neu, *Hethitische Keilschrift-Paläographie II (14/13 Jh. v. Chr.),* StBoT 21 (Wiesbaden: 1975).
49. It is undoubtedly because the contracts and administrative documents of Mesopotamia can be dated fairly easily by other means that paleography has remained underdeveloped. These texts often include a date. When they do not, their chronology can often be established by a prosopographical investigation.
50. For this lot of texts, still in part unpublished, see my "Les prêteurs et le palais: Les édits de *mîšarum* des rois de Babylone et leurs traces dans les archives privées," in *Interdependency of Institutions and Private Entrepreneurs (MOS Studies 2): Proceedings of the Second MOS Symposium (Leiden 1998),* ed. A. C. V. M. Bongenaar, PIHANS 87 (Leiden, 2000), 185–211 (200 and n. 52).
51. See B. R. Foster, "Archives and Empire in Sargonic Mesopotamia," in CRRAI 30, 46–52 (49).
52. For the influence of Eshnunna on the reform of writing in Mari at the time, see D. Charpin and N. Ziegler, *Mari et le Proche-Orient à l'époque amorrite: Essai d'histoire politique, Florilegium marianum V,* Mémoires de NABU 6 (Paris: 2003), 40 and n. 99.
53. T. 509 and 510, published by J.-M. Durand, "La situation historique des Šakkanakku: Nouvelle approche," *MARI* 4 (1985): 147–72.
54. At least before the introduction of the euro, when the traditional way of configuring the obverse and reverse of coins was abandoned.
55. That was rightly pointed out in M. W. Green, "The Construction and Implementation of the Cuneiform Writing System," *Visible Language* 15/4 (1981): 345–72.
56. Another question, which is still the object of debate, has to do with the direction of the writing. J. Marzahn has done very interesting experiments, which he explained in a still-unpublished paper given at a colloquium in Baghdad in March 2000.
57. See, for example, the plates in J. G. Westenholz et al., *Cuneiform Inscriptions in the Collection of The Bible Lands Museum Jerusalem, The Emar Tablets,* CM 13 (Groningen: 2000).
58. See M. Stol, *Letters from Yale,* AbB IX (Leiden: 1981), ibid., 126n197a.
59. K. Radner, "The Relation between Format and Content," 72.
60. The observations that can be made about "scribe's hands" also apply to the shape of the tablets. In that case, it seems to have been the scribe himself who fashioned his tablets.
61. K. R. Veenhof, "'Dying Tablets' and 'Hungry Silver': Elements of Figurative Language in Akkadian Commercial Terminology," in *Figurative Language in the Ancient Near East,* ed. M. Mindlin et al.(London: 1987), 41–75 (67n21).
62. B. Kienast maintains that the tablet was covered with a fine layer of flour before the envelope was formed (*ZABR* 2 [1996]: 2), but I confess I do not know whether analyses have been conducted on the fine white dust sometimes seen when an envelope is opened.
63. See, for example, the seal of Zimri-Lim on the envelope of the letter he sent to Tishulme, TH 72.15 (J.-M. Durand, LAPO 16 [Paris: 1997], 247), a photograph of which appears in my "The Writing, Sending, and Reading of Letters in the Amorite World," in *Babylonian World,* ed. G. Leick (New York: 2007), fig. 3.

64. See W. Sallaberger, *"Wenn Du mein Bruder bist, . . .": Interaktion und Textgestaltung in altbabylonischen Alltagsbriefen,* CM 16 (Groningen: 1999), 26.
65. Note that the text of the envelope almost always appears upside down in relation to that of the internal tablet. This makes it possible, in cases where only half of a document has been preserved, to have a complete text.
66. For a case of this kind, see D. Charpin, "Lettres et procès paléo-babyloniens," in *Rendre la justice en Mésopotamie,* ed. F. Joannès (Paris: 2000), 69–111 (72).
67. See K. Van Lerberghe and G. Voet, "On 'Quasi-Hüllentafeln,'" *NAPR* 6 (1991): 3–8.
68. Here I am summarizing my "Des scellés à la signature: L'usage des sceaux dans la Mésopotamie antique," in *Écritures II,* ed. A. M. Christin (Paris: 1985), 13–24.
69. According to Y. Metman, "Sigillographie," in *L'Histoire et ses méthodes,* ed. C. Samaran (Paris: 1961), 393–446 (393).
70. See, in general, the excellent introduction by D. Collon, *First Impressions: Cylinder Seals in the Ancient Near East* (1987; rev. ed., London: 2005). Two colloquia were devoted to these questions: McG. Gibson and R. D. Biggs, eds., *Seals and Sealing in the Ancient Near East,* BiMes 6 (Malibu, CA: 1977); and more recently, W. W. Hallo and I. J. Winter, eds., *Seals and Seal Impressions: Proceedings of the XLVe Rencontre Assyriologique Internationale Part II Yale University* (Bethesda, MD: 2001).
71. Sometimes the seal was rolled over the entire surface of the tablet.
72. Metman, "Sigillographie," 393.
73. For a study limited to a particular era, see W. F. Leemans, "La fonction des sceaux apposé à des contrats vieux-babyloniens," in *Mél. Kraus,* ed. G. van Driel, T. J. H. Krispijn, M. Stol, and K. R. Veenhof (Leiden: 1982), 219–44.
74. AbB XI (Leiden: 1986), 90: 18–19, 27–29.
75. See F. van Koppen, "Redeeming a Father's Seal," in *Mél. Walker,* ed. C. Wunsch (Dresden: 2002), 147–72.
76. Let me cite in particular the writings of D. Beyer, F. Blocher, G. Colbow, C. Reichel, D. Stein, and B. Teissier.
77. See, for example, A. Hattori, "Seal Practices in Ur III Nippur," in CRRAI 45/2, ed. W. W. Hallo and I. J. Winter (Bethesda, MD: 2001), 71–99.
78. I am thinking in particular of the pioneering study by J. Nougayrol on the "international" archives found in Ugarit, a good portion of which were composed elsewhere, particularly in the Hittite capital of Hattusha or in the city of Karkemish: J. Nougayrol, *Textes accadiens des archives sud (Archives internationales),* PRU 4 (Paris: 1956), 2–6. Unfortunately, Claude Schaeffer, the excavator of Ugarit, adopted the annoying habit of commenting personally on the material aspect of the tablets and of reserving the right to publish the photographs, which would have been welcome in Nougayrol's book; they have been reproduced in a dispersed manner, especially in C. F.-A. Schaeffer, "Matériaux pour l'étude des relations entre Ugarit et le Hatti. Recueil des sceaux et cylindres hittites imprimés sur les tablettes des archives Sud du palais de Ras Shamra," *Ugaritica* 3 (Paris: 1956): 1–92; and C. F.-A. Schaeffer, "Commentaires sur les lettres et documents trouvés dans les bibliothèques privées d'Ugarit," *Ugaritica* 5 (Paris: 1968), 607–768.
79. For an analysis of other examples, see S. Sanders, ed., *Margins of Writing, Origins of Culture: New Approaches to Writing and Reading in the Ancient Near East,* OIS 2 (Chicago: 2005).
80. See, for example, the study limited to sales contracts from the region between Sippar and Eshnunna at the beginning of the Old Babylonian period: A. Skaist, "The Sale

Contracts from Khafajah," in *Mél. Artzi*, ed. J. Klein and A. Skaist (Bar-Ilan: 1990), 255–76.

81. See M. Streck, *Das Amurritische Onomastikon der altbabylonischen Zeit. Band 1: Die Amurriter. Die onomastische Forschung. Orthographie und Phonologie. Nominalmorpologie*, AOAT 27/1 (Munster, 2000). See my review of that book in *AfO* 51 (2005–6): 282–92.
82. See N. Ziegler and D. Charpin, "Amurritisch lernen," in *Festschrift für Hermann Hunger zum 65. Geburtstag gewidmet von seinen Freunden, Kollegen und Schülern*, Wiener Zeitschrift für die Kunde des Morgenlandes 97 (2007): 55–77.
83. See G. Wilhelm, *Untersuchungen zum Ḫurro-Akkadischen von Nuzi*, AOAT 9 (Neukirchen-Vluyn: 1970). It is common in the history of writing for both the writing system and the language it notated to be borrowed. The adaptation of that writing system to the language of the borrowing people generally occurs only at a second stage. The Hurrians do not seem to have felt that need for their documents, as opposed to their correspondence (cf. note 84 in this chapter).
84. G. Wilhelm, "A Hurrian Letter from Tell Brak," *Iraq* 53 (1991): 153–68. That letter must of course be supplemented by the famous "Mitannian letter" sent to the pharaoh by the Mitannian king Tushratta and discovered in the Egyptian capital of the time, Tell al-'Amarna; see G. Wilhelm's translation in W. L. Moran, *The Amarna Letters* (Baltimore, MD: 1992), 63–71.
85. See T. Richter, "Qaṭna in the Late Bronze Age: Preliminary Remarks," *SCCNH* 15 (Bethesda, MD: 2005), 109–26.
86. See M. Dietrich, *The Neo-Babylonian Correspondence of Sargon and Sennacherib*, SAA 17 (Helsinki: 2003), no. 2. See chapter 1, note 73.
87. Cases in which cuneiform was written in ink on leather are very rare and occurred very belatedly (cf. note 31 in this chapter). Conversely, the number of extant clay tablets written in Aramaic continues to grow. New examples have recently been discovered in Tell Shioukh Fawqani near Karkemish and Tell Sheikh Hamad on the lower Habur; see A. Lemaire, *Nouvelles tablettes araméennes*, HEO 34 (Geneva: 2001).
88. See chapter 3.
89. J. N. Postgate, *Fifty Neo-Assyrian Legal Documents* (Warminster: 1976), unfortunately published without photographs for reasons of economy. A new, illustrated edition of this manual would be highly desirable.
90. See M. San Nicolò's "classic" *Die Schlussklauseln der altbabylonischen Kauf- und Tauschverträge* (1922; rev. ed. updated by H. Petschow, Munich: 1974).
91. A. Skaist, *The Old Babylonian Loan Contract: Its History and Geography* (Bar-Ilan: 1994). That attempt was unfortunately not very successful; see the reviews of M. Van de Mieroop, *JAOS* 116 (1996): 763–64; and D. Charpin, *AfO* 44/45 (1997–98): 347–49.
92. G. Kestemont, *Diplomatique et droit international en Asie occidentale, 1600–1200 av. J.C.* (Louvain-la-Neuve: 1974). Unfortunately, the title is such that many readers will read it as "diplomacy" rather than "diplomatics." In addition, translations of the texts are sometimes anachronistically "modern."
93. AbB IX, 264:7. See Sallaberger's interesting study, *"Wenn Du mein Bruder bist."*
94. F. R. Kraus, "Briefschreibübungen in altbabylonischen Schulunterricht," *JEOL* 16 (1959–62): 16–39; and Sallaberger, *"Wenn Du mein Bruder bist,"* 149–54.
95. S. Dalley et al., *The Old Babylonian Tablets from Tell al Rimah* (London: 1976), no. 107:12.

96. D. Charpin and J.-M. Durand, *Documents cunéiformes de Strasbourg conservés à la Bibliothèque Nationale et Universitaire* (Paris: 1981), no. 107:15.
97. AbB XI, 77:24–27.
98. K. Van Lerberghe and G. Voet, *Sippar-Amnānum: The Ur-Utu Archive. Volume 1,* MHET I Ghent: 1991), no. 77:26.
99. A. Finet, "Les symboles du cheveu, du bord du vêtement et de l'ongle en Mésopotamie," in *Eschatologie et cosmologie,* Annales du Centre d'Étude des Religions 3 (Brussels: 1969), 101–30.
100. See esp. K. Van Lerberghe and G. Voet, "An Old Babylonian Clone," in *Mél. De Meyer,* ed. H. Gasche, M. Tanret, C. Janssen, and A. Degraeve (Ghent: 1994), 159–68.
101. This phenomenon is proven by the archives of Ili-shukkal in Kutalla: see D. Charpin, *Archives familiales et propriété privée en Babylonie ancienne: Étude des documents de "Tell Sifr,"* HEO 12 (Geneva: 1980), 104.
102. See esp., for the Pre-Sargonic and Sargonic periods (twenty-fifth to twenty-third centuries BCE), the overview by G. Visicato, *The Power and the Writing: The Early Scribes of Mesopotamia* (Bethesda, MD: 2000). See also the more restricted approaches of P. Negri Scafa, "The Scribes of Nuzi," *SCCNH* 10 (Bethesda, MD: 1999), 63–80; and J. Ikeda, "Scribes in Emar," in *Priests and Officials in the Ancient Near East: Papers of the Second Colloquium on the Ancient Near East—The City and Its Life, Held at the Middle Eastern Culture Center in Japan (Mitaka, Tokyo) March 22–24, 1996,* ed. K. Watanabe (Heidelberg: 1999), 163–86. M. Muntingh's "The Role of the Scribe according to the Mari Texts: A Study of Terminology," *Journal of Semitics* 3 (1991): 21–53, already old, proves to be very disappointing. There are few monographs, but let me cite, as an example, B. Lion, "Dame Inanna-ama-mu, scribe à Sippar," *RA* 95 (2001): 7–32.
103. J. M. Sasson, "Shunukhra-Khalu," in *Mém. Sachs,* ed. E. Leichty, M. deJ. Ellis, and P. Girardi (Philadelphia: 1988), 329–51.
104. See my forthcoming book, *La Correspondance à l'époque amorrite.*
105. See, however, M. Tanret, "The Works and the Days . . . On Scribal Activity in Old Babylonian Sippar-Amnānum," *RA* 98 (2004): 33–62, and his note "Sheqels for the Scribe," *NABU* 2005/73.
106. See S. J. Lieberman, "Nippur: City of Decisions," in CRRAI 35, ed. M. deJ. Ellis (Philadelphia: 1992), 127–36 (130 and n. 18). That Assyriologist's premature death kept him from publishing the *Manual of Sumerian Legal Forms* he was preparing. See W. W. Hallo, "A Model Court Case concerning Inheritance," in *Mém. Jacobsen,* ed. T. Abusch (Winona Lake, IN: 2002), 141–54.
107. See B. Landsberger, *Die Serie ana ittišu,* MSL 1 (Rome: 1937).
108. See esp. the collection edited by K. R. Veenhof, *Cuneiform Archives and Libraries: Papers Read at the 30e Rencontre Assyriologique Internationale Leiden, 4–8 July 1983,* PIHANS 52 (Leiden: 1986); and, for the most recent periods, O. Pedersén, *Archives and Libraries in the Ancient Near East 1500–300* BC (Bethesda, MD: 1998). See also P. Matthiae, ed., *Gli archivi dell'Oriente Antico, Archivi e Cultura* 29 (1998); and M. Brosius, ed., *Ancient Archives and Archival Traditions: Concepts of Record Keeping in the Ancient World* (Oxford: 2003).
109. Think, for example, of the tablets illegally exhumed in Meskene (about 250 have currently been published) after the salvage excavations at the site—which had uncovered about 450 tablets—had come to an end (in 1976), not to mention the situation in Iraq since the end of the Gulf War.

110. See D. Charpin, *Le clergé d'Ur au siècle d'Hammurabi (XIXe–XVIIIe siècles av. J.-C.)*, HEO 22 (Geneva: 1986); and M. Van de Mieroop, *Society and Enterprise in Old Babylonian Ur*, BBVO 12 (Berlin: 1992).
111. See esp. L. Dekiere, "La généaolgie d'Ur-Utu, gala.maḫà Sippar-Amnānum," in Gasche et al., *Mél. De Meyer*, 125–41; and C. Janssen, "When the House Is on Fire and the Children Are Gone," in CRRAI 40 (Leiden: 1996), 237–46.
112. See, finally, C. Wunsch, *Das Egibi-Archiv I. Die Felder und Gärten*, CM 20 (Groningen: 2000); and K. Abraham, *Business and Politics under the Persian Empire: The Financial Dealings of Marduk-naṣir-apli of the House of Egibi (521–487 BC)* (Bethesda, MD: 2004).
113. See chapter 3.
114. See the various studies collected in F. Joannès, *Les phénomènes de fin d'archives en Mésopotamie*, *RA* 89 (1995).
115. M. G. Biga, "The Reconstruction of a Relative Chronology for the Ebla Texts," *OR* 72 (2003): 345–67.
116. From that standpoint, the title *State Archives of Assyria*, chosen for the corpus of neo-Assyrian documents—remarkable in other respects—published by the University of Helsinki since 1987 appears unfortunate.
117. See A. Archi's presentation in *Syrie, mémoire et civilisation*, ed. S. Cluzan et al. (Paris: 1994), 108–19 (with many photographs).
118. See Durand, LAPO 16, 25–40; and Charpin and Ziegler, *Mari et le Proche-Orient*, 1–28.
119. See S. Parpola's presentation, "The Imperial Archives of Nineveh," in Mattila, *Nineveh 612 BC*, 15–25.
120. There are exceptions, of course, as demonstrated for example by the archives of Ur-Utu found in his house of Tell ed-Dēr, ancient Sippar-Amnānum; see C. Janssen, "Inanna-mansum et ses fils: Relation d'une succession turbulente dans les archives d'Ur-Utu," *RA* 86 (1992): 19–52 (esp. 30–32). Another case is provided by S. W. Cole, *The Early Neo-Babylonian Governor's Archive from Nippur*, OIP 114 (Chicago: 1996).
121. See my "La fin des archives dans le palais de Mari," *RA* 89 (1995): 29–40.
122. A recent study has even placed in doubt the authenticity of that correspondence *as a whole*, arguing that all the letters are apocryphal; see F. Huber, "La correspondance royale d'Ur, un corpus apocryphe," *ZA* 91 (2001): 169–206. The analysis focuses primarily on the language of the documents: in the author's view, the Sumerian in the letters is too highly developed to date from the end of the third millennium BCE (see also D. Charpin, D. O. Edzard, and M. Stol, OBO 160/4 [Fribourg: 2004], 59–60n145).
123. The treaties discovered from before that time are draft agreements, not the text of the treaties actually concluded; see chapter 7.
124. See the translations discussed in G. Beckman, *Hittite Diplomatic Texts*, WAW 7.
125. S. Lackenbacher, LAPO 20 (Paris: 2002).
126. For the censuses attested in the Mari archives, see J.-M. Durand, LAPO 17 (Paris: 1998), 332–53.
127. The texts were published in R. M. Sigrist, *Les* sattukku *dans l'Ešumeša durant la période d'Isin et Larsa*, BiMes 11 (Malibu, CA: 1984).
128. D. Charpin, "Nouveaux documents du bureau de l'huile à l'époque assyrienne," *MARI* 3 (1984): 83–126; D. Charpin, "Nouveaux documents du bureau de l'huile (suite)," *MARI* 5 (1987): 597–99.

129. P. Matthiae, "The Archives of the Royal Palace G of Ebla: Distribution and Arrangement of the Tablets according to the Archaeological Evidence," in CRRAI 30, 53–71.
130. B. Lafont, "Les textes judiciaires sumériens," in *Rendre la justice en Mésopotamie. Archives judiciaires du Proche-Orient ancien (IIIe–Ier millénaires avant J.-C.)* (Paris: 2000), 35–68 (38n2).
131. French translation and commentary in D. Charpin, "Lettres et procès," 86–88; see chapter 5.
132. J. N. Postgate, "Administrative Archives from the City of Assur in the Middle Assyrian Period," in CRRAI 30, 168–83 (170 and n. 8).
133. M. Tanret, "As Years Went By in Sippar-Amnānum," in CRRAI 45/1, ed. T. Abusch, P.-A. Beaulieu, J. Huehnergard, P. Machinist, and P. Steinkeller (Bethesda, MD: 2001), 455–66.
134. J. M. Sasson, "Accounting Discrepancies in the Mari NÌ.GUB [NÍG.DU] Texts," in van Driel et al., *Mél. Kraus,* 326–41.
135. ARM X, 82. See commentary in my "L'archivage des tablettes dans le palais de Mari: Nouvelles données," in *Mél. Veenhof,* ed. W. H. van Soldt, J. G. Dercksen, N. J. C. Kouwenberg, and T. J. H. Krispijn (Leiden: 2001), 13–30.
136. ARM XXII, 428, 429.
137. AbB IV (Leiden: 1968), 22.
138. AbB XIII (Leiden: 1984), 46:11–16. For other references and a published example of a (dated) copy of a text held in the archives of the capital, see M. Stol, "A Rescript of an Old Babylonian Letter," in van Soldt et al., *Mél. Veenhof,* 457–65.
139. AbB IV, 118.
140. See my "Archivage et classification: Un exemple à Mari sous Zimrî-Lîm," in CRRAI 51, ed. R. D. Biggs, J. Myers, and M. T. Roth (Chicago: 2008), 1–13.
141. D. Charpin, "Un inventaire général des trésors du palais de Mari," *MARI* 2 (1983): 211–14.
142. See D. Charpin and J.-M. Durand, "Le tombeau de Yahdun-Lim," *NABU* 1989/27. The letter has now been quoted in extenso in French translation: N. Ziegler, "Aspects économiques des guerres de Samsî-Addu," in *Economie antique. La guerre dans les économies antiques,* ed. J. Andreau et al. (Saint-Bertrand-de-Comminges: 2000), 14–33.
143. Charpin, *Archives familiales et propriété privée.*
144. In particular, the use of seals without iconography, manufactured for the occasion (which Assyriologists call "bur-gul" seals, from the name of the stonecutter responsible for manufacturing them). See D. Charpin, "Noms de personnes et légendes des sceaux en Babylonie ancienne," in *L'écriture du nom propre,* ed. A. M. Christin (Paris: 1998), 43–55.
145. Sir L. Woolley and Sir M. Mallowan, *The Old Babylonian Period,* UE 7 (London: 1976).
146. See my *Le clergé d'Ur.*
147. A. H. Podany, *The Land of Hana: Kings, Chronology, and Scribal Tradition* (Bethesda, MD: 2002). On this subject, see my "Le 'royaume de Hana': Textes et histoire," *RA* 96 (2002): 61–92.
148. The only criticism that can be made of her is that she in some sense reinvented the wheel, since she is clearly one of the people doing diplomatics "without knowing it." She studied, first, "changes in physical attributes of the texts" ("size and shape," "seal impressions," and "paleography"), then "changes in the contents of the texts" (here her analysis is less rigorous, dealing successively with "institutions," "clauses,"

"practices regarding witnesses," "names," and "orthographic conventions"). Fortunately, a certain naiveté on her part in formulating the observations does not prevent them from retaining their full value.

149. E. Sollberger, "The Cruciform Monument," *JEOL* 20 (1968): 50–70.

150. M. A. Powell reconstituted an ingenious scenario, according to which the monument was to be attributed to Naram-Sin and not to Manishtushu (M. A. Powell, "Narām-Sîn, Son of Sargon: Ancient History, Famous Names, and a Famous Babylonian Forgery," *ZA* 81 [1991]: 20–30). That hypothesis has been invalidated by the manuscript discovered in the library of the temple of Sippar, excavated between 1985 and 1989 (F. N. H. Al-Rawi and A. R. George, "Tablets from the Sippar Library III: Two Royal Counterfeits," *Iraq* 56 [1994]: 135–48 [139–48]).

CHAPTER 3

1. D. O. Edzard, "Die *bukânum*-Formel der altbabylonischen Kaufverträge und ihre sumerische Entsprechung," *ZA* 60 (1970): 8–53. More recently, see M. Malul, "The *bukannum*-Clause: Relinquishment of Rights by Previous Right Holders," *ZA* 75 (1985): 66–77.
2. J. Bottéro, *Annuaire de l'École pratique des hautes études, IVe section, 1970–1971*, 112.
3. See CAD I/J, s.v. *isqu* A. mng. 1al'.
4. D. Charpin, *AFPP* (Paris: 1980), 176–78.
5. Within the context of divinatory practices, the clod of dirt functioned as a substitute for a city. When a diviner had to take omens regarding a city but was unable to go there in person, he required a clod of dirt from that city as support for his inquiry. See on this subject the remarks of J.-M. Durand, *Archives épistolaires de Mari* I/1, ARM XXVI/1, 41–43. That practice was similar to the taking of a lock of hair (*šartum*) and the fringe (*sissiktum*) of a garment for an oracular inquiry relating to an absent person (ibid., 40).
6. Such is the interpretation proposed by K. R. Veenhof, "An Old Babylonian Deed of Purchase of Land in the De Liagre Böhl Collection," in *Mél. Böhl*, ed. M. A. Beek, A. A. Kampman, C. Nijland, and J. Ryckmans (Leiden: 1973), 359–79 (esp. 364–68).
7. See S. Greengus, "Old Babylonian Marriage Ceremonies and Rites," *JCS* 20 (1966): 55–57; and cf. the Syrian practices attested in Aleppo especially (ARM XXVI/1, 10:15, commentary by J.-M. Durand, 103).
8. I am not persuaded by the arguments made by R. Westbrook against the theory expounded by S. Greengus; see R. Westbrook, *Old Babylonian Marriage Law, AfO Beiheft* 23 (Horn, Austria: 1988), 49–50.
9. S. Lackenbacher, "Note sur l'ardat-lilî," *RA* 65 (1971): 126 (obverse, II: 13–15), 153.
10. J. J. Finkelstein, "Cutting the *sissiku* in Divorce Procedure," *WO* 8 (1975–76): 236–40; K. R. Veenhof, "The Dissolution of an Old Babylonian Marriage according to *CT* 45, 86," *RA* 70 (1976): 153–64.
11. That aspect is missing from Westbrook's *Old Babylonian Marriage Law*. Here again, there is no direct evidence of this gesture, but only the parallel (very clear in my view) of texts describing the conclusion of an alliance between two kings (see chapter 7, sec. 3.3).
12. S. Lackenbacher, LAPO 20 (Paris: 2002), 328–33.
13. See F. Thureau-Dangin, "Trois contrats de Ras-Shamra," *Syria* 18 (1937): 245–55 (Lackenbacher, LAPO 20, 332) and the commentary by S. Lafont, "Nouvelles données sur la royauté mésopotamienne," *RHDFE* 73 (1995): 473–500 (487).
14. See the list composed by A. D. Kilmer, "Symbolic Gestures in Akkadian Contracts

from Alalakh," *JAOS* 94 (1974): 177–83 (esp. n. 24); and the references given in S. Greengus, "The Old Babylonian Marriage Contract," *JAOS* 89 (1969): 505–32 (515n7).

15. In what follows, I am summarizing my "'Manger un serment,'" in *Jurer et maudire: Pratiques politiques et usages juridiques du serment dans le Proche-Orient ancien*, ed. S. Lafont, *Méditerrannées* 10–11 (1997): 85–96, which the reader may consult for more details and textual references.
16. In Susa during the same period, someone who swore an oath "touched the head of the god"; see my note "'Manger l'*assakkum*' en Babylonie et 'Toucher le *kidinnum*' à Suse," *NABU* 2001/54.
17. See the detailed references in my "'Manger un serment.'"
18. ARM VIII, 195. See, more recently, K. R. Veenhof's review of E. Kutsch, *Salbung als Rechtsakt im Alten Testament und im Alten Orient*, *BiOr* 23 (1996): 308–13 (309b–21a).
19. See J.-M. Durand's commentary in *MARI* 1 (1982), 89. He proposes a new interpretation in his note "Tombes familiales et culte des Ancêtres à Emar," *NABU* 1989/112. He believes that the ritual in Emar that consisted of breaking bread upon the sale of a house is to be linked to the *kispum*, which would make it possible to reinterpret the examples from Mari: "It was certainly a festive moment when the transfer of property was celebrated, but it may have also been a rite through which the dead buried on the property were given their share, or at least a distorted memory of that ritual, when it was extended to realities other than a house (fields)." Durand himself raised the principal objection to his proposal, namely, that this clause appears only in texts regarding the sale of fields and not of houses.
20. They are attested from the third millennium BCE on; see the examples collected in I. J. Gelb, P. Steinkeller, and R. M. Whiting, *Earliest Land Tenure Systems in the Near East: Ancient Kudurrus*, OIP 104 (Chicago: 1991), 243–44, sec. 7.12.5.7; and P. Steinkeller, *Sale Documents of the Ur-III-Period*, FAOS 17 (Stuttgart: 1989), 143. See also, in general, M. Malul, *Studies in Mesopotamian Legal Symbolism*, AOAT 221 (Neukirchen-Vluyn: 1988), esp. 346–78, and chap. 7, "Ratification of a Deed of Sale" (though it overlooks the texts from *MARI* 1 [1982] and ARM XXII).
21. Text quoted in M. Kitz, "An Oath, Its Curse and Anointing Ritual," *JAOS* 124 (2004): 315–22; this article unfortunately overlooks my 1997 essay.
22. S. Parpola and K. Watanabe, *Neo-Assyrian Treaties and Loyalty Oaths*, SAA 2 (Helsinki: 1988), 52, sec. 72.
23. Ibid., 56, sec. 94.
24. Ibid., 51, sec. 523.
25. Veenhof, review of Kutsch, *Salbung als Rechtsakt im Alten Testament und im Alten Orient*, 313.
26. S. Démare-Lafont has reminded me, as a basis for comparison, of the ordeal by "bitter water" that the woman suspected of adultery is made to drink in Numbers 5:12–28: cf. S. Démare-[Lafont], "L'interprétation de Nb 5,31 à la lumière des droits cunéiformes," in CRRAI 33, ed. J.-M. Durand (Paris: 1987), 49–52 (esp. the bibliographical references, 49n1). J.-M. Durand has pointed out to me that the letter A. 350+ could be alluding to the punishment for perjury, when it is said (lines 10–11): "Zuzu filled himself with the water of the god and he died" (J.-M. Durand, LAPO 16 [Paris: 1997] 333). Cf. also the military oath among the Hittites (N. Oettinger, *Die Militärichen Eide der Hethiter*, StBot 22 [1976]). Many self-imprecations can be found in it, with comparisons such as, "just as yeast makes a loaf of bread swell, so anyone who violates the oath will burst and will meet a deadly fate" (8–9). A comparative

study could be undertaken on this subject. It would have to include Saint Paul, who declares: "Wherefore whosoever shall eat this bread, and drink this cup of the Lord, unworthily, shall be guilty of the body and blood of the Lord. . . For he that eateth and drinketh unworthily, eateth and drinketh damnation to himself" (I Corinthians 11:27, 29).

27. It is therefore clear why the term *asakkum* was also used to designate property set aside for the deity or the king (ARM I, 101:6; VII, 1005:2; XXII, 196:2; XXII, 234:7): anyone who seized it fell prey to the destructive force dormant within it. The letter ARM XXVI/1, 280, gives an excellent illustration. Batahrum's three sons died suddenly on the same day, and public rumor insinuated: "There is within that man [x minas] of silver, *asa* [*kkum* of the god/?king?]."

28. But note this sentence pronounced by the juror in an Old Babylonian lawsuit: "If anyone sees me in other dispositions, may they treat me [appropriately] for having held in contempt an oath by the king," *kīma nīš šarrim uṭappilu lū ipušūninni* (BM 13912, published by M. Anbar, *RA* 69 (1975), 121 no. 8: 14; translated in *Lettres et procès,* 96n51). The translation of the CAD, "(if I act contrary to the oath I am taking) let them treat me as if I had sullied the oath by the king" (I/J, 291b–292a), is unacceptable: the Akkadian preterit cannot be rendered as an irrealis mood. See the commentary on BM 13912 in J. M. Sasson, "Forcing Morals on Mesopotamian Society?" in *Mél. Hoffner,* ed. G. Beckman, R. Beal, G. McMahon (Winona Lake, IN: 2003), 329–40. For the expression *niš . . . ṭapālum* used positively, see ARM XXVI/2, 302:20.

29. Ninkarrak *murṣam kabtam asakum lemnam simmam marṣam . . . ina biniātišu lišāṣaššumma* (lines 50ff.).

30. BM 96998: 41–51 (text published with superb commentary by K. R. Veenhof, "Fatherhood Is a Matter of Opinion: An Old Babylonian Trial on Filiation and Service Duties," in *Mél. Wilcke,* ed. W. Sallaberger, K. Volk, and A. Zgoll [Wiesbaden:2003], 313–22); and see my note "Ṣurârum est-il le fils de son père? A propos d'un procès à Sippar-Amnânum," *NABU* 2005/3. See also, in general, E. Dombradi, *Die Darstellung des Rechtsaustrags in den altbabylonischen Prozessurkunden,* FAOS 20 (Stuttgart: 1996), 84–86, "Rituale vor den Göttersymbolen."

31. The two most frequent symbolic gestures are the immolation of an animal with which the perjurer has identified in advance, and the gesture of "striking one's throat" (*lipit napištim*): see chapter 7, sec. 3.

32. S. Çeçen and K. Hecker, "*Ina mātīka eblum.* Zu einem neuen Text zum Wegerecht in der Kültepe-Zeit," in *Mél. von Soden,* ed. M. Dietrich and O. Loretz (Neukirchen-Vluyn: 1995), 2:31–41. French translation by C. Michel, LAPO 19 (Paris: 2001), 150 no. 87 (but there is no reason to suppose that the goblet was filled with blood; any liquid sufficed for the analogy).

33. *FM* II, ed. D. Charpin and J.-M. Durand, Mémoires de NABU 3 (Paris: 1994), 122: 39–44 (adopting the translation of J. Sasson *apud* B. Lafont, "Relations internationales, alliances et diplomatie au temps des rois de Mari," in *Amurru* 2, ed. J.-M. Durand and D. Charpin [Paris: 2001], 250n162). See M. Guichard, "Au pays de la Dame de Nagar," in *FM* II, 235–72; and M. Guichard and D. Sevaliè, "Akîn-amar, Kabiya et la 'guerre de Bunû-Eštar,'" *NABU* 2003/6. For the role of the cup in alliance ceremonies, see B. Lafont, "Relations internationales, alliances et diplomatie au temps des rois de Mari,", 213–328 (267).

34. For other examples, see the references cited in D. Charpin, D. O. Edzard, and M. Stol, OBO 160/4 (Fribourg: 2004), 299.

35. See, more generally, M. Guichard, "Violation du serment et casuistique à Mari," in Lafont, *Jurer et maudire*, 71–84.
36. A.3354+, text quoted in my "Un traité entre Zimri-Lim de Mari et Ibal-pî-El II d'Ešnunna," Charpin and Joannès, *Mél. Garelli*, 139–66 (163).
37. That is the conclusion of Greengus's fundamental "The Old Babylonian Marriage Contract," 505–32.
38. See Westbrook, *Old Babylonian Marriage Law*.
39. See the example of the family of Ṣilli-Eshtar in Kutalla (Charpin, *Archives familiales*, 62–67).
40. D. Charpin and J.-M. Durand, *DCS* (Paris: 1981), 102a: 3, *ka-ni-ik ú-nu-tim ša* ha-la NP *ša i-na* dub *z*(*i*)*-it-tim la ša-ak-nu-ma*.
41. E. Prang, "Sonderbestimmungen in altbabylonischen Erbteilungsurkunden aus Nippur," *ZA* 70 (1981): 36–51.
42. Even when the witnesses were still alive, they sometimes forgot essential details of the transaction they had witnessed. That is the case for the witnesses to the marriage of Geme-Asalluhi. See BM 16764, edited by M. Jursa, "'Als König Abi-ešuh gerechte Ordnung hergestellt hat': Eine bemerkenswerte altbabylonische Prozessurkunde," *RA* 91 (1997): 135–45, translated with commentary in my "Lettres et procès paléo-babyloniens," 94–95, no. 49. The procedure for reconstituting lost originals, which made it possible to bring tablets "back to life" (*bulluṭum*) (see chapter 4, sec. 3.2), shows the limits of memory in the absence of written documents: in CT 47, 63, the names of the two neighbors to a plot of land were left blank (lines 14, 15).
43. See chapter 6.
44. J. J. Finkelstein, "Some New *Mišarum*-Material and Its Implications," *Mél. Landsberger*, ed. H. G. Güterbock and T. Jacobsen (Chicago: 1965), 233–46 (esp. 244); the copy of text BM 82064 is now in CT 48, 15. See my annotated translation of this text in "Lettres et procès paléo-babyloniens," 89–90, no. 45. Another example of a clod of dirt destroyed in place of a tablet appears in TIM IV, 40 (transcribed and translated by W. F. Leemans, *Mél. Garelli*, ed. D. Charpin and F. Joannès [Paris: 1991], 327); see also CT VI, 74a (MHET II/1, 44), pointed out by A. Goddeeris, OLA 109 (Louvain: 2002), 149.
45. Copy of this text in TCL I, 157; transcription and translation by F. Thureau-Dangin, *RA* 9 (1912): 21–24; legal commentary by E. Cuq with reference to the article previously cited.
46. On this subject, see G. Boyer, "La preuve dans les anciens droits du Proche-Orient," *Mélanges d'histoire du droit oriental* (Paris: 1965), 181–200; and, more recently, G. Cardascia, "Réflexions sur le témoignage dans les droits du Proche-Orient ancien," *RHDFE* 73 (1995): 549–57; as well as B. Kienast, "Mündlichkeit und Schriftlichtkeit im keilschriftlichen Rechtswesen," *ZABR* 2 (1996): 114–30.
47. See E. Dombradi, *Die Darstellung des Rechtsaustrags in den altbabylonischen Prozessurkunden*, FAOS 20, 88–89 (and, for the producing of witnesses, 86–88).
48. Complete translation of the text and commentary is in "Lettres et procès paléo-babyloniens," 77–78, no. 36.
49. Charpin, *Archives familales*, 142–44.
50. Copy in CT 47, 63; see the quotation from this text in chapter 4, sec. 3.2.
51. C. Wilcke, "Zu den spät-altbabylonischen Kaufverträgen aus Nord-Babylonien," *WO* 8 (1975–76): 254–85 (esp. 276–69); see also M. Tanret and K. De Graef, "Puzzling with Numbers: The Late Old Babylonian SI.BI Clause," *AfO* 50 (20003–4): 56–80.

52. For more details on that practice, see chapter 4.
53. "My tablets are in my father's hands; so long as my father does not come, I shall not pursue a lawsuit" (AbB XI [Leiden: 1977], 55).
54. R. Harris, "On the Process of Secularization under Hammurapi," *JCS* 15 (1961): 117–20.
55. The richest example is in the archives of Ur-Utu, discovered in his house at Sippar-Amnānum; see the bibliography in D. Charpin, D. O. Edzard, and M. Stol, OBO 160/4, 438–39.
56. The break assumed to have occurred between the Old Babylonian period and the Kassite period that followed may have been of lesser scope than is generally believed; see my "La commémoration d'actes juridiques: À propos des *kudurrus* babyloniens," *RA* 96 (2002): 169–91 (esp. 184–85).

CHAPTER 4

1. D. Charpin, *AFPP* (Paris: 1980), 156–59.
2. M. San Nicolò, *Die Schlussklauseln der altbabylonischen Kauf- und Tauschverträge* (1922; new ed., Munich: 1974), 128. See also E. Cuq, *Études sur le droit babylonien* (Paris: 1929), 196.
3. See the conclusion of my article in CRAAI 30 (1986),140.
4. See esp. K. Van Lerberghe and G. Voet, "On 'Quasi-Hüllentafeln,'" *NAPR* 6 (1991): 3–8; C. Janssen, H. Gasche, and M. Tanret, "Du chantier à la tablette. Ur-Utu et l'histoire de sa maison à Sippur-Amnānum," in *Cinquante-deux réflexions sur le Proche-Orient ancien offertes en hommage à Léon De Meyer,* ed. H. Gasche et al., MHEOP 2 (Ghent: 1994), 91–123 (96–110); M. Tanret, "The Fields and the Map: Of Ghosts and Fictive Neighbours," in CRRAI 44, ed. L. Milano, S. de Martino, F. M. Fales, and G. B. Lanfranchi (Padua: 2000), 157–62; and M. Tanret, C. Janssen, and L. Dekiere, *Chains of Transmission: A Search through Ur-Utu's Property Titles,* MHEM 2 (Ghent, forthcoming).
5. The English term "sales contract" is misleading from this standpoint, as is the French *contrat de vente;* the German *Kaufurkunde,* by contrast, corresponds exactly to the Babylonian expression.
6. K. R. Veenhof has published an Old Assyrian sales contract for a house in which the transfer of the previous deed is explicitly indicated (K. R. Veenhof, "Three Unusual Old Assyrian Contracts," in *Mél. Kienast,* ed. G. Selz (Munster: 2003), 693–705 (693, no. 1: 15–19).
7. Transcription and translation by C. Wilcke, "Zwei spät-altbabylonische Kaufverträge aus Kiß," *Mél. Kraus,* ed. G. van Driel, T. J. H. Krispijn, M. Stol, and K. R. Veenhof (Leiden: 1982), 471–72, no. 14. This text is obviously a draft, since the list of witnesses has been left blank and no seal was impressed in the left margin reserved for that purpose.
8. Let me add at present (2005) that the date at which these tables were lost is undoubtedly not fortuitous. It is now known that a royal *mīšarum* edict occurred in year 28 of Samsu-iluna: see D. Charpin, "Les prêteurs et le palais: Les édits de *mîšarum* des rois de Babylone et leurs traces dans les archives privées," in MOS 2 (Leiden: 2000), 185–211 (198–202). Moreover, it seems to me that this contract invalidates M. Tanret and K. De Graef's recent proposal that the small sum of money the purchaser paid above the price (designated as SI.BI) was an indemnification by the seller associated with the transfer of the earlier property deeds ("Puzzling with Numbers: The Late Old Babylonian SI.BI Clause," *AfO* 50 [2003–4]: 56–80). This

text, which they overlooked, includes a payment of money as SI.BI. See my note, "A nouveau la clause SI.BI," *NABU* 2005/71, and M. Tanret's reply, "Chain, Chain, Chain: On a Close Reading of YOS XIII, 96, Slaves and Animals," *NABU* 2005/72.

9. Transcription in *RA* 88 (1994): 80–81.

10. C. Janssen and M. Tanret propose to call these texts "certificates" (*Mél. De Meyer*, ed. H. Gasche, M. Tanret, C. Janssen, and A. Degraeve [Ghent: 1994], 96n21). The term is ambiguous, however. In fact, these are not "certificates of loss," since such documents would have had to be delivered to the person who lost the tablets (for examples of such certificates delivered to the owner of a seal who had lost his property, see F. van Koppen "Redeeming a Father's Seal," in *Mél. Walker*, ed. C. Wunsch [Dresden: 2002], 147–72). Here, conversely, the person who mislaid her property deeds pledged to transfer them should she find them again. The tablet was thus delivered to the purchaser to allow her to exercise her right to these tablets: it is a promise of restitution.

11. Transcription and translation in M. Schorr, VAB 5 (Leipzig: 1913), 281: see, finally, van Driel et al., *Mél. Kraus*, 466–68, no. 11.

12. R. Harris has argued on the basis of this text that a particular building of the cloister (*gagūm*) of Sippar held the archives of the *nadītum* ("The Organization and Administration of the Cloister in Ancient Babylonia," *JESHO* 6 [1963]: 121–57 [153–54]). Nothing authorizes such a conclusion, however; it was in the house of Aya-rishat, located inside the "cloister," that her two brothers were unable to find the tablets.

13. K. Van Lerberghe and G. Voet have managed to define more precisely what the *šurdē* (variant *serdē*) tablets were, which was still a mystery to me in 1983 (Van Lerberghe and Voet, "On 'Quasi-Hüllentafeln,'" 3–8). The oldest tablet to which it was possible to go back was designated the *ṭuppi ummātim*, while the tablets corresponding to later transactions (sale, inheritance, and so on) were designated either as such (*ṭuppi šimātim*, and so on), or under the general name *ṭuppi šurdē* (derived from form 3 of the verb *rēdūm*, "to follow"). See C. Janssen, CRRAI 40, ed. K. R. Veenhof (Leiden: 1996), 240ff.

14. Transcription and translation by Wilcke, van Driel et al., *Mél. Kraus*, 468–471, no. 13.

15. My transcription and translation of the text are in CRRAI 30, ed. K. R. Veenhof (Leiden: 1986), 123, where a more detailed commentary will be found.

16. Cf. R. Harris, *Ancient Sippar: A Demographic Study of an Old-Babylonian City (1894–1595 B.C.)*, PIHANS 36 (Leiden: 1975), 363.

17. Transcription and translation by Wilcke, van Driel et al., *Mél. Kraus*, 464, no. 10.

18. See the case of *BE* 6/1, 103, studied in my "Les prêteurs et le palais," 204n71.

19. H. Ranke, *Babylonian Legal and Business Documents from the Time of the First Dynasty of Babylon Chiefly from Sippar*, Babylonian Expedition 6/1 (Philadelphia: 1906), transcription and translation in Schorr, VAB 5, 92; see also Wilcke, van Driel et al., *Mél. Kraus*, 468, no. 12.

20. We now know that twenty-six years elapsed between the purchase of the plot and its resale, since M. Tanret has demonstrated that the year name "Ammi-ṣaduqa 17+b" corresponds to year 18 of that king (M. Tanret, "As Years Went By in Sippar-Amnānum," in CRRAI 45/1, ed. T. Abusch, P.-A. Beaulieu, J. Huehnergard, P. Machinist, and P. Steinkeller [Bethesda, MD: 2001], 455–66, esp. 458–59). The profit of 10 ⅓ shekels reaped by Hungullum is explained by the fact that he purchased a bare plot and resold a built-upon plot, rather than by a rise in the price of real estate during that period.

21. D. Owen, "Cuneiform Texts in the Collection of Professor Norman Totten," *Mesopotamia* 8–9 (1973–74): 10–14, no. 26.
22. Ibid., 26–29 (A. 32101).
23. See note 1 in this chapter.
24. Letter 7 118, in A. Ungnad, *Babylonian Letters of the Ḫammurapi Period*, University Museum, Babylonian Section 7 (Philadelphia: 1915); transcription and translation in AbB XI, 118. See also the commentary of San Nicolò, *Schlussklauseln*, 128.
25. For the very close connection between the payment of the purchase price and the drawing up of the sales contract, see TCL I, 221; and M. Anbar, "Textes de l'époque babylonienne ancienne," *RA* 69 (1975): 114, note to lines 7–11.
26. My interpretation differs from that of Wilcke in van Driel et al., *Mél. Kraus*, 480, no. 20; see my transcription in CRAAI 30, 128n25.
27. A complementary case is presented by K. Van Lerberghe (Van Lerberghe and Voet, "On 'Quasi-Hüllentafeln," 4–5). The seller explains that a field of twenty-four arpents had been divided in two. His father had bought twelve arpents and the chief merchant Ipqu-Annunitum had bought the rest; it was Ipqu-Annunitum who received the original deed of property.
28. See MHET II/6, 918, with commentary by S. Greengus, *JAOS* 121 (2001): 266b.
29. Letter 7 117, in Ungnad, *Babylonian Letters of the Ḫammurapi Period*, University Museum, Babylonian Section 7 (Philadelphia: 1915); transcription and translation in AbB XI, 7.
30. See R. Harris, "The *nadītu* Laws of the Code of Hammurapi in Praxis," *OR* 30 (1961): 163–69.
31. See Charpin, *Archives familiales*, 100.
32. Transcription and translation in CRRAI 30, 130n30.
33. The multiplicity of tablets can be explained in two ways. Either Adad-mushallim had not bought the field in question from a single holder but had engaged in several successive purchases of neighboring parcels, or he received a property deed from the former owner.
34. See the similar case cited in note 28 of this chapter.
35. See chapter 3.
36. V. Scheil, "Notules XXVI. L'expression Qatam nasâḫu 'retirer la main,'" *RA* 14 (1917): 95.
37. W. F. Leemans, "The Old Babylonian Business Documents from Ur," *BiOr* 12 (1955): 120b, text D. See, more recently, W. Farber, "Imgur-Sîn und seine beiden Söhne. Eine (nicht ganz) neu altbabylonische Erbteilungsurkunde aus Ur, gefunden wahrscheinlich in Larsa," in *Studies Presented to Robert D. Biggs. June 4, 2004. From the Workshop of the Chicago Assyrian Dictionary, Vol. 2*, Assyriological Studies 27, ed. M. Roth, W. Farber, M. W. Stolper, and P. von Bechtolsheim (Chicago: 2007), 65–79.
38. C.-F. Jean, *Š et A* 166 (Leemans, *BiOr* 12: 199, text C).
39. Leemans, *BiOr* 12:120a.
40. The authenticity of the adoption contract was sometimes contested, as in the case treated in CT 2, 47; for that affair, see R. A. Veenker, "An Old Babylonian Procedure for Appeal," *HUCA* 45 (1974): 8–9.
41. F. Thureau-Dangin, "Notes assyriologiques XVI. Un jugement sous le règne de Samsu-iluna," *RA* 9 (1912): 21ff.
42. Schorr, VAB 5, 317.
43. For the adoption of a young *nadītum* by her aunt, also a *nadītum*, see R. Harris,

"The *nadītu* Women," in *Mél. Oppenheim*, ed. M. W. Stolper (Chicago: 1964), 106–35 (124–25).

44. One of them with an unusual form; see B. Lion, "Un champ triangulaire dans un texte paléo-babylonien," *NABU* 2001/4.

45. For that symbolic gesture, see F. R. Kraus, review of E. Szlechter, *Tablettes juridiques de la 1re dynastie de Babylone conservées au Musée d'Art et d'Histoire de Genève*, *BiOr* 16, 122b and CAD Ṣ, 193b; to the references cited, add the text under consideration here and CT 47, 65a:15. That clause is found only in contracts relating to the adoption of a *nadītum* by one of her sisters, always preceding the clause "from the straw to the gold"; it is limited in time to the reign of Samsu-iluna. This type of pin (*ṣillūm*) was used to fasten a woman's clothing: a virgin was defined as "a young girl whose pin has not yet been opened by a handsome man" (CAD Ṣ, 193a).

46. My transcription of the text in CRRAI 30, 133n42. The text has since been republished in N. Yoffee, "Law Courts and the Mediation of Social Conflict in Ancient Mesopotamia," in *Order, Legitimacy, and Wealth in Ancient States*, ed. J. Richards and M. van Buren (Cambridge: 2000), 46–63 (note that "Zimri-Erra" is to be corrected to "Zimri-Erah").

47. C. Wilcke has commented on this text as follows: "in CT 47, 63 . . . sind aber die *ṭuppāt ummātim* neben der *ṭuppi aplūtim* und einer Klageverzichtsurkunde genannt. Darum ist mit einem engeren Begriff *ṭuppi ummātim* = Urkunde über Abmessung und Grenzen des Grundstücks und einem weiteren Begriff, der auch die Übertragung des Eigentums miteinschliesst, zu rechnen" (van Driel et al., *Mél. Kraus*, 480). In fact, it appears clearly that in this text, the *ṭuppāt ummātim* are not a *particular type* of document but rather the oldest property deeds.

48. K. R. Veenhof rightly pointed out to me that the reconstitution was based on the declaration of the previous witnesses (reading the envelope line 65', [*ṭup*]-*pa-šu an-ni-a-am a-na pí-i ši-*[*bu-tim ú-ba-al-li-ṭú-ma*], as "they 'brought [back] to life' his present tablet in accordance with the declaration of the witnesses"). "His present tablet" obviously designates CT 47, 63; the masculine possessive-*šu* probably refers to Ikun-pi-Sin (or Sin-ili?). Note that the memory of the witnesses was not complete, since in CT 47, 63 the names of the two neighbors of a plot of land were left blank (lines 14, 15).

For another example of the term *bulluṭum*, "bring (back) to life" in a similar context, see Di 1804: *ṭup-pu ša ik-nu-ku-ši-im* [*ih*]-*li-iq-ma* [*ṭup*]-*pa-am an-ni-a-am* [*ša*] PN *mu-us-sà* dumu PN_2 *id-di-nu-*⸢*ši úl*⸣*-ba-al-li-ṭú-ma ik-nu-ku-ši*, "the tablet that he had sealed for her was lost. Someone 'brought [back] to life' the present tablet, which her husband Inanna-mansum had given to her and sealed it for her" (unpublished text from Tell ed-Dēr, cited by C. Janssen, "Inanna-mansum et ses fils: Relation d'une succession turbulente dans les archives d'Ur-Utu," *RA* 86 [1992]: 19–52 [42n56]).

49. It is known that, on average, the *nadītum* enjoyed remarkable longevity; see Harris, *Mél. Oppenheim*, 122.

50. Transcription and translation by Wilcke, van Driel et al., *Mél. Kraus*, 435, 477, no. 17.

51. A notation of this kind can be explained by the sales restrictions sometimes existing on the property transferred as dowry to a nun or priestess (see note 30).

52. Transcription and translation by Wilcke, van Driel et al., *Mél. Kraus*, 475, no. 16.

53. See the diagram in CRRAI 30, 137.

54. R. Pientka-Hinz, "Ein spätaltbabylonischer Kaufvertrag aus Babylon," in Wunsch, *Mél. Walker*, 201–15; see my remarks in *RA* 97 (2003): 186. Note as well, in Sip-

par, the sales contract for field VS 29, 15; dating from the end of the reign of Ammi-ṣaduqa (ca. 1626 BCE), it recalls two previous transactions going back to year 18 of Ammi-ṣaduqa (1629 BCE) and year 2 of Abi-eshuh (1710 BCE). See H. Klengel, "Eine altbabylonische Kaufurkunde betreffend Feld von 'Stiftsdamen' des Gottes Šamaš in Sippar," in *Mél. Röllig*, ed. B. Pongratz-Leisten, H. Kühne, and P. Xella (Neukirchen-Vluyn: 1997), 163–70.

55. I am in no way claiming that this was a trait peculiar to Old Babylonian common law, to which I have intentionally limited the present inquiry. See, for example, P. Maidman, "A Nuzi Private Archive: Morphological Considerations," *Assur* 1/9 (1979): 1–8. For the continuation of Old Babylonian practices in the Kassite period, see my "La commémoration d'actes juridiques: À propos des *kudurrus* babyloniens," *RA* 96 (2002 [2004]): 169–91.
56. That expression therefore does not designate merely the old sales contracts, contrary to what R. Harris argued in "Biographical Notes on the *nadītu* Women of Sippar," *JCS* 16 (1962): 1–12 (1n3).
57. W. von Soden, *AHw* (Wiesbaden: 1965–1981), 1414b.
58. As indicated by Wilcke, van Driel et al., *Mél. Kraus*, 451n49.
59. C. Wilcke review of H. Klengel, *Altbabylonische Texte aus Babylon* (*ZA* 80 [1990]: 306) has rejected that etymology, which I proposed in CRRAI 30, 138. He remarks that *ummatum* in the singular form is attested in TCL XVIII, 105:14–15 (*ka-ni-ka-at é šua-ti s[e-e]r-d[i]-a-am ù um-ma-ta* [see now AbB XIV, 159, and the note of K. R. Veenhof, 216, s. v. *serdûm*]). As a result, however, he is obliged not to take into account the full grapheme attested elsewhere: "Wie die explicite Pluralschreibung *um-ma-a-tim* zu erklären ist, wird man besser offen lassen" (Wilcke, review of Klengel, *Altbabylonische Texte aus Babylon* 306). Since then, a new piece of evidence has surfaced that must be taken into account: the use of the term *ammatum* in the *kudurrus* to designate a type of property deed. The Explicit Malku 1 series gives *ammatu* as a synonym for *ummu*, "mother"; it seems to me that this confirms my previous proposal (see *RA* 96 [2002]: 178).
60. See my "Les décrets royaux à l'époque paléo-babylonienne, à propos d'un ouvrage récent," *AfO* 34 (1987): 36–44. Such a translation is confirmed by a passage from the epic of Lugalbanda: "The days passed, the months grew longer, *mu ama-ni-ir ba-gi*$_4$, the year returned to its starting point" (lines 259–60). See chapter 6, note 23.
61. In CRRAI 30, 138n52, I criticized C. Wilcke for establishing a link between *ṭuppāt*/*kanikāt ummātim* and what he called the "Quasi-Hüllentafeln," that is, the particular form taken by deeds of property in Babylonia in the last third of the reign of Samsu-iluna. Instead of enclosing the tablet in an envelope that reproduced the text of the contract and provided extra space for the seals, a margin intended for the seal impressions was set aside directly on the tablet. Wilcke returned to that question in *ZA* 80 (1990): 305.
62. Particularly in the case of dowries, which can be explained by the restrictions on sales affecting that category of property; see note 30 of this chapter.
63. See H. Klengel, "Untersuchungen zu den sozialen Verhältnissen im altbabylonischen Dilbat," *AoF* 4 (1976): 63–110 (esp. 67–78); and, more recently, S. G. Kosthurnikov and N. Yoffee, "Old Babylonian Tablets from Dilbat in the Ashmolean Museum," *Iraq* 48 (1986): 117–30.
64. W. F. Leemans, *Legal and Economic Records from the Kingdom of Larsa*, SLB 1/2 (Leiden: 1954), 7.
65. See my review article of S. I. Feigin's *Legal and Administrative Texts of the Reign of*

Samsu-iluna, YOS 12 (New Haven, CT: 1979), in *BiOr* 38 (1981): 533 and 546–47; and my "Notices prosopographiques, 2: Les descendants de Balmunamhe," *NABU* 1987/36.

66. After my oral presentation in Leiden (1983), M. Van de Mieerop rightly observed that this hypothesis may have been valid for contracts dealing with real property but that it would be more difficult to explain the preservation of contracts dealing with slaves on that basis. See now C. B. Dyckhoff, "Priester und Priesterinnen im altbabylonischen Larsa. Das Amtsarchiv als Grundlage für prosopographische Forschung," in CRRAI 47, ed. S. Parpola and R. M. Whithing (Helsinki: 2002), 123–27; I do not agree, however, with Dyckhoff's analysis of the provenance of texts resulting from the looting of Larsa before Parrot's excavations.
67. See chapter 3.
68. It is sometimes possible, however: see the case of Alum in sec. 1.3 of this chapter.

CHAPTER 5

1. See in particular M. Roth, "Mesopotamian Legal Traditions and the Laws of Hammurabi," *Chicago Kent Law Review* 71/1 (1995), 13–39.
2. For an overview of Hammurabi's reign, see my *Hammu-rabi de Babylone* (Paris: 2003), 210–18, which outlines a few of the themes developed in the present chapter. Currently, the best translation of the Code of Hammurabi is by M. Roth in *Law Collections from Mesopotamia and Asia Minor*, WAW 6 (Atlanta: 1995), 71–142. J. Bottéro's "Le 'Code' de Hammurabi," *Annali della Scuole Normale Superiore di Pisa* 12 (1982): 409–44 (reprinted in his *Mésopotamie. L'écriture, la raison et les dieux* [Paris: 1987], 191–23, and translated into English as *Mesopotamia: Writing, Reasoning, and the Gods* [Chicago: 1992]), provides a good overall approach. In the twenty-five years since it was written, new documents have come to light, making it possible to reconsider certain points from a new vantage point; it is these aspects that I have emphasized here. Complementary approaches can be found in E. Lévy, ed., *La codification des lois dans l'Antiquité. Actes du colloque de Strasbourg 27–29 novembre 1997*, Travaux du Centre de Recherche sur le Proche-Orient et la Grèce antiques 16 (Paris: 2000), esp. contributions by M. T. Roth, "The Law Collection of King Hammurabi: Toward an Understanding of Codification and Text" (9–31), R. Westbrook, "Codification and Canonization" (33–47), S. Lafont, "Codification et subsidiarité dans les droits du Proche-Orient ancien" (49–64), and R. Yaron, "The Nature of the Early Mesopotamian Collections of Laws: Another Approach" (65–76).
3. Note, however, that the Code of Lipit-Eshtar, of which only copies on tablets exist, must also have had a monumental form. The king of Isin declares in its epilogue: "The day I established justice [*nì-si-sá*] in Sumer and Akkad, I erected this stela" (M. Roth, *Law Collections*, 34; cf. 35n1, which notes the existence of "two fragments of a stone stela that could be Lipit-Ishtar's original monument"). It is likely that this was also true for the other texts of the same kind.
4. V. Scheil, "Textes élamites sémitiques 2e série. Code des lois de Hammurabi (Droit Privé), roi de Babylone, vers l'an 2000 av. J.C.," MDP IV (Paris: 1902), 11–162, pl. 3–15. The stela of the code had just been found, during the Susa excavations in December 1901 (two large fragments forming the base) and January 1902 (upper part). A photograph of the 1902 discovery is reproduced in B. André-Salvini, *Le Code de Hammurabi* (Paris: 2003), 8 (fig. 2).
5. The inauguration of the room took place on Wednesday, November 5, 2003.

6. The traditional numbering skips from sec. 65 to sec. 99; it thus counts 282 laws in all, which is no doubt a few too many.
7. M. Roth, *Law Collections,* 13–22; and C. Wilcke, "Der Kodex Urnamma (CU): Versuch einer Rekonstruktion," in *Mém. Jacobsen,* ed. T. Abusch (Winona Lake, IN: 2002), 291–333.
8. See Roth, *Law Collections,* 23–35.
9. Ibid., 57–70.
10. See esp. J. J. Finkelstein, "The Laws of Ur-Nammu," *JCS* 22 (1969): 66–82 (81).
11. The Sumerian terms *nin-dingir, lukur,* and *nu-gig* designate three categories of consecrated women; *lukur* corresponds to the Akkadian *nadītum.*
12. The Sumerian in this passage was misunderstood until a comparison was made with the text of sec. 180 of the Code of Hammurabi; see my note "Le § 22 du 'code' de Lipit-Eštar," *NABU* 1989/113. My interpretation was revised with slight modifications by Roth in *Law Collections,* 30, whose translation I adopt here.
13. AbB XIII (Leiden: 1994), 12, translation and commentary by D. Charpin, "Lettres et procès paléo-babyloniens," in *Rendre la justice en Mésopotamie,* ed. F. Joannès (Vincennes: 2000), 69–111 (esp. 85, no. 41).
14. I am omitting the exposition of the first case submitted to the king; see the publications cited in the previous note.
15. That is, "If you refuse to sell your goods to reimburse me." Here we see very clearly how incurring a debt led to the alienation of one's patrimony—and how debtors attempted to mount a resistance against that development. An excellent example of a sale of land by an insolvent debtor has been studied by E. Woestenburg on the basis of MHET II/3, 442: see *AfO* 44/45 (1997–98): 354. See also note 31 in chapter 6.
16. It must be understood that the nun-*nadītum*'s father and brothers pledged in writing to support her during her lifetime.
17. The *ilkum* was a service (military or other) performed by an individual in the king's behalf. In return, the king granted possession of a piece of land (a field, and possibly a house and orchard); see my *Hammu-rabi de Babylone,* 164, 252.
18. Text edited by C. Janssen, "Samsu-iluna and the Hungry *nadîtums,*" *NAPR* 5 (1991): 3–40. French translation in D. Charpin, "Lettres et procès," 86–88, no. 43. See S. Lafont's commentary, "Les actes législatifs des rois mésopotamiens," in *Auctoritates. Xenia R. C. Van Caenegem Oblata. La formation du droit et ses auteurs,* ed. S. Dauchy et al., Wetenschappelijk Comité voor rechtsgeschiedenis koninklijke Academi voor wetenschappen, letteren en schone kunsten van België, Iuris Scripta Historica 13 (Brussels: 1997), 3–27, esp. 22–27.
19. See K. R. Veenhof's recent article "The Relation between Royal Decrees and Laws in the Old Babylonian Period," *JEOL* 35/36 (1997–2000): 49–84.
20. See ibid., 57.
21. I depart here from the position taken by F. R. Kraus ("Ein zentrales Problem des altmesopotamischen Rechtes: Was ist der Codex Hammu-rabi?" *Genava* 8 [1960]: 283–69), who sees the code as a compilation of exemplary royal decisions.
22. The best study of the literary procedure of variation is B. L. Eichler's "Literary Structure in the Laws of Eshnunna," *Mél. Reiner,* ed. F. Rochberg Halton (New Haven, CT: 1987), 71–84. For the illusion of exhaustivity sought in composing the Code of Hammurabi, see R. Westbrook, "Codex Ḫammurabi and the Ends of the Earth," in CRRAI 44. ed. L. Milano, S. de Martino, F. M. Fales, and G. B. Lanfranchi (Padua: 2000), 101–3.
23. See Roth, *Law Collections,* 72.

24. Despite the existence of the official status of a sort of "accuser"; cf. my note, "Qabbâ'um 'délateur'?" *NABU* 1993/23.
25. For that problematic, see S. Lafont, "Un 'cas royal' à l'époque de Mari," *RA* 91 (1997): 109–19.
26. E. Leichty, *The Omen Series* Šumma Izbu, TCS IV (New York: 1970), 203 (YOS 10, 56, i, 34–35).
27. I develop this next paragraph in my "Codes de lois et recueils divinatoires," *NABU* 2006/1.
28. As the passages in the first (or second) person show; I have placed these quotations in italics.
29. See, for example, U. Koch-Westenholz: "Extispicy was a very direct way of questioning the gods about particular events and their intentions or their decisions in any particular matter, what the Babylonians called their 'judgements'" (*Babylonian Liver Omens,* CNIP 25 [Copenhagen: 2000], 13).
30. For a good presentation of these compilations of omens, see J. Bottéro, "Symptomes, signes, écriture en Mésopotamie ancienne," in *Divination et rationalité,* ed. J.-P. Vernant et al. (Paris: 1974), 70–197 (esp. 84–85).
31. I note only this general remark by J. J. Finkelstein, who observes that the collections of laws "may be learned forms of speculation and improvization [*sic*] in the manner of later talmudic and scholastic learning, and, as was more obviously the case, in the divinational 'sciences' of Mesopotamia itself" ("Sex Offenses in Sumerian Laws," *JAOS* 86 [1966]: 355–72 [esp. 368]).
32. See Leichty, *The Omen Series* Šumma Izbu, 23; and, more generally, U. Koch-Westenholz's description of how the canonical series known through first-millennium BCE manuscripts were constituted on the basis of the Old Babylonian precursors: "They may well have developed gradually from Old Babylonian 'forerunners,' like some of the lexical compendia, merely involving some additional material and systematization" (*Babylonian Liver Omens,* 20).
33. Bottéro, *Mésopotamia,* 160–61.
34. See Koch-Westenholz, *Babylonian Liver Omens,* 15 (regarding the diviners of the Old Babylonian era): "The diviner, guided by his experience and his knowledge of the general rules of extispicy, could describe and interpret actual livers and phenomena that were not recorded in the series."
35. See the two cases submitted to Samsu-iluna examined in note 14 of this chapter.
36. See M. Roth, "Hammurabi's Wronged Man," *JAOS* 122 (2002): 38–45 (who discusses the previous interpretations).
37. See also, very recently, CAD Š/II, 1992, 166a *"narî šaṭram li-iš-ta-ás-si-ma awâtija šūqurātim lišmēma"* (let him [have] my inscribed monument read and let him listen to my priceless words); the factitive is added in brackets. Note as well the translation "may he have read to him" in Westbrook, "Codex Ḫammurabi and the Ends of the Earth," 101. M. Roth had translated it "let him have my inscribed stela read aloud to him" (*Law Collections,* 134); in her 2002 article (cited in note 36 of this chapter), she changed it to "may he read aloud my inscribed stela" (39), but without explaining the change in her interpretation. R. Borger had correctly translated it "meine beschriftete Stele möge er lesen" (TUAT I.1 [Gütersloh: 1982], 76). C. Wilcke, for his part, translated and annotated Hammurabi's wish as "daß der 'geschädigte Bürger, der von einem Reichtsfall betroffen ist [*sic: ša awātam iraššû*], meine Stele ganz genau laut lesen [oder sich vorlesen lassen: Gtn und Štn gleichlautend] und meine überaus

kostbaren Worte hören' soll" (Abusch, *Mém. Jacobsen,* 299, in the middle of the long note 26).

38. G. R. Driver and J. C. Miles, *The Babylonian Laws Volume II: Transliterated Text Translation Philological Notes Glossary* (Oxford: 1955), 286.
39. See chapter 1.
40. Unfortunately, the original locations of these fragments—like the location of the large stela—are unknown: they were in their entirety part of the Babylonian booty taken to Susa by an Elamite king from the twelfth century BCE. See J. Nougayrol, "Les fragments en pierre du Code Hammourabien (I)," *JA* (1957): 339–66; (II) *JA* (1958): 143–55; and the photographs reproduced in B. André-Salvini, *Le Code de Hammurabi,* 52–53 (figs. 49–51).
41. Note that this obligation was common to all the sovereigns of the era. A remarkable formulation of it is found in a prophecy addressed by the god Addu of Aleppo to Zimri-Lim, king of Mari: "Listen to that single word of mine! When someone who faces trial appeals to you, saying: 'A wrong has been done me,' stand up and render a judgment for him; respond to him forthrightly. That is what I desire of you" (J.-M. Durand, *Le Culte d'Addu d'Alep et l'affaire d'Alahtum, FM* VII [Paris: 2002], 135, no. 38: 6'–11'). What was at issue here was simply direct contact between the plaintiff and the sovereign, as the small size of the kingdom of Mari allowed. Note that the correction of *hablāku* for *habtāku* proposed by Roth ("Hammurabi's Wronged Man," 44) is ruled out by paleography (cf. the photo published by J.-M. Durand, *Le culte d'Addu d'Alep,* 133).
42. A reproduction can be found, for example, in B. Legras, *Lire en Égypte, d'Alexandre à l'Islam* (Paris: 2002), 28 (fig. 3).
43. For a good summary of the debate, see S. Démare(-Lafont), "La valeur de la loi dans les droits cunéiformes," *Archives de philosophie du Droit* 32 (1987): 335–46. See also, more recently, R. Westbrook, "Biblical and Cuneiform Law Codes," *RB* 92 (1985): 247–64, as well as two studies in H. J. Gehrke and E. Wirbelauer, eds., *Rechtskodifizierung und soziale Normen im interkulturellen Vergleich,* ScriptOralia 66, Reihe A, Altertumwissenschaftliche Reihe Bd. 15 (Tübingen: 1994): B. Kienast, "Die Altorientalischen Codices zwischen Mündlichkeit und Schriftlichkeit" (13–26), and J. Renger, "Noch einmal: Was war der 'Kodex' Ḫammurapi—ein erlassenes Gesetz oder ein Rechtsbuch?" (27–58). C. Wilcke replied to Renger's article in his essay in Abusch, *Mém. Jacobsen,* 298–300 (the very long note 26).
44. Such, for example, is the point of view defended by J. J. Finkelstein in "Ammiṣaduqa's Edict and the Babylonian 'Law Codes,'" *JCS* 15 (1961): 91–104 (103).
45. The excavations of Larsa, for example, have shown that this was not a vain wish. The neo-Babylonian kings Nebuchadnezzar and Nabonidus in the sixth century BCE said they had rebuilt the temple of Ebabbar according to the ancient plans (see D. Charpin, "Les découvertes épigraphiques de la campagne 1985 à Larsa," in *Larsa, 10e campagne, 1983, et 'Oueili, 4e campagne, 1983. Rapport préliminaire,* ed. J. L. Huot [Paris: 1990]). In fact, the excavations have revealed a succession of superposed walls measuring more than eighteen meters deep.
46. Code of Hammurabi, sec. 32.
47. AbB IX, 32.
48. See AbB XIII, 12, discussed in note 13 of this chapter.
49. See M. Stol, *BiOr* 56 (1999), col. 672 (and, more recently, D. Charpin, D. O. Edzard, and M. Stol, OBO 160/4 [Fribourg: 2004], 789). Note the cautiousness of M. Stol's

formulation: "The school letter *illustrates* a rule *like* CH § 28." A. Goddeeris does not adopt the hypothesis of a school exercise (A. Goddeeris, OLA 109 [Louvain: 2002], 293n289), contrary to K. R. Veenhof in AbB XIV, no. 98 ("probably a school letter"; cf. 91n98.a).

50. The first text was published by G. Dossin, TCL XVII, 44 (AbB XIV, 98, translated here); the second by J. R. Kupper, "Lettres de Kiš," *RA* 53 (1959): 180 (D 46). The proper names are not the same in the two letters. In the second copy, there is only one son and the end of the text, poorly preserved, appears to be different in part. For other examples of school letters of the same type, see F. R. Kraus, "Briefschriebübungen im altbabylonischen Schulunterricht," *JEOL* 16 (1959–62): 16–39; and W. Sallaberger, *"Wenn Du mein Bruder bist . . .": Interaktion und Textgestaltung in altbabylonischen Alltagsbriefen,* CM 16 (Groningen: 1999), 149–54.

51. Letter A. 3529, edited by R. F. G. Sweet, in *On Prices, Moneys, and Money Uses in the Old Babylonian Period* (Ph.D. diss., University of Chicago, 1958), 104–5; cf. Roth, *Law Collections,* 6, 10n1. Note that this letter belongs to a group of letters and administrative texts dating from the reign of Samsu-iluna, which come from the city of Damrum, near ancient Kish (see Sweet, *On Prices, Moneys, and Money Uses,* 105–7 and 203–4n88; "Kisik" should be corrected to "Damrum," which we now know to have been the reading for HI.GAR^{ki}). For the city of Damrum, see Charpin, Edzard, and Stol, OBO 160/4, 89–91.

52. Even if, as Sweet thinks, it was the employer who was alluding to the stela because the wage recommended in the code was lower than that demanded by the workers.

53. For that notion, cf. my "Le juste prix," *NABU* 1999/79.

54. See F. Malbran-Labat, *Les inscriptions royales de Suse* (Paris: 1995), 32–33, no. 12. The title of shepherd, which Attu-hushu was the only Susian sovereign to have used, characterizes the exercise of justice by a Mesopotamian king. The title is in this case linked to the local deity, Inshushinak. For the sort of "parenthesis" constituted by the reign of Atta-hushu, see M. J. Steve, F. Vallat, and H. Gasche, "Suse," in *Supplément au dictionnaire de la Bible* 73 (Paris: 2002), 446.

What interests me in the case of Attahushu is the mention of a stela erected on the marketplace. That differs from the support used for the other "price lists" known for that era, which were generally found on foundation documents, hence inaccessible to the ordinary person. For these price lists, see esp. J. Renger, "Patterns of Non-institutional Trade and Non-commercial Exchange in Ancient Mesopotamia at the Beginning of the Second Millennium BC," in *Circulation of Goods in Non-palatial Context,* ed. A. Archi, Incunabula Graeca 82 (Rome: 1984), 31–124 (esp. 91–94).

55. For an example of a passage quoted from an edict in a letter, see chapter 6, sec. 2.1.

56. For the activities of diviners in the Old Babylonian period, see J.-M. Durand, *Archives épistolaires de Mari I/1,* ARM XXVI/1, part 1; U. Jeyes, *Old Babylonian Extispicy: Omen Texts in the British Museum,* PIHANS 64 (Leiden: 1989).

57. See, for example, S. M. Freedman, *If a City Is Set on a Height: The Akkadian Omen Series* Summa Alu ina Mēlê Šakin. *Volume 1: Tablets 1–21,* OPSNKF 17 (Philadelphia: 1998), 8–10. For an example of an *implicit* quotation of a compendium, see note 28 of this chapter.

58. See V. A. Hurowitz, "Hammurabi in Mesopotamian Tradition," in *"An Experienced Scribe Who Neglects Nothing": Ancient Near East Studies in Honor of Jacob Klein,* ed. Y. Sefati et al. (Bethesda, MD: 2005), 497–532.

59. The code of Ur-Nammu was, of course, recopied after the twenty-first century in Old

Babylonian schools, but we do not have any manuscript dating from after the mid-second millennium BCE.

60. For the latter case, see my "Les soldats d'Assurbanipal ont-ils détruit le Code de Hammu-rabi lors du sac de Suse?" *NABU* 2003/77.
61. Note from this standpoint the contradiction in J. Bottéro's argument. He wishes to define "what Ḫammurabi's 'Code' could have represented in the eyes of its author and his fellow citizens and contemporaries at the time it was composed" (*Mesopotamia,* 157). Yet a few pages later, he uses the fact that it was still being recopied in the first millennium BCE as an argument against the idea that it was a legislative text: "Therefore, if the Mesopotamians indefinitely recopied this work word for word after these events and at least for a millennium later, we have to adjust to the idea that it was because they saw in it something other than a text that was, so to say, normative and legislative" (160). This was obviously a *change of status* for the text, which was surely not received in the first millennium BCE as it had been during Hammurabi's lifetime.
62. W. G. Lambert, "The Laws of Hammurabi in the First Millennium," in *Mél. Finet,* ed. M. Lebeau and P. Talon (Louvain: 1989), 95–98.
63. Let me emphasize that this is certainly not Marduk, the god of Babylon, as Bottéro writes (*Mesopotamia,* 157). That hypothesis, which goes back to Gadd (*Ideas of Divine Rule in the Ancient Near East* [London: 1948], 90–91), and was followed by Falkenstein (*ZA* 51 [1955]: 262), Koršec (HdO 1/III, 95n2), and others, has to be abandoned: Gadd quite simply forgot the rays coming out of the god's shoulders.

    U. Seidl has recently asked whether the scene might represent Hammurabi before the god Shamash, or whether we ought rather to posit that the king is being represented before *the cult statue* of the god ("Das Ringen um das richtige Bild des Šamaš von Sippar," *ZA* 91 [2001]: 120–32 [esp. 120–21]). For the iconography of the Louvre stela and the symbolism of the ring and the circle that the god Shamash holds in his hand, see E. Ascalone and L. Peyronel, "Two Weights from Temple N at Tel Mardikh-Ebla, Syria: A Link between Metrology and Cultic Activities in the Second Millennium BC?" *JCS* 53 (2001): 1–12 (7n20).
64. The solar aspects of the figure of the "just king" will some day have to be studied systematically; see chapter 6, sec. 3.1.

CHAPTER 6

1. For the term "shepherd" applied to the king in the context of the "redress" (*mīšarum*) edicts, see B. Landsberger, *JNES* 14 (1955): 146.
2. See D. O. Edzard, "'Soziale Reformen' in Zweistromland bis ca. 1600 v. Chr.: Realität oder literarischer Topos?" *Acta Antiqua Academiae Scientiarum Hungaricae* 22 (1974): 145–56.
3. These texts, edited and annotated, can be found in F. R. Kraus, *Königliche Verfügungen in altbabylonischer Zeit,* SD 11 (Leiden: 1984).
4. In addition to the text edited by F. R. Kraus in *Königliche Verfügungen,* 154–60, see the fragment now published by W. W. Hallo, "Slave Release in the Biblical World in Light of a New Text," *Solving Riddles and Untying Knots: Biblical, Epigraphic, and Semitic Studies in Honor of Jonas C. Greenfield,* ed. Z. Zevit, S. Gitin, and M. Sokoloff (Winona Lake, IN: 1995), 79–93.
5. Edict of X, edited by F. R. Kraus in *Königliche Verfügungen,* 160–62.
6. Edited by F. R. Kraus in *Königliche Verfügungen,* 163–83; I adopt his paragraph numbering below for the edict of Ammi-ṣaduqa.

7. See R. Pientka's very useful *Die spätaltbabylonische Zeit: Abiešuḫ bis Samsuditana. Quellen, Jahresdaten, Geschichte,* Imgula 2 (Munster: 1998).
8. On this case, see my "La Babylonie de Samsuiluna à la lumière de nouveaux documents," *BiOr* 38 (1981), col. 517–47 (esp. col. 520).
9. See M. Stol, review of S. I. Feigin, *Legal and Administrative Texts of the Reign of Samsu-iluna, JAOS* 102 (1982): 162b.
10. See my "Marchands du palais et marchands du temple à la fin de la Ie dynastie de Babylone," *JA* 270 (1982): 25–65, with additions in "Économie et société à Sippar et en Babylonie du nord à l'époque paléo-babylonienne," *RA* 99 (2005): 148–50. See also M. Stol, "Wirtschaft und Gesellschaft in altbabylonischer Zeit," in D. Charpin, D. O. Edzard, and M. Stol, OBO 160/4 (Fribourg: 2004), 641–975 (esp. chap. 18).
11. See chapter 7, notes 2–4.
12. Note that the receipts found in the archives of the interested parties in Sippar or in other cities were written in Babylon (see my "Marchands du palais," 29, 38, 42–46).
13. They are important for us because they attest to the existence of many edicts that would otherwise have remained unknown; a list of them has been compiled by F. R. Kraus, *Königliche Verfügungen,* chap. 2–5.
14. NBC, 6311 (emphasis added); I indicated to W. W. Hallo the link between this letter and the text of the edict (cf. *Mél. Greenfield,* 82n15). He quoted it in part and discussed it before it was published in O. Tammuz, "Two Small Archives from Lagaba," *RA* 90 (1996): 121–33 (esp. 125–26). That letter belongs to a batch of documents from Lagaba in central Babylonia, which dates from the reign of Samsu-iluna (see my "Les prêteurs et le palais: Les édits de *mîšarum* des rois de Babylone et leurs traces dans les archives privées," MOS 2 [Leiden, 2000], 185–211 [esp. 195–96]).
15. It is reproduced above in italics. As always in the ancient East, the quotation is not word-for-word accurate; for this problem, see my *La correspondance à l'époque amorrite* (forthcoming).
16. See Charpin, "La Babylonie de Samsuiluna à la lumière de nouveaux documents," col. 535–36 (archives L).
17. All these cases were collected and discussed in my "Les prêteurs et le palais"; see also my "Les prêteurs et le palais (suite)," *NABU* 2001/51; my article in *RA* 99 (2005), esp. 139, 149–51, 154–75; and my "Données nouvelles sur la vie économique et sociale de l'époque paléo-babylonienne," *OR* 74 (2005): 409–21.
18. For Syria (from Mari to Alalah via Terqa), see D. Charpin, "L'*andurârum* à Mari," *MARI* 6 (1990): 253–70 (esp. 262–63, 266). For Anatolia, see K. Balkan, "Cancellation of Debts in Cappadocian Tablets from Kültépé," in *Mél. Güterbock,* ed. K. Bittel, P. H. J. Houwin Ten Cate, and E. Reiner (Istanbul: 1974), 29–41 (esp. 33). Note the similarity between these clauses and the *prosbol* of Israelite documents from the early Christian era, stipulating that the debtor renounce the advantage of the sabbatical year.
19. For *ana šīmim* loans, see *JA* 270 (1982): 40n36. As for *ana harrānim* loans, let us note the frequency of that specification, for example, in the archives of Etel-pi-Marduk, dating from the reign of Samsu-ditana and found in Babylon (see my "Un quartier de Babylone et ses habitants," *BiOr* 42 [1985], col. 272).
20. For this type of loan, see my "À propos des contrats d'embauche pour la moisson," *NABU* 1993/59; and VS 29, 63 and 73 (*RA* 99 [2005]: 150). This labor could also include molding bricks. For an example of a text combining the two types of reimbursement, see YOS 12, 224, in my "Les prêteurs et le palais," 205n74.
21. The CAD translates *andurārum* in this context as "manumission (of private slave)"

(A/2, 115); von Soden renders it as "Zustand der Lastenbefreiung, Freistellung von Abgaben" (W. von Soden, *AHw* [Wiesbaden: 1965–1981], 50b).

22. I developed that new interpretation of *andurārum* in "Les décrets royaux à l'époque paléo-babylonienne, à propos d'un ouvrage récent," *AfO* 34 (1987): 36–44.
23. J.-M.Durand has pointed out a passage to me from the epic of Lugalbanda that confirms this sense of the Sumerian *ama*: "the days passed, the months grew longer, the year returned to its starting point (*ama*)" (lines 259–260). The *PSD* placed the passage under the rubric of "transferred meaning" but translated it literally as "the year returned to its mother" (A/3, 203a).
24. As in the case of debts, a list has been compiled by F. R. Kraus in *Königliche Verfügungen*, chap. 2–5.
25. This text was published by J. J. Finkelstein, "Some New *Mîsharum* Material and Its Implications," *Mél. Landsberger*, ed. H. G. Güterbock and T. Jacobsen (Chicago: 1965), 233–46, republished by F. R. Kraus, AbB VII (Leiden: 1977), 153; French translation and commentary in my "Lettres et procès paléo-babyloniens," in *Rendre la justice en Mésopotamie*, ed. F. Joannès (Paris: 2000), 91–92, no. 47.
26. See my "Les prêteurs et le palais," 202; that date seems more likely to me than the accession to the throne of Abi-eshuh, as C. Wilcke proposed in *Mél. Kraus*, ed. G. van Driel, T. J. H. Krispijn, M. Stol, and K. R. Veenhof (Leiden: 1982), 481n69.
27. Another allusion to the application of the *mīšarum* in year 28 of Samsu-iluna comes from Nippur: a text mentions that "the king cancelled the tablets of exchange of real property" (PBS 8/2, 226; see Kraus, *Königliche Verfügungen*, 75, and my "Les prêteurs et le palais," 198). In Sippar, a lawsuit concerning a house measuring 2 *sar* contains an allusion to a royal decision, dated Samsu-iluna 17, that restored the real estate alienated by soldiers-*rēdûm*, *bā'irum*, and other service providers (*ilkum ahûm*): see MHET II/3, 462, and E. Woestenburg's commentary, *AfO* 44/45 (1997–98): 355.
28. For the Sasiya family, see D. Charpin, *AFPP* (Geneva: 1980), 28–34; for the Ku-Ningal family, see my *Le clergé d'Ur au siècle d'Hammurabi* (Geneva: 1986), 70–75.
29. Other archives even document the situation in Larsa a few years earlier (year 25 of Rim-Sin, that is, 1798 BCE); cf. E. Bouzon, "Die soziale Bedeutung des *ṣimdat-šarrim*-Aktes nach den Kaufverträgen der Rim-Sin-Zeit," in *Mél. von Soden*, ed. M. Dietrich and O. Loretz (Neukirchen-Vluyn: 1995), 2:11–30.
30. VS 7, 156; on other points in this difficult text, see F. R. Kraus, *Königliche Verfügungen*, 85.
31. E. Woestenburg has studied, on the basis of MHET II/3, 442, a very fine example of a plot of land sold after a debt could not be repaid: *AfO* 44/45 (1997–98): 354. For other examples, see my article in *RA* 99 (2005): 138–39.
32. On this subject, see D. Charpin, "La politique immobilière des marchands de Larsa à la lumière des découvertes épigraphiques de 1987 et 1989," in *Larsa, travaux de 1987 et 1989*, ed. J. L. Huot (Beirut: 2003), 311–22.
33. It is clear that the measures were not restricted to the Crown lands, despite what S. Richardson has recently claimed in "Trouble in the Countryside *ana tarṣi* Samsuditana: Militarism, Kassites, and the Fall of Babylon I," in CRRAI 48, ed. W. H. van Soldt, R. Kalvelagen, and D. Katz (Leiden: 2005), 273–89 (279–82)
34. For the year names, see in general M. J. A. Horsnell, *The Year Names of the First Dynasty of Babylon* (Hamilton, ON: 1999); for the name of year 2 of Abi-eshuh, see my review of VS 22 in "Un quartier de Babylone et ses habitants," col. 274–75. Note that Ammi-ṣaduqa's accession to the throne constitutes an exception, since the

mīšarum is commemorated in the name of year 1; no doubt Ammi-ditana died very early in the last year of his reign.

35. AbB XII, 172:8'–10' (which dates to Abi-eshuh's accession to the throne).
36. Word for word, "he washed the dirty hair of the country." For the justification for that translation, see my "Les prêteurs et le palais," 185n1. For mourning upon the king's death, see my "'Le roi est mort, vive le roi!' Les funérailles des souverains amorrites et l'avènement de leur successeur," in *Mél. Stol*, ed. R. van der Spek (Bethesda, MD: 2008), 69–95. The explanation proposed by S. Greengus, that "torches were used as a rapid signal, initially, to alert the population" (*JAOS* 108 [1988]: 153b) does not seem convincing to me.
37. TCL XVII, 76; see K. R. Veenhof, AbB XIV, 130.
38. See J. J. Finkelstein, "Ammiṣduqa's Edict and the Babylonian 'Law Codes,'" *JCS* 15 (1961): 102 (with a slightly different opinion).
39. See my "Les prêteurs et le palais," 202–3. In addition, a *mīšarum* likely took place in year 15 of Samsu-ditana (*RA* 99 [2005]: 150–51).
40. See the antithetical articles by F. R. Kraus and J. J. Finkelstein in *Mél. Landsberger*, ed. H. G. Güterbock and T. Jacobsen (Chicago: 1965).
41. A good exposition of the sabbatical year can be found in R. de Vaux, *Ancient Israel: Its Life and Institutions,* trans. John McHugh (New York: 1961), 173–75.
42. See, for example, N. P. Lemche, "The Manumission of Slaves—the Fallow Year—the Sabbatical Year—the Yobel Year," *Vetus Testamentum* 20 (1976): 38–59, and "*Andurârum* and *Mîšarum:* Comments on the Problem of Social Edicts and Their Application in the Ancient Near East," *JNES* 38 (1979): 11–22. See, more recently, E. Otto, "Soziale Restitution und Vertragsrecht. Mīšaru(m), (an)-durāru(m), kirenzi, parā tarnumar, šemiṭṭa und derôr in Mesopotamien, Syrien in der Hebräischen Bibel und die Frage des Rechtstransfers im alten Orient," *RA* 92 (1998): 125–60.
43. In fact, the biblical regulation explicitly foresaw that case: "Beware that there be not a thought in thy wicked heart, saying, The seventh year, the year of release, is at hand; and thine eye be evil against thy poor brother, and thou givest him nought" (Deuteronomy 15:9). But there is nothing like that in the Old Babylonian edicts.
44. TCL I, 15. According to the persuasive interpretation of Kraus (*Königliche Verfügungen,* 74 and n. 167), we are to understand the creditor's words to the debtor ironically: "The probabilities that I will recover that debt are so poor that you may just as well take my money immediately." See also the translation of K. R. Veenhof, AbB XIV, 15 (from which I deviate slightly for line 20).
45. If, at least, we allow ourselves a comparison here to what happened in Lagid Egypt. The context for the "amnesties" of the Ptolemies was clearly that of peasant revolt. Like the *mīšarum* of the Babylonian kings, "nothing in the orders of the Ptolemies fundamentally calls into question the essential origin of the problem" (C. Préaux, *Nouvelle Clio* 6 [Paris: 1978], 398).
46. That example of canceling debts is to be added to my study in *MARI* 6, cited in note 18 of this chapter.
47. F. R. Kraus, *Ein Edikt des Königs Ammi-ṣaduqa von Babylon,* SD 5 (Leiden: 1958).
48. F. R. Kraus, "Ein Edikt des Königs Samsu-iluna von Babylon," in Güterbock and Jacobsen, *Mél. Landsberger,* 225–31. An additional manuscript (NBC, 8618), also very incomplete, has been published more recently by Hallo, "Slave Release in the Biblical World in Light of a New Text," 79–93.
49. I am summarizing here the second part of my "Les décrets royaux à l'époque paléo-babylonienne, à propos d'un ouvrage récent," 41–44.

50. For that restitution, see my "L'édit d'Ammi-ṣaduqa: Nouvelle lecture (sec. 10, B iii:25)," *NABU* 2003/79.
51. Charpin, Edzard, and Stol, OBO 160/4, 330.
52. I have also proposed an interpretation of sec. 20–21 in the same vein; see my "Les décrets royaux à l'époque paléo-babylonienne," 43–44.
53. We have only a few paragraphs from the edict of Samsu-iluna, but they are *word-for-word* identical to the text promulgated nearly a century later by Ammi-ṣaduqa: from a historical perspective, the order must obviously be reversed.
54. See my "Marchands du palais et marchands du temple à la fin de la Ie dynastie de Babylone," *JA* 270 (1982): 59n80.
55. So it was for the title *šakkanakkum*, which was no longer used after the reign of Abi-eshuh.
56. See AbB XI, 113; AbB XIII, 89; commentary in my "Les prêteurs et le palais," 185–86.

CHAPTER 7

1. See chapter 5.
2. See my "Un quartier de Babylone et ses habitants," *BiOr* 42 (1985): 265–78.
3. A. Falkenstein, "Eine Inschrift Waradsins aus Babylon," *BaM* 3 (1964): 25–40 (esp. 25).
4. See the bibliography in D. Charpin, D. O. Edzard, and M. Stol, OBO 160/4 (Fribourg: 2004), 428–29; and O. Pedersén, *Archive und Bibliothek in Babylon. Die Tontafeln der Grabung Robert Koldeweys 1899–1917*, ADOG 25 (Saarwellingen: 2005).
5. For Suma-la-El (and not Sumu-abum) as founder of the first dynasty of Babylon, see Charpin, Edzard, and Stol, OBO 160/4, 81–86.
6. See ibid., 361–63.
7. For a general introduction, see B. Lafont, "Relations internationales, alliances et diplomatie au temps des rois de Mari," in *Amurru* 2, ed. J.-M. Durand and D. Charpin (Paris: 2001), 213–328; a summary in English appears in "International Relations in the Ancient Near East: The Birth of a Complete Diplomatic System," *Diplomacy & Statecraft* 12/1 (2001): 39–60.
8. See B. Lafont, "Messagers et ambassadeurs dans les archives de Mari," in CRRAI 38, ed. D. Charpin and F. Joannès (Paris: 1992), 167–83.
9. ARM II, 23 (J.-M. Durand, LAPO 17 [Paris: 1998], 590): 7–8.
10. ARM II, 70 (J.-M. Durand, LAPO 16 [Paris: 1997], 352): 4'–11'.
11. ARM XXVI/2, 370:4'–9'.
12. ARM XXVI/2, 361:13–19 (the restitution at the beginning of line 17 should be corrected to [*mu-ki*]-*lu*). Throughout this chapter, italics in quotations indicate that the correct translation is uncertain.
13. ARM XXVI/2, 363:27–30.
14. Unpublished text A. 4474+: 11–14.
15. ARM II, 23 (Durand, LAPO 17, 590): 9–11.
16. ARM XXVI/2, 384.
17. ARM II, 23 (Durand, LAPO 17, 590): 3'–6'.
18. Unpublished text M. 10728 (the beginning of the letter is missing).
19. See A. 2968+: 9–20; text published by M. Guichard, "'La malédiction de cette tablette est très dure!' Sur l'ambassade d'Itûr-Asdû à Babylone en l'an 4 de Zimrî-Lîm," *RA* 98 (2004): 13–32.
20. ARM II, 76 (Durand, LAPO 16, 404): 5–38.

21. See B. Lafont, "Messagers et ambassadeurs," CRRAI 38, 177–80, as well as the observations of Durand, LAPO 16, 69–73.
22. ARM XXVI/2, 392:4–9.
23. See A. 2968+:34–73; text published by M. Guichard, "'La malédiction de cette tablette est très dure!'" 13–32.
24. Unpublished text A. 258:30–44.
25. ARM XXVI/2, 366.
26. See the letter from Ibal-pi-El A. 486+, published by P. Villard, "Parade militaire dans les jardins de Babylone," *FM* [I], ed. J.-M. Durand, Mémoires de *NABU* 1 (Paris: 1992), 137–52 (Durand, LAPO 17, 579).
27. Unpublished text A. 4252: "Yamhad's troops arrived here. The day after they arrived, they entered for the meal in the presence of Hammurabi." The reverse enumerates the presents-*qiršum* given as a function of rank. See also the unpublished text A. 1982, quoted in ARM XXVI/2, 174n. f.
28. See ARM XXVI/1, 101 n. b, and XXVI/2, 307 n. a, as well as Durand, LAPO 16, 169.
29. Unpublished text A. 4256.
30. For these omen consultations, see Charpin, Edzard, and Stol, OBO 160/4, 244–46.
31. ARM XXVI/1, 104:5–17.
32. ARM XXVI/1, 104:3'-5'.
33. That is the case for the *totality* of letters written by Ibal-pi-El in Babylonia, which date from the war against Elam; for more details, see CDOG 2, 118–19n26.
34. Cf. ARM XXVI/2, 371:18.
35. Cf. ARM XXVI/2, 370:46'–47'.
36. See ARM II, 29 (Durand, LAPO 16, 288).
37. Unpublished text A. 430+.
38. For the presence of a deaf person at this interview, see my commentary in ARM XXVI/2, 140n7. For the Mari palace, note as well the mention of a "deaf man" (*sukkukum*) among the king's intimates who swore an oath in year 2 of Zimri-Lim (ZL 1'); see J.-M. Durand, "Précurseurs syriens aux protocoles néo-assyriens: Considérations sur la vie politique aux Bords-de-l'Euphrate," in *Mél. Garelli*, ed. D. Charpin and F. Joannès (Paris: 1991), 13–72 (esp. 41 [M. 6822: 3']).
39. Quoted by J. Sasson, *Mél. Birot*, ed. J.-M. Durand and J.-R. Kupper (Paris: 1985), 246.
40. For later examples, see P. Girardi, "Declaring War in Mesopotamia," *AfO* 33 (1986): 30–38 (the documentation from Mari, which was published later, could not be taken into account in that article).
41. For more details, see CDOG 2, 121–23; D. Charpin and N. Ziegler, *FM* V, Mémoires de NABU 6 (Paris: 2003), 216–22; Charpin, Edzard, and Stol, OBO 160/4, 210–26.
42. Text edited and commented on by J.-M. Durand, "L'empereur d'Élam et ses vassaux," in *Mél. De Meyer*, ed. H. Gasche, M. Tanret, C. Janssen, and A. Degraeve (Ghent: 1994), 15–22 (A. 6 [Durand, LAPO 17, 556]).
43. A. 1314 (Durand, LAPO 16, 251), published by G. Dossin, "Une lettre de Iarîm-Lim, roi d'Alep, à Iašûb-Iaḫad de Dîr," *Syria* 33 (1956): 63–69 (Recueil G. Dossin [Louvain: 1983], 180–86).
44. It was placed into doubt by J. M. Sasson, "Yarim-Lim's War Declaration," in Durand and J.-R. Kupper, *Mél. Birot*, 237–56. But see, in support of its authenticity, Durand, LAPO 16, 385.
45. See M. Guichard, "Les aspects religieux de la guerre à Mari," *RA* 93 (1999): 27–48.
46. For details on the events, see *FM* V, 231–32, and Charpin, Edzard, and Stol, OBO 160/4, 317–23.

47. ARM XXVI/2, 372:27–40.
48. See P. Steinkeller, "A History of Mashkan-shapir and Its Role in the Kingdom of Larsa," in *The Anatomy of a Mesopotamian City*, ed. E. Stone and P. Zimansky (Winona Lake, IN: 2004), 26–42.
49. ARM XXVI/2, 385: 8'–15'.
50. See F. Lerouxel, "Les échanges de présents entre souverains amorrites au XVIIIe siècle d'après les Archives royales de Mari," in *FM* VI, ed. D. Charpin and J.-M. Durand, Mémoires de NABU 7 (Paris: 2002), 413–64.
51. CTN IV, 63; on this subject, see my remarks in *RA* 91 (1997): 188–90 and in Charpin, Edzard, and Stol, OBO 160/4, 244–45, and the new edition of this text by W. G. Lambert, *Babylonian Oracle Questions*, MC 13 (Winona Lake, IN: 2007).
52. See my *AFPP*, 188–89.
53. For more details, see Charpin, Edzard, and Stol, OBO 160/4, 323–24.
54. See my remarks in *AfO* 44/45 (1997–98): 341a. Complete translation and commentary in "Lettres et procès paléo-babyloniens," 86, no. 42. See also K. R. Veenhof's analysis, "The Relation between Royal Decrees and Laws in the Old Babylonian Period," *JEOL* 35/36 (1997–2000): 49–84 (esp. 78).
55. See on this point my "Une alliance contre l'Elam et le rituel du *lipit napištim*," in *Mél. Perrot*, ed. F. Vallat (Paris: 1990), 109–18.
56. The animal was usually a baby donkey (see B. Lafont, "Relations internationales, alliances et diplomatie au temps des rois de Mari,", 262–71), but sometimes another animal (see my note, "Le sacrifice des chèvres lors d'alliances sous le règne de Zimri-Lim," *NABU* 2008/48).
57. J.-M. Durand, "Assyriologie," *Annuaire du Collège de France* (2000–1), 693–705 (esp. 696–702).
58. See D. Charpin, "Une alliance contre l'Elam et le rituel de *lipit napištim*," Vallat, *Mél. Perrot*, 109–18. Let me add to that file the letter from Ibal-pi-El ARM II, 29, based on the new interpretation by Durand, LAPO 16, 288.
59. Unpublished text M. 6072:4–9.
60. A. 4626 (Durand, LAPO 16, 286): 16–21. Since I published this text in *Mél. Perrot*, I have been able to locate a fragment that constitutes the beginning of the letter and gives the name of its sender.
61. See J.-M. Durand, "Fragments rejoints pour une histoire élamite," in *Mél. Steve*, ed. L. De Meyer, H. Gasche, and F. Vallat (Paris: 1986), 111–28. The text (M. 6435+) was retranslated in Durand, LAPO 16, 290.
62. We do not have the complete text, only a summary: "I swear that I will not make peace with the lord of Elam."
63. ARM XXVI/2, 372:5–22.
64. ARM I, 37 (Durand, LAPO 16, 280): 19–27.
65. A. 405.
66. References are helpfully collected in B. Lafont, "Relations internationales, alliances et diplomatie au temps des rois de Mari," 283–93.
67. ARM XXVI/2, 372:55–60.
68. A. 2968+:4'–9'; published by M. Guichad, "'La malédiction de cette tablette est très dure!'" 13–32.
69. On this point, see my remarks in Charpin, Edzard, and Stol, OBO 160/4, 80–86; and, independently, A. Goddeeris, "The Emergence of Amorite Dynasties in Northern Babylonia during the Early Old Babylonian Period," in CRRAI 48, ed. W. H. van Soldt, R. Kalvelagan, and D. Katz (Leiden: 2005), 138–46.

70. In the archives discovered at the palace of Shehnā/Shubat-Enlil (Tell Leilan), both the royal correspondence and five contemporary treaty texts have been discovered; see J. Eidem, *Royal Letters and Treaties from the Lower Town Palace,* YTLR (New Haven, CT, forthcoming); and the information collected in Charpin, Edzard, and Stol, OBO 160/4, 349–51.
71. See the conclusion of this chapter.
72. This is the famous case of the "journey to Ugarit"; see the indications in *FM* V, 214–16. Note as well that Samsi-Addu and Dadusha, king of Eshnunna, seem to have met in Agade to conclude an alliance (N. Ziegler, *FM* V, 90–91).
73. For more details on this point, see my "Guerre et paix à l'époque amorrite," CRRAI 52, ed. H. Neumann, R. Dittmann, A. Schuster Brandis, and C. Eder (Wiesbaden: forthcoming).
74. Despite an erroneous indication in *RIME* 4, 753, no treaty from Tell Leilan includes a seal impression (cf. *RA* 86 [1992]: 89).
75. For these divine symbols, see chapter 3, sec. 1.3.
76. For this gesture consisting of tying together the fringe of the spouses' garments during a wedding, see chapter 3, sec. 1.1.
77. A. 3354+, text quoted in my "Un traité entre Zimri-Lim de Mari et Ibal-pî-El II d'Ešnunna," Charpin and Joannès, *Mél. Garelli,* 139–66 (163).
78. *ARM* XXVI/2, 449:55.
79. Namely, the treaty between Hammurabi and Zimri-Lim against Elam (M. 6435+ [Durand, LAPO 16, 290], 5, cited in note 61 of this chapter), and the one concluded between Atamrum and Zimri-Lim (A. 96 [Durand, LAPO 16, 291], 4).
80. See D. Charpin, "L'évocation du passé dans les lettres de Mari," in CRRAI 43, ed. J. Prosecky (Prague: 1998), 91–110.
81. See the Hittite treaty engraved on a bronze tablet and weighing 5 kilograms found in Bogazköy (H. Otten, *Die Bronzetafel aus Bogazköy: Ein Staatsvertrag Tutḫalijas IV,* StBOT Beiheft [supplement] 1 (Wiesbaden: 1988). The Egyptian-Hittite treaty was recopied onto a silver tablet, though the text known to us is preserved only on clay; see E. Edel, *Der Vertrag zwischen Ramses II. von Ägypten und Ḫattušili III. von Ḫatti,* WVDOG 95 (Berlin: 1997). For other references, see G. Beckman, *Hittite Diplomatic Texts,* WAW 7 (Atlanta: 1996), 103.
82. G. Beckman, *Hittite Diplomatic Texts,* 86 no. 18, sec. 16 (three times a year in this case).
83. S. Lafont, "L'arbitrage en Mésopotamie," *Revue de l'arbitrage* 4 (2000): 557–90 (esp. 572–74).
84. See ARM XXVI/2, 449:49; cf. D. Charpin and J.-M. Durand, "La suzeraineté de l'empereur (Sukkalmah) d'Elam sur la Mésopotamie et le 'nationalisme' amorrite," in CRRAI 36, ed. L. De Meyer and H. Gasche (Ghent: 1991), 59–66 (esp. 61).
85. ARM XXVI/2, 468: 8'–9'.
86. They were published or republished by J. R. Kupper, ARM XXVIII, 1, 3–5.
87. ARM XXVI/2, 375:4–20.
88. For the most recent overview of that question, see my "La fin des archives dans le palais de Mari," *RA* 89 (1995): 29–40.
89. ARM XXVI/2, 384, quoted in chapter 1, note 16.
90. ARM II XXVI/1, 102:20'.
91. ARM II, 24+ (Durand, LAPO 17, 586): 15.
92. ARM XXVI/1, 40:5.
93. ARM XXVI/2, 81:6', 20'.

94. A.3274 (cf. M. Guichard, "Les relations diplomatiques entre Ibal-pi-El II et Zimri-Lim: Deux étapes vers la discorde," *RA* 96 [2002]: 109–42 [127–32]). Significantly, this was an intercepted letter that was not intended for the king of Mari.
95. See N. Ziegler, *Le Harem de Zimrî-Lîm, FM* IV (Paris: 1999).
96. We do not even know the name of Hammurabi's principal wife. The letters from Mari reveal only the names of two of his sons; see B. Lion, "Des princes de Babylone à Mari," *FM* II, ed. D. Charpin and J.-M. Durand, Mémoires de NABU 3 (Paris: 1994), 221–34.
97. ARM XXVI/2, 449:12–23, following J.-M. Durand's translation, *FM* [I], 30.

CHAPTER 8

1. See the lists in D. Charpin and N. Ziegler, *FM* V, Mémoires de NABU 6 (Paris: 2003), 263–71, and D. Charpin, D. O. Edzard, and M. Stol, OBO 160/4 (Fribourg: 2004), 392–402.
2. Letter from Itur-Asdu, A. 482, quoted in G. Dossin, "Les archives épistolaires du palais de Mari," *Syria* 19 (1938): 117–18 (Recueil G. Dossin [Louvain: 1983], 114–15]); see D. Charpin and J.-M. Durand's commentary, "La prise du pouvoir par Zimri-Lim," *MARI* 4 (1985): 323n131.
3. See J.-M. Durand, "Unité et diversités au Proche-Orient à l'époque amorrite," in CRRAI 38, ed. D. Charpin and F. Joannès (Paris: 1992), 97–128.
4. See B. Lafont, "Le Proche-Orient à l'époque des rois de Mari: Un monde sans frontières?" in CRRAI 44, ed. L. Milano, S. de Martino, F. M. Fales, and G. B. Lanfranchi (Padua: 2000), 49–55.
5. There are no recent studies devoted specifically to this word; F. Pintore's article "*Pat(t)um* nelle lettere di Mari," *Oriens Antiquus* 8 (1969): 265–79, already old, is concerned primarily with the notion of *āl pāṭim* ("border city"). Within the context of an invasion, *pāṭum* could designate "the front": see ARM XXVI/1, 156:14 (cf. 324n. c) and *ARM* XXVI/2, 447:19'. See also the observations in J.-M. Durand, "Assyriologie," *Annuaire du Collège de France* (1999–2000): 701–20 (707–8); and the entry *pāṭu* in the CAD P, 305–10.
6. See, for example, AbB XI (Leiden: 1986), 92:5'.
7. The paragraph deals with the indemnification of a man who had been the victim of thieves: "The city and the mayor in the territory [*erṣetum*] or on the border [*pālaṭum*] from which the act of robbery was committed will have to compensate him for the property he lost" (sec. 23).
8. See B. Lion, "Les governeurs provinciaux du royaume de Mari à l'époque de Zimrî-Lîm," in *Amurru* 2, ed. J.-M. Durand and D. Charpin (Paris: 2001), 141–201.
9. Particularly M. Liverani; see esp. his *Prestige and Interest: International Relations in the Near East, ca. 1600–1100 B.C.*, HANE/S 1 (Padua: 1990), 89.
10. See J.-M. Durand's remark in J.-M. Durand, LAPO 17 (Paris: 1998), 515–16.
11. See *FM* V, 181 and 202.
12. Samsi-Addu's letter to the local king defined Shusharra as "my border city" (*āl pāṭī*) (J. Eidem and J. Laessoe, *ShA* 1 [Copenhagen: 2001], 15:11), which, as such, had to to lodge and reprovision a garrison to assure the protection of the entire kingdom.
13. IM 95200: xiv 11–xv 4; see D. Charpin, "Données nouvelles sur la région du Petit Zab au XVIIIe siècle av. J.-C.," *RA* 98 (2004): 151–78 (154 and commentary, 156–57).
14. ARM V, 58 (J.-M. Durand, LAPO 16 [Paris: 1997], 422).
15. See letter A. 162, published in my "Sapîratum, ville du Suhûm," *MARI* 8 (1997): 341–66 (354, no. 4).

16. ARM XIV, 117 (Durand, LAPO 16, 396).
17. A text indicates that the circulation of goods intended for one's own consumption was not taxed: "At present, ten men of Yabliya went to Mari to buy grain. May my lord not detain them: these people are not merchants, they are making purchases for their own subsistence, the tax collector [*mākisum*] must not tax them!" This is in a letter from the governor of Yabliya, Hammanum, which I shall soon publish (A. 1307).
18. See the translation of these texts in J.-M. Durand, LAPO 18 (Paris: 2000), nos. 862–903. On the *miksum,* cf. C. Michel, "Le commerce dans les textes de Mari," in *Amurru* 1, ed. J.-M. Durand (Paris: 1996): 385–426 (407–8), and sec. 2.2 of this chapter.
19. AbB II, 84. See W. F. Leemans, *Foreign Trade in the Old Babylonian Period,* SD 6 (Leiden: 1960), 105–9.
20. ARM XIV, 52 (Durand, LAPO 18, 920).
21. See K. R. Veenhof, *Aspects of Old Assyrian Trade and Its Terminology,* SD 10 (Leiden: 1972), esp. part 4, "Smuggling," 305–42. An anthology of the principal letters relating to contraband can be found in C. Michel, *Correspondance des marchands de Kanish* (Paris: 2001), 238–66.
22. The unpublished letter A. 4285+ mentions a Babylonian general, Hammanum, who has just arrived in Hit (lines 8–9). I therefore diverge from the interpretation of M. Guichard, "Le sel à Mari," 187n92.
23. A. 815:5–18, quoted in M. Guichard, "Le sel à Mari (III). Les lieux du sel," in *FM* III, ed. D. Charpin and J.-M. Durand, Mémoires de NABU 4 (Paris: 1997), 167–200 (187 and n. 91).
24. ARM XXVII, 26:15–19.
25. ARM XXVI/1, 253:4–10, 15'–18'.
26. On this subject, see D. Charpin and J.-M. Durand, "Aššur avant l'Assyrie," *MARI* 8 (1997): 367–92 (esp. 377–81).
27. See the edition of this text by D. Charpin, "Tell Mohammed Diyab, une ville du pays d'Apum," in *Tell Mohammed Diyad, campagnes 1987 et 1988,* ed. J.-M. Durand (Paris: 1990), 117–22 (retranslated by Durand, LAPO 16, 333). The expression *ina šepātim* in line 6 is elucidated in M. Guichard, "Le Šubartum occidental à l'avènement de Zimrî-Lîm," in *FM* VI, ed. D. Charpin and J.-M. Durand, Mémoires de NABU 7 (Paris: 2002), 119–65 (162–63).
28. See *FM* V, 37, 180, as well as the recent studies of J.-M. Durand, especially in the *Annuaire du Collège de France* (1999–2000, 2000–1, and 2001–2); see also his "Peuplement et sociétés à l'époque amorrite. (I) Les clans bensim'alites," in CRRAI 46, ed. C. Nicolle (Paris: 2004), 111–98.
29. ARM V, 17+ (Durand, LAPO 17, 490).
30. S. Çeçen and K. Hecker, "*Ina mātika eblum.* Zu einem neuen Text zum Wegerecht in der Kültepe-Zeit," in *Mél. von Soden,* ed. M. Dietrich and O. Loretz (Neukirchen-Vluyn: 1995), 2:31–41 (French translation in Michel, *Correspondance des marchands de Kanish,* 150, no. 87). This text is of further interest in that it demonstrates the monopoly enjoyed by Assyrian merchants. The treaty stipulates that the Anatolian prince was banned from trading with "Akkadian" merchants, that is, natives of Babylonia.
31. On this subject, see Charpin and Durand, "Aššur avant l'Assyrie," 378 and n. 82; see also chapter 6, sec. 2.2.
32. See the cases studied in Charpin and Durand, "Aššur avant l'Assyrie," 381. Several texts from Mari show that the merchant district (*kārum*) was the object of a separate

census: see C. Michel, "Le commerce dans les textes de Mari," 415; and my forthcoming "Artisans et marchands dans l'armée de Mari."

33. Unpublished letter A.4435, to be published by N. Ziegler.
34. Under the reign of Zimri-Lim, this was the chief merchant Iddiyatum, alias Iddin-Numushda (cf. my note in *NABU* 1989/59); see also the set of letters collected by J.-M. Durand, LAPO 18, 25–39.
35. See F. Joannès, ARM XXVI/2, 320n. c. K. R. Veenhof has observed that such an obligation did not exist when Assyrian trade with Cappadocia was most active (the so-called *kārum* II period).
36. ARM XXVI/2, 443:1–32.
37. Contrary to the impression created for some by a superficial reading of the document, this text absolutely does not show that a queen could stand in for her husband during his absence. It is exactly the reverse: Atamrum's wife says that she cannot assume responsibility for letting through merchants whose arrival was not officially announced. In Atamrum's absence, she wrote to his suzerain, Zimri-Lim, king of Mari, so that that the king would make a decision.
38. ARM XIII, 34 (Durand, LAPO 17, 696).
39. ARM XIV, 9 (Durand, LAPO 16, 343).
40. ARM XIV, 36 (Durand, LAPO 16, 393).
41. Letter A. 2746, to be published in my *La correspondance à l'époque amorrite* (forthcoming).
42. See "La circulation des commerçants des nomades et des messagers dans le Proche-Orient amorrite (XVIIIe siècle av. J.-C.)," 62n40.
43. See the examples collected and analyzed in Charpin and Durand, "Aššur avant l'Assyrie," 379–80.
44. A. 16 (Durand, LAPO 18, 912).
45. A. 2776, published by D. Charpin and J.-M. Durand, "Aššur avant l'Assyrie," 383–84.
46. Letter Kt n/K 504, published by C. Günbatti, "The River Ordeal in Ancient Anatolia," in *Mél. Veenhof*, ed. W. H. van Soldt, J. G. Dercksen, N. J. C. Kouwenberg, and T. J. H. Krispijn (Leiden: 2001), 151–60.
47. The Sumerogram is notated GABA.RÁ, rather than the usual RÁ.GABA; vol. 4 of the CAD includes the reference (*s.v. rakbû*, 106a), even while expressing doubt "a *r.* (?)."
48. A. Goetze, "Fifty Old Babylonian Letters from Harmal," *Sumer* 14 (1958): 1–76 and pl. 1–24 (esp. 23–24, no. 5 [IM 51251]). [Translator's note:] The translation is my own.
49. See J. Renger, "Flucht als soziales Problem in der altbabylonischen Gesellschaft," in *Gesellschaftsklassen in Alten Zweistromland und in den angrenzenden Gebieten—XVIII. Rencontre assyriologique internationale, München, 29. Juni bis 3. Jul 1970*, ed. D. O. Edzard (Munich: 1972), 167–82, (esp. 177); see also D. C. Snell, *Flight and Freedom in the Ancient Near East*, CHANE 8 (Leiden: 2001), 55–56.
50. D. Charpin, "Un traité entre Zimri-Lim de Mari et Ibâl-pî-El II d'Ešnunna," in *Mél. Garelli*, ed. D. Charpin and F. Joannès (Paris: 1991), 139–66 (esp. 161–62); and my note "La visite des messagers d'Ešnunna à Mari," *NABU* 1992/101. Text republished in Durand, LAPO 16, 282.
51. The term used is *nēberum*: the site of Mashkan-shapir has now been identified as Tell Abu Duwari, which was on the Tigris at the time (see P. Steinkeller, "New Light on the Hydrology and Topography of Southern Babylonia in the Third Millennium," *ZA* 91 [2001]: 22–84).

52. Unpublished letter A. 914: 5–20. I shall publish this letter in a future volume of ARM, which will include the correspondence of Ibal-pi-El, to which this document belongs.
53. For the situation on the northern border of the kingdom of Larsa in the area of Mashkan-shapir, see explicitly letter AbB IX (Leiden: 1981), 74:9.
54. Line 21; the missing word is probably not "Elam," since the Elamite emperor was residing in Eshnunna at the time. I prefer to insert *a-na* [lú-sukkal].
55. A. 266, published by J.-M. Durand, "La Cité-État d'Imâr à l'époque des rois de Mari," *MARI* 6 (1990): 39–92 (republished in Durand, LAPO 16, 298). For a detailed commentary on the political situation, see my "Babylone face au conflit entre Alep et Qaṭna d'après les archives royales de Mari" (forthcoming).
56. See esp. letter M. 5431, published and annotated by F. Joannès, "Une mission secrète à Ešnunna," in CRRAI 38, 185–93.

CONCLUSION

1. See, in this respect, K. R. Veenhof, "'Modern' Features in Old Assyrian Trade," *JESHO* 40/4 (1997): 333–66.
2. D. Charpin, "Maisons et maisonnées en Babylonie ancienne de Sippar à Ur. Remarques sur les grandes demeures de notables paléo-babyloniens," in CRRAI 40, ed. K. R. Veenhof (Leiden: 1996), 221–28 (esp. 222).
3. See H. Vanstiphout, "Enmerkar's Invention of Writing Revisited," in *DUMU-E$_2$-DUB-BA-A, Studies in Honor of Å. W. Sjöberg,* ed. H. Behrens, D. Loding, and M. T. Roth (Philadelphia: 1989), 515–24; P. Michalowski, *Letters from Early Mesopotamia,* WAW 3 (Atlanta: 1993), 2; J. J. Glassner, *Écrire à Sumer. L'invention du cunéiforme* (Paris: 2000), chap. 1 (translated into English as *The Invention of Cuneiform: Writing in Sumer* [Baltimore, MD: 2003]).
4. I will soon publish the archives of Alammush-nāṣir, which date from the middle of Samsu-iluna's reign and give a very clear example of that behavior. Some of his letters to his steward Nabi-Shamash have already been published (cf. AbB XIV [Leiden: 2005], xxi, sec. f). On this archival lot, cf. note 51 in chapter 5.
5. AbB VIII, 109.
6. Information communicated by A. Fadhil during the RAI in Münster, July 2006.
7. See chapter 3, sec. 2.1.
8. J.-M. Durand, "La vengeance à l'époque amorrite," in *FM* VI, ed. D. Charpin and J.-M. Durand, Mémoires de NABU 7 (Paris: 2002), 39–50.
9. This information surfaced in the context of the trial of Shamash-tappe, known through AbB XIV, 207: "the father of sons cannot adopt his slave" (lines 20–22).
10. See chapter 6.
11. Unpublished letter A. 2446: (7): *al-kam a-na-ku ù at-ta pí-am a-na pí-im* (8) *i ni id-bu-ub.*
12. J. Eidem and J. Laessoe, *ShA* 1 (Copenhagen: 2001), 65:5–11.
13. AbB XI, 94:9: *ka-ni-ku lu-ú qú-ru-um-ma* KA *lu ša-ki-in.*
14. See my *Le clergé d'Ur au siècle d'Hammurabi* (Geneva: 1986), chap. 6. The case of the "library" of Me-Turan is unclear because of the initial catastrophic decision to publish the "literary" texts without taking any interest in the archives found in the same building, as A. Cavigneaux has acknowledged ("A Scholar's Library in Meturan? With an Edition of the Tablet H 72 [Texts of Tell Haddad VII]," in *Mesopotamian Magic: Textual, Historical, and Interpretative Perspectives,* ed. T. Abusch and K. van der Toorn, AMD 1 [Groningen: 1999], 251–73).

15. K. R. Veenhof, "'Dying Tablets' and 'Hungry Silver': Elements of Figurative Language in Akkadian Commercial Terminology," in *Figurative Language in the Ancient Near East,* ed. M. Mindlin, M. J. Geller, and J. E. Wansborough (London: 1987), 41–75.
16. "When . . . [the judges] reviewed the trials of the people of Sippar, 'listened' to the purchase tablets for the fields, houses, and gardens, and broke those that were invalidated by the *mīšarum*" (AbB VII, 153: 7–9).
17. As we saw in chapter 4, that is the expression appearing on tablets that take note of the nontransfer of previous deeds of property.
18. We thus find, in AbB XII, 32: 38: *pí-ia la i-sà-ra-ar,* "may my mouth not become a liar."
19. Let me note the title L. Oppenheim gave to a paragraph in his *Ancient Mesopotamia* relating to religions: "Why a 'Mesopotamian Religion' Should Not Be Written" (A. L. Oppenheim, *Ancient Mesopotamia: Portrait of a Dead Civilization* [Chicago: 1964], 172). He wanted thereby to draw attention to the danger of not understanding what was irreducible about Mesopotamian religion with respect to our usual approach to religion(s).

INDEX